Break-Glass

Helmut Petritsch

Break-Glass

Handling Exceptional Situations in Access Control

With a Foreword by Prof. Dr. Günther Pernul

 Springer Vieweg

Dr. Helmut Petritsch
Walldorf, Germany

Dissertation, University of Regensburg, 2014

ISBN 978-3-658-07364-0   ISBN 978-3-658-07365-7 (eBook)
DOI 10.1007/978-3-658-07365-7

The Deutsche Nationalbibliothek lists this publication in the Deutsche Nationalbibliografie; detailed bibliographic data are available in the Internet at http://dnb.d-nb.de.

Library of Congress Control Number: 2014950445

Springer Vieweg
© Springer Fachmedien Wiesbaden 2014

Printed on acid-free paper

Springer Vieweg is a brand of Springer DE.
Springer DE is part of Springer Science+Business Media.
www.springer-vieweg.de

Foreword

Break-glass is a mechanism to handle exceptional situations in access control. Under emergency situations users should be able – to a certain extent – to request exceptional privileges to achieve tasks which could not be accomplished otherwise. Afterwards, after the emergency situation has been resolved, authorities responsible for auditing a security policy should be able to check if the exceptional access can be justified.

In this book the author develops a break-glass concept which is orthogonal to existing access control techniques. As such, the break-glass does not rely on specific properties of a given access control model. This is in contrast to other approaches which mainly try to integrate exception-handling into a particular access control model. Grounded on requirements stemming from real-world application cases and legal requirements, the author develops a comprehensive generic break-glass model consisting of a three-step process: pre-access, at-access, and post-access. Each of the process steps is thoroughly analyzed and the major components and players identified. In addition, much effort is devoted to the post-access break-glass analysis with the focus on developing an analysis infrastructure in order to support validity checks and perform the auditing of the exceptional access. All the findings of the author are evaluated and partly tested by a prototype implementation under almost real-world conditions.

In addition to break-glass, this book also describes state-of-the-art achievements in a wider range of topics, such as authorization systems, XACML-based authorization policies, role-based access control systems, software architectures and the form of their representation. The focus of the book is on the technical and organizational issues. This book is mainly recommended for readers who are interested in its valuable contributions to research, but also for those looking for a comprehensive summary of the state of the art of break-glass and related technologies.

Prof. Dr. Günther Pernul
Department of Information Systems
University of Regensburg, Germany

Contents

List of Figures

List of Listings

1 Introduction

1.1 Motivation

Information Technology (IT) systems comprise fine-grained Access Control (AC) mechanisms, commonly following the *least privilege principle* [93]: restricting privileges of users to what is needed to fulfill their tasks. AC policies are machine readable rules used to enforce those privileges at runtime. Hence, for the definition of policies, all processes and scenarios which make up the benefit of the IT system have to be modeled in order to be able to define machine readable and enforceable policies. Thus, policies have to be defined beforehand in machine readable form and remain static at runtime.

A prerequisite for this approach is that any possible scenario or process which could be executed in the future has to be modeled to derive the required privileges and translate them into machine readable form, i. e., AC policies. This, however, causes two problems. First, it is expensive or even impossible to foresee all possible scenarios and exceptions [40, 76, 87, 89]. Second, it is hard to fully express privileges in machine readable form [52, 64, 89]: one would have to formalize everything that could influence the AC decision and collect all required information about the state of the environment the IT system is operating in, in order for the decision making component to work properly. Jackson [64] argues that, in oder to build a machine, one needs to formalize the requirements, which are "conditions over phenomena of the environment." However, this formalization can only be a "sufficiently faithful approximation" [64] and there is an inherent mismatch between the physical environment and the formalization thereof. Hence, not all privileges can be expressed in machine readable form. Hence, *it is not possible to make* AC *policies complete and correct.* For example, it is hard to formalize moral considerations; laws and legal regulations are not unambiguous but have to be interpreted by judges during lawsuits on a case by case basis; for an IT system it is hard to assess if a specific situation has occurred, e. g., if a physical object is present and in a specific state. Overall, the correctness of an AC decision relies on both the correctness and completeness of both the AC policies and the system information at runtime.

Although more and more fine-grained AC models, policy languages and techniques to gather security requirements have been developed, it is not possible to define fully correct policies, causing a mismatch between what a user is empowered to do and what he is permitted to do [52]. For example, current AC models are not able to ensure compliance with laws and legal regulations such as Basel II [12] or Sarbanes-Oxley Act (SOX) [99]. This can be seen in the increasing number of faults in [37, 78, 108] and costs for [57, 102] audit certificates which should ensure compliance in a post-hoc fashion.

Consequently, when defining AC policies, one has to balance the trade-off between the effort for policy development, too lax policies, and too restrictive policies, i. e., a trade-off between costs for policy development, the risk of revealing confidential data, and the potentially lost benefit. Increased effort and costs during development and maintenance of policies allow to define more accurate policies, but never fully correct ones. Policies that are too lax increase the risk of misuse and enable people to do more things than they are allowed to do. However, policies that are too restrictive increase the less apparent risk of hindering people from doing their work, causing, at best, merely higher costs and loss of benefit or, at worst, irrevocable damage.

As solution, we will present an approach called *Break-Glass*, which allows users to override a denying decision: if the user confirms that he requires access, he is exceptionally permitted to proceed with his work, but all his actions are recorded, and he will be held responsible in case he misused the responsibility granted by Break-Glass. We will present a generic Break-Glass model, and discuss our solution along the whole life-cycle of Break-Glass.

With Break-Glass, the user is explicitly empowered to make a – preliminary – decision: the user may have knowledge of the situation which the IT system does not possess. At the same time, the user has to take responsibility for his decision. The final AC decision is deferred to a post-access phase, where irresponsibly acting users are punished. Given the availability of Break-Glass as exception mechanism, regular access can be more constraining: Break-Glass can grant exceptional privileges in exceptional situations, while regular AC mechanisms are granting regular privileges in a restrictive way. Hence, Break-Glass is not only a mechanism to extend access rights, but also allows to make (regular) privileges more restrictive.

This concept of exceptional access with punishment of misuse is well-known in the non-IT world, e. g., breaking a pane of glass to raise a fire alarm, breaking the glass of a window to provide and make an emergency exit, or pulling emergency brakes for trains and moving staircases. Also, within an IT system, deferring the final AC decision to a post-access phase has some advantages. First, the evaluation can be done or supported by a natural person, which allows to include hard to encode rules. Second, the evaluation can be done for a concrete situation and, therefore, possible scenarios do not have to be predicted. Third, the evaluation is not time-critical as in terms of milliseconds at runtime. Fourth, information may be available post-access which was not available at-access.

A common motivation for Break-Glass or *"need for security override"* [45] can be found in the health care domain. Here, the discrepancy between the need to protect sensitive data vs. the need to access data to save patients' health and lifes is immediately understandable. Too lax policies are a problem, e. g., [19] argues that too lax policies are causing data breaches, e. g., reporters of the Sunday Times "were able to gain access to the private medical records [...] by paying a small fee to a commercial agency." [45] When medical data of celebrities or politicians get public (e. g., as reported by [4]), this is likely to be detected. However, if a curious neighbor is causing the same incident, it will most likely not get public and hence not be detected [4]. Following the study of [62], there is an increasing number of leakages of patient data: in 2012, 27% of all respondents of the study reported a security breach within 12 months (13% in 2008), and "56% of respondents indicated that the source of the breach was unauthorized access to information by an individual employed by the organization at the time of the breach." Within the study, missing attention was identified as the element putting most risk on data confidentiality, and the area of security policies and procedures was the one with most observed deficiencies. Hence, we see that defining accurate AC policies for health care applications is still a challenging task. Restrictive polices may be too restrictive once in a while, and policy engineers may choose to make policies less restrictive than it would technically be possible, as a denied access may cause harm to patients.

Exception mechanisms for health care systems are not only demanded by physicians and other professionals (e. g., [4, 45, 66, 91]), but also part of legal requirements for the health care domain. The United States (US) Health Insurance Portability and Accountability Act (HIPAA) Administrative Simplification [82] (i. e., HIPAA Part II) defines, among other things, how to treat individually identifiable health information. IT systems processing patient data in the US have to be compliant with this law. According to HIPAA [82], a procedure for granting access in emergencies is required, i. e., §164.312(a)(2)(ii) "Emergency access procedure (Required). Establish (and implement as needed) procedures for obtaining necessary electronic protected health information during an emergency." Furthermore, professional users should be enabled to make decisions if and which data (to which extent) should be accessible during an emergency situation, i. e., §164.510(b)(3), in "an emergency circumstance, the covered entity[1] may, in the exercise of professional judgment, determine whether the disclosure is in the best interests of the individual," where disclosure "means the release, transfer, provision of, access to, or divulging in any other manner of information outside the entity holding the information."

The Berlin data protection commissary (Berliner Beauftragter für Datenschutz und Informationsfreiheit) states in his annual report of 2009 [19] (in German) that only users who are involved in the treatment of a patient may be permitted to access a patient's health record. However, emergency access ("Notfallzugriff") with post-access evaluation has to be possible. Although this is only a recommendation and not legally binding, it shows that implementing some kind of exception mechanism is in the interest of the patient. Only if such an exception mechanism is in place, regular privileges can be reduced to follow the least privilege principle, while in exceptional situations access to required data can be achieved.

Break-Glass is not restricted to or only relevant for the health care domain. Bartsch [11] shows how Break-Glass can be used to reduce inefficiencies of authorization mechanisms. Bartsch argues that permissions are assigned along the most common processes, but "every once in a while, employees need higher privileges than assigned by default to complete the work at hand" [11]. Similar, Zhao and Johnson [113] argue that "control should not become a barrier to value creation. Anecdotal evidence suggests that many users bypass annoying security rules in order to accomplish their tasks." For this, subjects can override (escalate) a given base level of privileges when needed, while subjects abusing this mechanism are penalized. Also, large business software vendors offer certain mechanisms to increase privileges in exceptional or emergency situations, e. g., SAP's product "Governance, Risk Management, and Compliance (GRC)" (help.sap.com/grc) including a component called "Superuser Privilege Management (SPM)" [98] (formerly known as Firefighter), or Oracle's Role Manager [83].

Existing research is either specific to given implementations or AC models and hence not comparable, or covers only the adoption of the AC model used for Break-Glass, i. e., omiting succeeding questions such as behavior at runtime or investigations of Break-Glass accesses in the post-access phase.

Simple solutions, such as distributing accounts with higher privileges [66, 98], or engineering solutions for specific applications [50], solve only the problem that is specific to the targeted application. More generic solutions

---

[1]Meaning the accessing subject which has to comply with the privacy and security rules

introduce Break-Glass as extension to an existing or new AC model, typically tackling the definition of exceptional privileges. While such approaches aim at defining new AC models or new versions of existing AC models, we belief that instead of introducing one of "the next 700 access control models" [10] it is essential that Break-Glass is defined as orthogonal concept on top of existing AC models. For this, a generic concept of Break-Glass which models the characteristics of Break-Glass independently from any specific AC model will be presented. Up to now, there is no common concept which could reflect such generic Break-Glass characteristics or would allow for a comparison of existing Break-Glass approaches. Our Break-Glass model is generic in the sense that it defines Break-Glass on top of existing AC models, and the introduced characteristics will allow to compare existing Break-Glass approaches.

But even defining such a Break-Glass model does not solve all problems. Two further central building blocks for Break-Glass will be presented: *user confirmation* and *post-access evaluation*. By user confirmation we are referring to the requirement that users have to confirm that they are using exceptional privileges and that they will be held responsible if those privileges are misused. As users are held responsible for the potential damage they are causing, they should receive some information about the extent of their override, which allows them to weigh the potential benefit against the potential damage. We will present some techniques used for user information.

Post-access evaluation is needed to ensure the functioning of a key requirement: punishment of incorrectly behaving users. If misbehavior is not detected and punished, the Break-Glass mechanism is likely to be misused. Although it is a common statement that such post-access evaluation has to be done, we are not aware of any work that shows how this work can be supported, or how the investigation can be automated. In fact, most solutions only define an AC model which allows for Break-Glass. We think that the success of Break-Glass heavily relies on good support of the auditor, as the effort (i. e., costs) which is caused by Break-Glass is heavily influenced by the (manual) audit costs. Thus, Break-Glass can only be successful, if post-access evaluation causes only reasonable effort; otherwise, the problem of writing correct AC policies is only moved to a later point in time, leaving the primary problem unsolved. We will present techniques for investigations and automated post-access evaluation.

In the rest of this chapter, we will introduce a "running example" (section 1.2) which we will use throughout the thesis to explain use cases and techniques. We will present the applied methodology in section 1.3 and give an overview of the thesis structure in section 1.4.

1.2 Running Example

As running example we have chosen a scenario from the health care domain, as in this case, the discrepancy between protection need of sensitive data vs. need of data to save patients' health and life is immediately understandable. We will demonstrate in our running example that, while defining fine-grained and restrictive privileges for the regular case, Break-Glass enables the modeling exceptional privileges without the need to model all possible exceptional situations in detail.

To make the scenario as close to the real world as possible, we have chosen a mixture of two approaches on how to handle data in the health care domain. First, in the context of the British National Health Service (NHS) program, Becker [14] presented a formal policy for an electronic health record service. The second approach is i.s.h.med, which is a Siemens product based on SAP patient management. In both cases, traditional Role Based Access Control (RBAC) concepts are recognized as not sufficient for the application domain of health care scenarios. Thus, additionally to RBAC, a notion for expressing a relationship between patient and treating health care professional is introduced, and only if such a Treatment Relationship (TR) exists, the health record of the patient can be accessed. Taking a TR into account is a common approach, e. g., [19, 45].

We have explicitly chosen an AC model which cannot be classified as one standard AC model such as RBAC. In its basic representation, one could name it "RBAC/TR model." We will demonstrate Break-Glass along this scenario on top of the AC model used, but note that this is only done to demonstrate the application of our Break-Glass model along a concrete example: the presented Break-Glass approach does not rely on this underlying AC model or the scenario sketched in the running example.

1.2.1 Regular Use Case

In our running example, access is only permitted if there is an existing (ongoing) TR: patients (or agents, which are persons authorized by a patient to act on behalf of the patient) have to give their consent to a treatment. Health records have a header with labels which indicate the content, and prohibit physicians without the required qualification to see them (e. g., an eye specialist may not see the results of a gynecological investigation). Especially sensitive records (e. g., records containing information about an abortion or an attempted suicide) may be hidden ("*sealed*") and only become visible if the patient granted the right to see it to a specific physician or department, with exception of the creator of the record, who can always see records created by him. Nurses are permitted to view general information (e. g., name and birth date), work on administrative data (e. g., room number), and view medication data for the ward round in the morning, i. e., between 6 a.m. and 12 p.m. Physicians can create health records, but the header of a health record can only be modified by the creator. Headers which are not sealed can be seen by all physicians. The full entry can only be read and modified by physicians with the according qualification. Additionally, physicians have full access to medication data. Also for physicians, a TR has to exists in any case before the listed rules can be applied.

Those rules are used to formulate regular privileges: in the regular case, a patient comes to his General Practitioner (GP) or the hospital, giving his consent to a treatment, e. g., by providing his insurance card, and, potentially, a Personal Identification Number (PIN). From here, the patient may be referred to a specialist, requesting a diagnosis and thereby implicitly creating a TR. By this, the consulted specialist has the right to access the health record of the patient, and his nurse is allowed to see data required for administrative tasks (e. g., make an appointment or accounting purposes).

Regular privileges will allow access for such regular cases, and protect data from being accessed in other cases. However, there are a lot of scenarios which differ from the regular case. For example, suppose the following three scenarios which do not follow the regular case but are, however, in the best interest of the patient and should therefore be possible to execute:

Scenario 1: A patient is referred to another department within the hospital for an additional diagnosis. Usually, this referral is entered into the system, first, for accounting reasons, and, second, to document the TR with the consulted department in order to activate the required privileges. However, after a pileup on the motorway a lot of patients require immediate first treatment, and thus, the patient is sent on his way for the external diagnosis without entering this referral into the system and, therefore, no access rights are granted to the other department. Hence, at the other department no patient data can be viewed, and the diagnoses cannot be entered into the system.

Scenario 2: A patient comes to a casualty department in a hospital but he (or his agent) is not able to provide the required consent to establish the TR. There are a variety of reasons, e. g., he may not have his insurance card with him, he may be unconscious, there may be no (authorized) agent with him, the card reader may have a problem reading the card, etc. Thus, the patient cannot be registered with the system, and no data if the patient can be viewed or entered.

Scenario 3: A nurse has to prepare an infusion which has some ingredients
that are known to be capable of causing allergic reactions. Usually,
a doctor is responsible for determining a treatment and, therefore,
also has to check for a known allergy, but the physician is busy with
another urgent task and therefore (verbally) instructs the nurse to
make this check. As the nurse does not have the permissions to check
for a known allergy, she has to wait until a physician becomes available.

In all three exemplary cases, access will be denied as they are clearly
out-of-the-regular cases and are hence not covered by regular privileges. This
has the effect that, first, the patient will not receive the treatment he or she
needs, and, second, the data have to be entered later, e. g., for accounting
reasons, hereby causing additional effort.

As those accesses would serve the interest of the patient, it should be
possible to execute them. However, defining regular privileges which would
permit them is hard: first, it would require high effort to define all possible
exceptional situations beforehand. Second, it is hard to define machine
readable rules which cover all exceptional situations, e. g., an IT system
will hardly be in the position to detect if there is an unconscious patient,
determine his identity and create an according TR in the system. Also,
if there is an exceptional situation in a department justifying a specific
relaxation of policies, or if there is a verbal instruction from a physician to
a nurse, is hard to determine for an IT system.

Those scenarios should demonstrate that it is hard and expensive to
capture all possible deviations of the regular case, i. e., there may be situations
which cannot be foreseen (with reasonable effort), especially for seldom
executed processes or if the workflow changes frequently. But even if a
situation can be foreseen, for an IT system it may be hard to determine
if such a situation is currently ongoing or not. Furthermore, it is hard to
define actions which are capable to compensate the irregular situation (e. g.,
how could the IT system react if there is a problem with the card reader).

1.2.2 Break-Glass Use Case

The use of traditional AC mechanisms leaves the persons responsible for
protecting data with a hard choice. Either they define AC policies in a
potentially too restrictive way. This could cause harm to patients' health or,
in worst case, life. Or, they define the access control policies in a potentially
too lax way, i. e., allowing every access which could help in saving the patients'
health and life. But, in this case, the risk of disclosure of sensitive data is
high, risking their organization's reputation and compliance with legal rules.

Break-Glass provides the solution: regular privileges are defined to capture regular cases in a fine-grained manner as described above. Exceptional privileges are defined where it is not possible to decide beforehand if an access has to be permitted or denied. Note that this explicitly excludes privileges, where it can be decided beforehand that they must not be granted, from the exceptional privileges. We would like to demonstrate with three Break-Glass examples what such exceptional privileges and their integration in an application can look like:

Break-Glass Example 1: Break-Glass per Action

Like in scenario 1, suppose a physician, Carol, has to make a diagnosis for a physician from another department. However, as the requesting department is overburdened with work, the referral was not entered into the system as usual. Consequently, she does not have the required regular privileges to access the patient's data. Instead of being blocked due to missing privileges when accessing some required data, a Break-Glass notification is shown to Carol:

Missing privileges: the patient is currently under treatment in this hospital but not under you or your department. You can

- *Break the Glass and proceed immediately*
  WARNING: Your actions will be recorded, misuse will be punished!
- *Abort*

As Carol is aware of the fact that the referral was not entered into the system, and she is confident that the access is legitimate, she executes the request, i.e., breaks the glass. By doing so, the access is marked as Break-Glass access, i.e., causing an investigation in the post-access phase.

Break-Glass Example 2: Creating a Preliminary Assignment

Like in scenario 2, a patient, Bob, is brought to the casualty department in a hospital, but he cannot provide his consent for a TR as he is unconscious, and his wife as his agent is not available to give the consent for him. During first aid, the insurance and identity cards have been found. Therefore, a physician, Alice, is able to identify the patient. She decides to create an exceptional relationship and starts the according action in the user interface, receiving a notification

You have to provide a short statement why the patient consent is missing! WARNING: This and all follow-up actions will be recorded, misuse will be punished!

She provides a short statement that the patient is unconscious and there is no agent who could provide consent, and confirms the message. The system stores two things: first, Bob has an unconfirmed TR within the department of Alice, and, second, Alice has confirmed that she is working on a preliminary TR. After providing the required information and confirmation, Alice is able to see the patient's data as if a regular relationship would exist. As long as she is retrieving data based on the unconfirmed TR, her background is colored red.

During the treatment of Bob, another subject from the department of Alice, Carol, has to review some data about the patient. As she would have access if there was a regular TR, she receives a notification:

Warning: Patient consent is still missing! If you want to work with a preliminary assignment you have to confirm!

WARNING: This and all follow up actions will be recorded, misuse will be punished!

When Carol confirms this message, it is stored that, in addition to Alice, Carol has confirmed that she is working on a preliminary treatment. As for Alice, the background of her desktop is colored red.

Break-Glass Example 3: Requesting Override Information

Like in scenario 3, a nurse, Dave, follows the (verbal) order of a physician, Alice, and tries to check a patient's health record for known allergies. This is beyond his regular tasks and therefore not permitted. However, Break-Glass is possible, and he receives a notification:

You are not permitted to access the requested data. When breaking the glass, you are leaving your regular responsibilities and both the patient and your supervisor(s) will be notified. You can

- *Break the Glass and proceed immediately*
  WARNING: Your actions will be recorded, misuse will be punished!
- *Receive some override information before Breaking the Glass*
- *Abort*

As Dave is not sure if he should break the glass, he wants to receive some override information first and chooses the second option. As response, the system returns three users who are close to him and permitted to execute the requested task, giving him an idea how large his override would be. One of the people listed is Alice, the physician who gave him the order. Dave is now sure that he is acting correctly and leaves a message in the optional text field, stating that he is working on Alice's order.

1.2.3 Post-Access Investigations

Every single Break-Glass access will have to be investigated to detect misuse and therefore ensure that misbehaving users can be punished. For this, the investigator will have to inspect every single Break-Glass access and estimate if using Break-Glass was justifiable. If this has to be done without support from the authorization infrastructure, Break-Glass will cause high effort.

We will demonstrate how at least some Break-Glass accesses can be evaluated in an automated manner using policy-driven analysis. For example, an auditor will be able to sort out all Break-Glass accesses which are based on a preliminary TR, if a regular TR is established within the next, e. g., 24 hours. Also, once determined to be permissible, certain "types" of Break-Glass accesses will be evaluated in a more efficient way than if one would have to start from scratch.

1.3 Methodology

A commonly accepted paradigm for information system research is the *design science* approach as proposed by Hevner et al. [61]. Here, design science is characterized as "fundamentally a problem-solving paradigm" that "seeks to extend the boundaries of human and organizational capabilities by creating new and innovative artifacts." [61] Following the research questions discussed in section 10.2, this is what we want to achieve with this thesis. We follow Peffers et al. [84] by discussing how we implemented the six activies they present as design science methodology:

- *Problem identification and motivation:* The scientific problem and the need for a solution, i. e., the motivation to solve the problem, have to be presented.
- *Objectives for a solution:* The objectives for a solution has to be infered from the problem definition.
- *Design and development:* The contribution able to fulfill the presented requirements has to be developed, where contributions can be "constructs, models, methods, or instantiations" [84]. This includes the architecture and functionality of the solution.
- *Demonstration:* "Demonstrate the use of the artifact to solve one or more instances of the problem." [84]
- *Evaluation:* "Observe and measure how well the artifact supports a solution to the problem." [84]
- *Communication:* The problem, its relevance and the found solution have to be published.

Problem Identification and Motivation

We motivated the general problem in section 1.1, where we also identify the problems current AC techniques have with exceptional situations. As one of our objectives is to provide a generic Break-Glass model, we investigated the identified problem by doing a review and survey of the related work. This contains not only existing scientific contributions, but we also investigate case studies and available products.

Objectives for a Solution

Based on the related work, we present the requirements and principles for a holistic Break-Glass approach in section 3.1. Here, we will further detail the problems which have to be solved when providing both a generic Break-Glass model and a holistic Break-Glass approach. We will argue that, although a generic Break-Glass model helps in providing a holistic Break-Glass approach, the model itself does not define a complete solution, and define the requirements for a holistic approach.

Design and Development

In the Chapters 3 to 6 we will describe our core research contributions: our generic Break-Glass model (chapter 3) and how the four fundamental principles of Break-Glass (section 3.1) can be ensured throughout the whole lifecycle (Figure 3.1) of Break-Glass.

Pre-access (chapter 4), with *governance* we refer to the tolerated empowerment given to users. At-access (chapter 5), both the *accessibility* of Break-Glass for user, and the *awareness* of users that they are using exceptional mechanisms, have to be ensured. Post-access (chapter 6), it has to be possible to make user *accountable* for illegitimate accesses. All phases rely on the preceding phases and are based on the Break-Glass model.

Demonstration

We demonstrate the solution with the introduction of the corresponding concepts, i. e., within Chapters 3 to 6, along the running example presented in section 1.2. We furthermore present a prototypic implementation of the presented concepts in chapter 7.

Evaluation

Following [84], we compare the functionality of our approach with the solution objectives in section 9.1. The generalizability property of our approach is evaluated by, first, classifying existing work along our solution and demonstrate how our approach can be used to simulate existing Break-Glass models in chapter 8 and how they can be categorized (section 9.2). Second, we demonstrate how our Break-Glass model can be applied to existing AC models in section 9.3. We furthermore present a prototypic implementation in chapter 7.

Communication

We have published intermediate results in [27, 28, 29, 32, 33]. Furthermore, we are planning to publish subsequent papers discussing contributions not yet published on scientific conferences, workshops or journals.

1.4 Thesis Structure

After presenting the background in chapter 2, the main structure of this thesis is aligned with the life cycle of a Break-Glass access as depicted in Figure 3.1. chapter 3 will introduce a *generic Break-Glass model*. This model is the foundation for the following three phases: in the *pre-access* phase, described in chapter 4, we will show how to define Break-Glass policies. In the *at-access* phase, described in chapter 5, users have to be notified about the Break-Glass access, and information has to be recorded for post-access investigations. Finally, in the *post-access* phase Break-Glass accesses have to be investigated to separate legitimate from illegitimate accesses (chapter 6). Along this structure, three main concepts are introduced: the *generic Break-Glass model* in chapter 3, the differentiation of *policy permissions vs. policy state* in subsection 4.1.2, and the *versioning* concept in subsection 5.2.1.

Our generic Break-Glass model with the concept of *extension* and *refinement* relationships between policies and a *lattice evaluation algorithm* used to enforce those relationships is presented in chapter 3. The abstract Break-Glass model (section 3.2) is instantiated with the core model (section 3.3), which is based on positive (i. e., PERMIT) permissions. As extension to the core model, we define a constraints model (section 3.4) which allows to define both positive and negative (i. e., DENY) permissions (i. e., constraints). Naturally, the policy extension concept defined for the abstract model is valid for both the core and the constraints model.

While we see the abstraction from AC models for our generic Break-Glass framework in chapter 3 as the greatest possible abstraction, for the following three phases described in Chapters 4 to 6 we are introducing the differentiation between *policy permissions* and *policy state* (subsection 4.1.2). This allows to model all kinds of relationships and assignments, e. g., role assignments for assigning roles to users, relationships between patients and physicians for fine-grained authorization (subsection 4.1.5), or, assigning a "frame" which remains "broken" for a specific time-frame to implement stateful Break-Glass (subsection 4.2.3). The described policy state management (subsection 4.1.3) allows us to model administrative controls, i. e., the definition of a (meta) policy which controls changes to the policy.

The *versioning* concept (subsection 5.2.1) is introduced with the at-access phase to record at-access information and make it available post-access for analysis. Together with the policy state concept, versioning is the foundation for the techniques presented for the analysis infrastructure and the *policy-driven analysis* in chapter 6.

We will introduce the background of our work in chapter 2. In chapter 8 we will present the related work and discuss how existing approaches can be modeled with our approach. Furthermore, we will present a classification of Break-Glass in section 9.2.

We will present four lines of evaluation. First, the requirements identified for Break-Glass (section 3.1) will be compared with the properties of our solution in section 9.1. Second, we will compare our generalized Break-Glass Model with existing Break-Glass models in chapter 8, and classify them along our model in section 9.2. Third, to demonstrate the generalizability of our approach, we will apply Break-Glass to some existing AC models in section 9.3. Fourth, a prototypic implementation (chapter 7) shows the feasibility of the approaches presented in this thesis.

As core contributions we see our generic Break-Glass model which allows to implement Break-Glass independently from the underlying AC model as well as to represent a wide range of existing Break-Glass models, demonstrating that Break-Glass is an orthogonal concept and independent from any specific AC model. Our Break-Glass model is used along the whole life-cycle of a Break-Glass access, for which we introduce two further concepts. First, a distinction between *policy permissions* and *policy state* which allow to model privileges and administrative controls. Second, the concept of *versioning* allows to restore the security relevant system state for every point in time. We will discuss our contributions in more detail in chapter 10. Parts of this thesis have already been published, i. e., section 3.3 is based on [27], section 5.1 is based on [32], and section 6.2 is based on [29].

2 Background

In this chapter, we will introduce the background needed throughout this thesis. First, we will discuss some basic definitions in section 2.1. In section 2.2, we will introduce our generic notion of an Access Control (AC) model, some basic concepts, and some AC models that will be used in order to evaluate the generalizability of our approach. You may also have a look at Appendix A, presenting the terminology used in this thesis.

2.1 Information Security

This section summarizes some common security foundations and is based on Bishop *"Computer Security – Art and Science"* [25]. We will only sketch the most important concepts required later in this thesis, for a more complete discussion please refer to Bishop [25]. Please note that, for a consistent terminology, we will use terms as defined in Appendix A also for citations.

There are three principles which are considered to be the foundations for information security: confidentiality, integrity, and availability. We will follow Bishop [25] in the definition of those three concepts:

Definition 1. *Let S be a set of subjects and let R be some resource. Then R has the property of* confidentiality *with respect to S if no member of S can obtain information about R [25, p. 96].*

Informally, subjects being part of S are not allowed to see R, e. g., defining the set S as all entities not required to know R for their work. Thus, confidentiality is a principle "that information is not made available or disclosed to unauthorized individuals, entities, or processes" [1], where even knowledge over the existence of R is information about R.

Definition 2. *Let S be a set of subjects and let R be some information or a resource. Then R has the property of* integrity *with respect to S if all members of S trust R [25, p. 96].*

Informally, integrity is a principle "of safeguarding the accuracy and completeness of assets" [1]. It describes the trustworthiness subjects can have on resources or information. It can be applied in different ways, for example, as *data integrity* for information not changed on storage or not modified during transmission, or *origin integrity*, e. g., authenticity. Mechanisms to assure integrity fall into two classes: *prevention* mechanisms detect unauthorized changes at-access and can forestall unauthorized changes in the first place, i. e., *prevent* that the system moves to a state where integrity is hurt; *detection* mechanisms may detect unauthorized changes only post-access, i. e., that a system moves to a state where integrity is hurt can be *detected* but not prevented.

Definition 3. *Let S be a set of subjects and let R be a resource. Then R has the property of* availability *with respect to S if all members of S can access R [25, p. 96].*

Thus, availability describes the ability of subjects to consume resources as planned, i. e., is the principle "of being accessible and usable upon demand by an authorized entity" [1]. Unavailability may lead to unplanned and unintended behavior. Attempts to block availability, called Denial of Service (DoS) attacks, are not only hard to prevent, but it may also be hard to detect it, e. g., to differentiate between high load and an attack.

Definition 4. *A secure system is a system that starts in an authorized state and cannot enter an unauthorized state [25, p. 95].*

The abstract goal is to be able to make a system secure. Security policies define what is considered to be secure.

Definition 5. *A security policy is a statement that partitions the states of the system into a set of authorized, or secure, states and a set of unauthorized, or non-secure, states [25, p. 95].*

Business systems manage and use confidential data and hence, have to implement confidentiality, integrity, and availability. Thus, the overall goal is to make those systems *secure*, requiring *security policies* and according mechanisms to enforce those policies, i. e., to forestall that a system can reach an unauthorized state.

The most basic questions which have to be solved are who is authorized to observe (read) what to ensure confidentiality, and who is authorized to alter (write) what to ensure integrity.

Definition 6. Authentication *is the binding of an identity to a subject [25, p. 309].*

Authentication is a technique to ensure *origin integrity*, i. e., assure that the accessing subject can be identified unambiguously. The kind of authentication being sufficient has to be defined by the security policy, e. g., requiring username and password or an authentication with cryptographic means.

Definition 7. Authorization *or* Access Control (AC) *is a technique to ensure confidentiality and a prevention mechanisms for unauthorized changes, which is a subset of data integrity.*

AC contributes to two basic security concepts: confidentiality and integrity. AC does not necessarily cover full integrity, i. e., an access may be authorized but still violate data integrity. This is why AC models are sometimes divided into confidentiality, integrity, and hybrid models. Also, AC relies on authentication as the authorization is dependent on the accessing subject. We will discuss AC in more detail in section 2.2.

Definition 8. Accountability *or* non-repudiation *is a property which ensures that a subject cannot dispute to have executed some action.*

This general property can be ensured on different levels and by different means, e. g., using cryptography to create signatures, or logging actions without letting subjects alter those logs.

The implicit goal of AC is to fulfill the *least privilege principle*, i. e., defining security policies which implement least privilege. If additional rights for specific tasks are required, those should be relinquished immediately on completion [25].

Definition 9. *The* principle of least privilege *states that a subject should be given only those privileges that it needs in order to complete its task [25, p. 343].*

Another well-known (and in most cases implicitly applied) principle is the *default deny principle* which states that all accesses not explicitly permitted are implicitly denied per default. The inverse *default permit principle*, i. e., all accesses not explicitly denied are implicitly permitted per default, is technically possible but rather exotic.

2.2 Access Control

2.2.1 Concepts

Discretionary vs. Mandatory Access Control

One very common categorization of AC model properties (or "patterns" [94], or meta models) is the differentiation between Discretionary Access Control (DAC) and Mandatory Access Control (MAC). In DAC subjects have control over resources, i. e., the discretionary to delegate permissions to other subjects. Thus, a subject "may, at his own discretion, determine who is authorized to access the objects he creates" [94]. The Trusted Computer System Evaluation Criteria (TCSEC) [81] (also known as *Orange Book*) define that DAC "shall define and control access between named users [i. e., subjects] and named objects [i. e., resource] [...]. The enforcement mechanism [...] shall allow users to specify and control sharing of those objects." As concrete example for such a DAC enforcement mechanism the concept of groups as used in file systems is mentioned. In contrast, Mandatory Access Control (MAC) (sometimes called *Non-Discretionary Access Control*) does not give this discretionary, but defines controls that are not under the control of subjects. DAC and MAC are not AC models itself, but AC models can follow one or both of them, i. e., the distinction is a conceptual one.

The AC models used by an Operating System (OS), e. g., for permissions on files, are often considered to be DAC models: a resource (e. g., a file or process) created by a subject (e. g., a user or a process) is owned by the creating subject, which has full control over the resource, e. g., can destroy it or grant other subjects access to it. Every element can be both resource and subject, e. g., a user (resource) can be created by a process (subject), or a process (resource) can be created by a user (subject). A common example for a MAC model are Multi-Level Security (MLS) systems, for which the Bell-La Padula model discussed later is one of the most prominent examples. DAC and MAC can be combined: for example, the Bell-La Padula model explicitly defines both MAC and DAC controls[1]. An example for a MAC concept implemented in operating systems is that only root can open sockets on ports below port 1024.

---

[1]The Bell-La Padula model is commonly referred as pure MAC model, as the MAC part is precisely modeled and the DAC part could be exchanged as long as it meets some requirements.

Delegation

Barka and Sandhu [9] characterizes delegation as a process where "some active entity in a system delegates authority to another active entity in order to carry out some functions on behalf of the former." Zhang et al. [111] identify three types of delegations: 1. backup of role, i. e., if some job function needs to be maintained by others, e. g., during absence; 2. decentralization of authortransferedity, i. e., job functions are assigned from higher to lower job positions; 3. collaboration of work, i. e., grant each other permissions to shared resources. Crampton and Khambhammettu [42] distinguish between *grant* and *transfer* delegation. For grant delegation, both the delegator (i. e., the subject possessing some permission) and the delegatee (i. e., the subject receiving some permissions) hold the delegated permission. For transfer (or *proxy* [53]) delegation, the permission is transferred and not duplicated, i. e., the delegated permission is no longer available to the delegator. Furthermore, it has to be noted that between *administrative* and *user* delegation is differentiated, e. g., Firozabadi et al. [53] differentiate between the delegation of permissions and the delegation of the right to delegate permissions.

Overall, the concept of delegation allows to modify the rights of individuals at runtime and hence allows authorized subjects to adapt required permissions of other subjects according to the current, possibly exceptional, situation. Overall, delegation is a very powerful and broad concept. For example, DAC models implicitly implement a delegation concept, as the owner of a resource can define which other users may access this resource, i. e., he may delegate some permissions to others. Consequently, there are a wide variety of concepts and models how delegation can be modeled and implemented, which will not be discussed due to space limitations.

Separation of Duty

The Separation of Duty (SoD) principle states that two actions may not be executed by the same subject. Depending on the context, there may be a scope defined where this constraint has to be valid. In the context of process models, where SoD constraints are commonly defined, the scope can be a process instance, and the actions are tasks of the process. A common example for an SoD constraint is an invoice process, where the approval has to be implemented according to the *four eyes principle*, stating that two persons have to work on an invoice to be approved. Here, for the two tasks "acquire invoice" and "approve invoice" a SoD constraint can be defined, assuring the compliance with the four eyes principle.

AC models implementing SoD, e. g., Role Based Access Control (RBAC) as discussed in subsection 2.2.2, may differentiate between Static Separation of Duty (SSoD) and the more powerful Dynamic Separation of Duty (DSoD). For SSoD, it has to be assured that the defined privileges permit subjects to either execute the one or the other task. Thus, SSoD can be guaranteed through the assignment of permissions, and is static in the sense that it depends only on the permissions and not on the dynamic context of the application. While this does not cause overhead at runtime, it has limitations, as, e. g., there has to be a strict separation between salesmen creating invoices, and salesmen approving invoices. This is a harder constraint than the four eyes principle would require. Furthermore, in its strict interpretation the whole history of permission assignments has to be taken into account. This can cause problems when changing permissions (i. e., the assumption of static permissions does not hold), e. g., an employee moving from an executive to a controlling department. SSoD can be defined on top of, e. g., RBAC (discussed in the next subsection 2.2.2) by defining a SoD constraint between two roles. When assigning roles, it has to be assured that existing SoD constraints are not hurt.

In contrast, Dynamic Separation of Duty (DSoD) allows for more fine-grained definition of constraints, as a scope can be defined in which the constraints have to be enforced. This requires access to the system history, however, the system history may be implicitly or explicitly part of the system state (e. g., it is stored who created an invoice). Thus, to enforce DSoD at runtime, some contextual information (system history or system state) is required. For example, to ensure that the same subject cannot approve and create an invoice, it may be saved who created an invoice. The concepts of the Chinese Wall model [26] (separate resources to avoid conflict of interest) can be interpreted as implementing the SoD concept. As SoD is not in the discretion of subjects, SoD is a MAC pattern [41].

Binding of Duty (BoD) is a related concept and in some sense the opposite. It states that if one task was executed by a subject, another task has to be executed by the same subject. There is no differentiation between static and dynamic BoD, as static BoD does not make sense as it would require that permissions can only assigned to a single subject.

Obligations

We are using obligations are a concept to express conditions which have to be met but cannot be enforced by the decision making, central authority, and hence have to be enforced in a distributed way. An important distinction is the point in time when an obligation is enforced. *Pre-obligations* [39, 95] can and have to be enforced before the access. *Post-obligations* on the other hand can only be fulfilled after the access. Here, the system needs to monitor the fulfillment or satisfaction of obligations and take consequences or compensatory actions if this is not the case [23]. A related concept is the *advice*, introduced with XACML 3.0. An advice only defines what could be done, i. e., advices do not have to be enforced. This allows to model "hints" for client applications, i. e., the enforcing component may (but is not bound to) enforce the advice.

2.2.2 Access Control Models

There are a lot of AC models, both in scientific literature and commercial products. Providing a complete overview and comparison of all existing AC models would clearly exceed the frame and scope of this work. Thus, we tried to pick some models to represent some aspects of existing models. We are aware of the fact that this reflects a personal opinion. However, it is sometimes argued that all AC models can be reduced to a common basis, e. g., see [10, 35, 59] for publications dealing with this research question. We will now define a rather abstract definition of AC models.

In general, AC models describe how to map an AC request $Q \in \mathcal{Q}$ to an AC response $N \in \mathcal{N}$, i. e., $\mathcal{Q} \rightarrow \mathcal{N}$. A request Q typically contains the triple (S, R, A), with subject $S \in \mathcal{S}$, resource $R \in \mathcal{R}$, and action $A \in \mathcal{A}$. However, a request may contain fewer or further elements, depending on the concrete AC model. A response N comprises usually $\mathcal{D} \times 2^{\mathcal{O}}$, i. e., consists of a decision $D \in \mathcal{D}$ and, optionally, a, possibly empty, set of obligations $2^{\mathcal{O}} \subseteq \mathcal{O}$. We require the set $\mathcal{D}$ to contain at least the two distinctive elements PERMIT and DENY, i. e., $\{\text{PERMIT}, \text{DENY}\} \subseteq \mathcal{D} \wedge \text{PERMIT} \neq \text{DENY}$.

For the evaluation of a request Q, the

- security state $\sigma_{\text{sec}} \in \Sigma_{\text{sec}}$ captures the security relevant state of the system (i. e., the AC configuration), where σ_{sec} is an instance out of all possible security states Σ_{sec} accepted by the AC model,
- system state $\sigma_{\text{sys}} \in \Sigma_{\text{sys}}$ captures the functional state of the application or system, e. g., the formalized state of the environment, where σ_{sys} is

a concrete instance out of all possible system states Σ_{sys} accepted by the AC model,

may be required. Hence, one can define the implementation of an AC model as Access Control Function (ACF) taking a request Q, security state σ_{sec} and system state σ_{sys} as input, and returning an AC decision D with optionally a set of obligations $2^{\mathcal{O}}$, i.e.,

$$\text{ACF} : \mathcal{Q} \times \Sigma_{sec} \times \Sigma_{sys} \rightarrow \mathcal{D} \times 2^{\mathcal{O}} \tag{2.1}$$

An AC model may further define a way to define *administrative controls*. Such administrative controls (or administrative policies) allow to change the behavior of the ACF by changing the security state σ_{sec}.

Definition 10. *An* administrative control *regulates changes to the security relevant system state, i.e., defines controls for policy administration.*

Thus, we define a more general ACF_a:

$$\text{ACF}_a : \mathcal{Q} \times \Sigma_{sec} \times \Sigma_{sys} \rightarrow \mathcal{D} \times 2^{\mathcal{O}} \times \Sigma_{sec} \tag{2.2}$$

ACF_a allows to transform the security state into a new security state. For AC models which consider administrative controls as outside of the primary AC model, the ACF is sufficient. AC models using administrative controls are, e.g., models using delegation mechanisms which includes DAC models.

Access Control Matrix

The "simplest framework for describing a protection system" [25] is the *access control matrix model*, first introduced by Lampson [69] and refined by Graham and Denning [58], which we will describe here. In this model, permissions $P \subseteq \mathcal{P}$ for every subject $S \in \mathcal{S}$ on every resource $R \in \mathcal{R}$ are stored in a two-dimensional matrix M. Rows are labeled by subject names, and columns by resource names, i.e., $M[S, R]$ specifies the permissions of subject S upon resource R. Subjects are also treated as resources. The set of available permissions $\mathcal{P}$ which can be assigned depends on the applied context, common examples are *read, write, append, execute, owner* and *control*. One subject may get assigned several permissions $P \in \mathcal{P}$ for one resource, thus, the fields of the matrix contains a subset $P \subseteq \mathcal{P}$, e.g., {*read, write*}, or an empty set if the subject does not have any permissions on the corresponding resource.

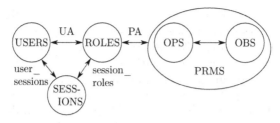

Figure 2.1: The Core RBAC model [2].

For administering the entries in M, the access control matrix follows the DAC pattern. Permissions $P \in \mathscr{P}$ can be marked with the *copy-flag*. The two permissions $\{owner, control\} \in \mathscr{P}$ have a special meaning. The copy-flag, denoted as asterisk $*$, allows a subject to copy (i. e., delegate) permissions to another subject. The permission *owner* for a resource R allows the holder of this permission to delegate and retract any permission to and from all other subject for this resource R. The permission *control* can be assigned only to fields in $M[S, R]$ where R is a subject, and allows to retract any permission from the controlled subject. The term Access Control List (ACL) refers to an approach to store the column of the matrix with the resource it protects, the term Identity Based Access Control (IBAC) can be used to characterize models managing privileges on an individual (subject) basis [63].

Role Based Access Control

Role Based Access Control (RBAC) is a well-known and established access control model, both in research and commercial systems [55]. While the concept of RBAC was already existing (e. g., Ferraiolo and Kuhn [49]), the most citet publication regarding RBAC is Sandhu et al. defining RBAC defined in [96] (RBAC96), which can be seen as the basis for the American National Standards Institute (ANSI) RBAC standard [2]. The general idea of RBAC is to group permissions (i. e., the right to execute a specific action on a specific resource) in *roles*, so that the (technical) RBAC roles reflect the (organizational) roles people can take in an organization. [2] defines four model components:

Core RBAC (see Figure 2.1) defines the fundamental data elements: subjects (USERS) are assigned to roles (ROLES), defining the user assignment (UA). Permissions (PRMS) are the approval to perform actions (operations/OPS) on resources (objects/OB), and are assigned to roles, defining the permission assignment (PA). Sessions (SESSIONS) define an activated subset of roles for a user.

Hierarchical RBAC extends Core RBAC with a notion of a role hierarchies (RH) defining inheritance relations upon roles. If role r_1 inherits from r_2, the permissions of r_1 are a superset of the permissions of r_2, i.e., $r_1 \geq r_2$. If r_1 (r_2) is the *immediate descendant* (*ascendant*) of r_2 (r_1), one can write $r_1 \gg r_2$. By convention, a diagram would show the more powerful (*senior*) role r_1 towards the top, and the less powerful (*junior*) role r_2 towards the bottom [96]. The *General Role Hierarchy* allows to define an arbitrary partial order (i.e., allowing for multi inheritance), whereas the *Limited Role Hierarchy* allows only a single immediate descendant and is therefore not supporting multiple inheritance[2].

Static Separation of Duty (SSoD) RBAC defines constraints on the user assignment (UA), i.e., SSoD prevents the assignment of roles to users which would hurt a SoD constraint. Thus, SSoD can be enforced at configuration time by administrative controls.

Dynamic Separation of Duty (DSoD) RBAC defines constraints on the activation of roles and therefore the assignment to SESSIONS, i.e., DSoD prevents the activation of a role which would hurt a SoD constraint. SSoD RBAC and DSoD RBAC can be subsumed under the term Constrained RBAC. For both SSoD and DSoD, the constraints allow to define a role set rs and a number $n, n \geq 2$, and no user may possess n roles out of rs at the same time. For example, rs could be defined as r_1, r_2, and $n = 2$. For SSoD, no user may have assigned both r_1 and r_2 in UA. In case of DSoD he may not activate both r_1 and r_2 for a session.

There are a number of further models which extend RBAC with further concepts, e.g., obligations [112], or allow to define different types of constraints, e.g., [3, 20, 21, 105]. Fuchs et al. [55] provide a survey about vast amount of RBAC-based models. For this thesis, we will limit ourself to [2] due to space reasons.

Multi-Level Security

Multi-Level Security (MLS) models follow the MAC pattern, its most prominent example is the Bell-La Padula model (although it is not a pure MLS model and therefore not a pure MAC system). The original conceptual

---

[2]There are some errors in the formal definition of [2] reported by, e.g., Li et al. [70]. We cited the corrected definitions.

model presented in La Padula and Bell [68] (based on the mathematical foundations presented in Bell and La Padula [15]) was adapted to be able to implement the needs of the Multics OS [18] resulting in what is considered today as the Bell-La Padula model [16].

The Bell-La Padula model maps a request Q with (S, R, A), consisting of subject S, resource R, and action (access attribute) A, to a decision D (i. e., a response N without obligations) with $D \in \{\text{PERMIT}, \text{DENY}, \text{ERROR}, ?\}$. Two types of access are differentiated: *observe* (i. e., extraction of information) and *alter* (i. e., insertion of information), resulting in four actions (access attributes) $\{A_r, A_a, A_w, A_e\} = \mathscr{A}$:

- A_r (read): observation with no alteration,
- A_a (append): alteration with no observation,
- A_w (write): both observation and alteration, and
- A_e (execute, or sometimes empty): neither observation nor alteration

In the Bell-La Padula model, MAC and DAC patterns are combined, and both, the MAC and the DAC part have to permit the access. For DAC, an access control matrix records the permissions in which a subject is permitted to access a resource. The AC matrix entries are a subset of $\mathscr{A}$, i. e., $A \in \mathscr{A}$ corresponds to $P \subseteq \mathscr{P}$. Also, any interpretation or other form of an access control matrix which records all the necessary information is acceptable.

The MAC part defines security levels. Informally, the goal is to ensure that, first, subjects can read information only from their security level or below and, second, forestall *information flow* from higher to lower levels. More formally, a security level L consists out of two parts (C, K):

- the classification (or clearance or sensitivity) $C \in \mathscr{C}$, where $\mathscr{C}$ is a linear (i. e., totally) ordered set $\mathscr{C} = \{C_1, C_2, ..., C_q\}$ with $C_1 > C_2 > ... > C_q$, and
- categories $K \subseteq \mathscr{K}$ are a set of labels $\mathscr{K} = \{K_1, K_2, ..., K_r\}$.

A security level L_u *dominates* L_v, written $L_u \infty L_v$, if and only if $C_u \geq C_v$ and $K_u \supseteq K_v$. The relation ∞ defines a partial order (i. e., a lattice) on all security levels $L \in \mathscr{L}$. Note that the lattice is defined through (and can be derived from) the definition of $\mathscr{C}$ and $\mathscr{K}$.

Informally, one can read $L_u \infty L_v$ as "L_u has at least the same or a higher security level as L_v." For example, let us assume a set of classifications: *top secret* (C_{TS}), *secret* (C_S), *confidential* (C_C), and *unclassified* (C_U) with $C_{TS} > C_S > C_C > C_U$. Furthermore assume categories for *Air Force* (K_A), *Navy* (K_N), and *Coast Guard* (K_C), i. e., $\mathscr{C} = \{K_A, K_N, K_C\}$. A security level $(C_S, \{K_A, K_C\})$ dominates security levels where both classification and categories are dominated, e. g., $(C_S, \{K_A\})$, $(C_C, \{K_A, K_C\})$, or $(C_S, \{K_A, K_C\})$, but does hence neither dominate $(C_{TS}, \{K_A, K_C\})$ nor

$(C_C, \{K_N, K_C\})$. The security level $(C_{TS}, \{K_A, K_N, K_C\})$ dominates all
other security levels.

Subjects and resources are assigned to a security level L. The maximum
security level of a subject S_i is denoted as $f_S(S_i)$, the security level of a
resource R_j is denoted as $f_R(R_j)$. Based on this, there are two properties
defined:

- The *simple security property* or *ss-property* states that for every *observing* request $Q(S, R, A)$ (i. e., where $A \in \{A_r, A_w\}$) the security level of the subject must dominate the security level of the resource, i. e., $f_S(S) \infty f_R(R)$. Thus, a subject cannot read information from higher levels. This is why the ss-property is described as *no reads up*.

- The *⋆-property* states that for every subject S having simultaneous alter access to a resource R_a and observe access to a resource R_o, $f_R(R_a) \infty f_R(R_o)$ has to hold, i. e., the security level of the altered resource R_a has to dominate the security level of the observed resource R_o. Thus, if information can be observed from one resource, it must not be possible to copy this information to a resource on a lower level, hence the ⋆-property is described as *no writes down*.

As the ⋆-property has to be valid for all simultaneous observe and alter
accesses, during the implementation for the Multics OS it became obvious
that the ⋆-property causes multiple checks at runtime to ensure this property.
"Based on an engineering short cut" [18], every subject S has a *current
security level*, denoted as $f_C(S)$. While the ss-property is not affected by
this change, the ⋆-property can be refined to:

- $f_S(S) \infty f_C(S)$, i. e., the maximum security level of the subject must dominate the current security level of the subject.
- For observation with no alteration (A_r): $f_C(S) \infty f_R(R)$, i. e., the current security level of the subject must dominate the resource security level.
- For alteration with no observation (A_a): $f_R(R) \infty f_C(S)$, i. e., the resource security level must dominate the current security level of the subject.
- For both observation and alteration (A_w), both conditions for A_r and A_a have to be valid, hence, $f_R(R) = f_C(S)$, i. e., the resource security level has to be the same as the current security level of the subject.

For the implementation of the Multics OS, the ⋆-property still caused
problems for processes such as a scheduler, as it needs write access on
processes with different levels (and therefore violating $f_R(R) = f_C(S)$ for
A_w). For this, *trusted subjects* are not subjected to the restrictions under
the original ⋆-property. Still, trusted subjects must not copy information

from higher to lower levels, i. e., are not involved in "communication paths." Informally, a process can be made a trusted subject, if it can be split into sub tasks which individually do not violate the $\star$-property.

Clark-Wilson Model

While MLS models are considered as confidentiality models, the Clark-Wilson model [41] is considered as integrity model. There are further common integrity models such as the the Biba model [24], or Lipner's integrity matrix model [72]. We will discuss the Clark-Wilson model as representative for integrity models, as it is the most recent and most citet one, and it "models many commercial systems more realistically than previous models," [25], i. e., there is a close relationship to today's Business Process Models (BPMS). Furthermore, we will need this model to discuss one of the contribution in the related work, i. e., see discussion of Povey [87] in section 9.3.

Two notes regarding integrity models: first, it is often argued that models implementing confidentiality are required for military scenarios, whereas models implementing integrity are for commercial application. We see this more as a rough distinction of the main focus of a model rather than an exclusive ability. Second, it is sometimes challenged if integrity models are AC models or rather an orthogonal concept, as authorization is sometimes only considered as not violating confidentiality. However, we see authorization as a subset of integrity (see Definition 7).

The model presented in Clark and Wilson [41] is, in essence, designed to forestall fraud and error, and is based on two core concepts: the Separation of Duty (SoD) principle (see section 2.2.1) and transactions, which are considered to be the basic operations. Here, transaction does not only include the concept of an atomic operation (e. g., during a transaction the system may be in an invalid state), but also the logging and recording of changes to critical data for later investigations, e. g., as done with double entry bookkeeping. SoD is needed as a computer system cannot gather information from the real world, but rely on users to provide correct information. While SoD cannot eliminate fraud, as employees may collude, it still "has proved very effective in practical control of fraud." [41]

They define four basic requirements for a system to assure integrity:[3]
1. authenticate subjects so that their actions can be controlled and audited;

---

[3]In 1987, Clark and Wilson talk about programs which could be seen as the equivalents to tasks or transactions in today's Business Process (BP) and Enterprise Resource Planning (ERP) systems. Also, the "data center" can be seen as the (central) authority managing such a BP system.

2. specific resources can be manipulated only through a restricted set of tasks, where a central authority can ensure that those meet the well-formed transaction rules; 3. authorization is done on the level of tasks, where the authority can ensure that the defined SoD constraints are met; and 4. the system must log which subject executed which task. Furthermore, Clark and Wilson define two further requirements they have in common with confidentiality models: 1. the system must contain mechanisms ensuring that the security requirements are enforced; and 2. those mechanisms must be protected against tampering or unauthorized changes, i. e., providing administrative controls. Thus, to ensure integrity, data can only be manipulated by specific tasks, which have to stick to specific rules. Subjects user are not permitted to manipulate a data item directly, but only authorized to execute tasks. Thus, instead of defining controls on data directly, "the user is constrained by what programs he can execute, and the manner in which he can read or write data items is implicit in the actions of those programs" [41]. Based on this, four terms are introduced:

- *Constrained Data Items* (CDI) are resources under integrity control.
- *Unconstrained Data Items* (UDI) are resource not under integrity control.
- *Integrity Verification Procedures* (IVP) can test that CDIS comply to (integrity) contraints, i. e., check if the system is in a *valid state*.
- *Transformation Procedures* (TP) implement well-formed transactions, i. e., change the system from one valid state to another. Operations may result in an inconsistent state, but (well-formed) transaction must preserve consistency.

Based on these four elements, nine rules (five *Certification* and four *Enforcement* rules) are defined, which ensure that integrity constraints defined upon TPs can be enforced. The general idea is that TPs are certified to manipulate specific CDIs, i. e., ensure the IVPs to be successful, and log changes to an append-only log-CDI. The system has to maintain a list, defining which (authenticated) subject is authorized to execute which TP on which CDI, and enforce those authorizations. Both, the certification of TPs, and the maintenance of the list, i. e., the administrative controls, have to ensure integrity constraints.

Attribute Based Access Control

For Attribute Based Access Control (ABAC), there is no commonly accepted definition as for RBAC. In ABAC, privileges on resources are granted based on attributes assigned to subjects, and hence allows to decouple the AC decision from the identity of the accessing subject: the AC decision relies solely on "properties" the subject has, and not on its identity. Although this concept makes ABAC especially relevant in the context of web services [67, 106], ABAC can be seen as generalization of other AC models [63, 88]. Hu et al. [63] characterize the key difference between ABAC and other models such as RBAC or ACL as "the concept of policies that express a complex Boolean rule set that can evaluate many different attributes." [63] The eXtensible Access Control Markup Language (XACML) as one of the most prominent languages expressing ABAC policies will be discussed later in subsection 2.2.4.

Attribute-based Encryption

Attribute-based Encryption (ABE) [22, 92] is an asymmetric cryptographic primitive which generalizes Identity-based Encryption (IBE) [56]: while in IBE, a user is described by a single string associated with his identity, in ABE a group of receivers is described by a combination of several descriptive attributes. User are "described" by such attributes (e. g., job description and status) and receive the private keys related to those attributes. For encryption, attributes can be combined in logical and $\wedge$ and logical or $\vee$ expressions and hence formulate an attribute policy. The cryptographic primitive ensures that data can only be decrypted if the receiver fulfills the attribute policy, i. e., has (the private keys to) a set of attributes which can fulfill the boolean expression.

In current ABE implementations, the policy itself is cryptographically bound to the data object, but can still be read by any receiver [86]. Moreover, using ABE, a sender does not need to know the public keys of the recipients. Thus, messages can be encrypted before any receiver must own the required decryption keys. Albeit, a trusted third party, called attribute authority, must be able to produce any possible private key. Thus, ABE allows to implement sticky policies which can be enforced by cryptographic means.

2.2.3 Distributed Access Control Systems

In distributed systems, the making of decisions and their enforcement is split into components distributed throughout the system (see Figure 2.3). A coarse-grained distinction is to separate the Policy Decision Point (PDP), i. e., the component implementing the Access Control Function (ACF) and returning an AC decision, and the Policy Enforcement Point (PEP), which enforces the AC decision within the protected application. The PEP is

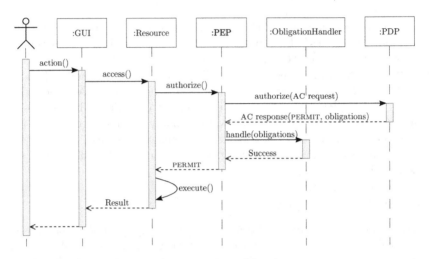

Figure 2.2: An access control request granted by the PDP.

embedded into the application context, queries the PDP for an AC decision and enforces the returned response, eventually including obligations.

At runtime, users have to be authenticated, i.e., the accessing subject has to be identified (see Definition 6, p.16). Here, different approaches can be used. For examples, user credentials can be stored locally at the protected resource or checked with a central Identity Provider (IDP), e.g., using Single Sign On (SSO) protocols such as Security Assertion Markup Language (SAML) (www.oasis-open.org/committees/security) or OpenID (openid.net), or protocols for distributed identity management such as the System for Cross-domain Identity Management (SCIM) (simplecloud.info). We will not discuss authentication in more detail, but only assume that subjects can be authenticated in a way so that the PEP can use authentication information to formulate AC requests.

Figure 2.2 shows the sequence of an access as it is handled by PEP and PDP. The user triggers an action in the Graphical User Interface (GUI) which causes an access to some resource. The resource uses a PEP to check if the request is permitted. There may be implementation variants where the PEP is implemented, e.g., as filter which enforces AC decisions before the resource is accessed. In case the response from the PDP contains some obligations, the PEP has to trigger the enforcement by the obligation handler. If the AC decision is PERMIT and all obligations can be enforced, access can be granted, otherwise, access should be denied and a corresponding message should be

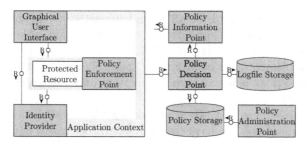

Figure 2.3: A distributed security architecture.

displayed to the user. There may be variants how AC decisions beyond PERMIT and DENY have to be enforced, and how obligations are handled which depend on the actual AC model and implementation. Furthermore, there may be variants how the PDP resolves context information from the policy storage and the Policy Information Point (PIP). We will discuss such a flow along Figure 4.4 in subsection 4.1.2.

The PDP, as implementing component of the ACF, requires two types of information: first, the security state σ_{sec}, i.e., an AC configuration such as AC policies, role assignments, etc., which are stored in the Policy Storage (see Figure 2.3). Second, the system state σ_{sys}, i.e., information about the state of the application, other systems or the state of the environment, provided by the Policy Information Point (PIP). The PDP *resolves* σ_{sec} and σ_{sys} information as required during evaluation, e.g., following a poll approach. The PDP's AC decision is returned to the PEP. The Obligation Handler (being part of the PEP) will enforce the obligations attached to the AC decision. The Policy Administration Point (PAP) is used to administer the policy storage, e.g., change the rules, or add new role assignments, and administrative controls have to be enforced. AC requests and particularly changes to the security state – stored in the policy storage – have to be logged. In section 4.1 we will discuss how the PDP can resolve security state (σ_{sec}) and system state (σ_{sys}) information at runtime.

2.2.4 XACML

The eXtensible Access Control Markup Language (XACML) is a general purpose language for expressing and querying AC policies, i.e., implementing the ACF and defining how to formulate a request Q for this ACF. XACML is standardized by the Organization for the Advancement of Struc-

tured Information Standards (OASIS) and currently in version 2.0 [80], for
version 3.0 a preliminary Committee Specification is available (www.oasis-
open.org/committees/xacml/). XACML is designed to be generic (i. e., it
allows the implementation of various AC models or combinations thereof),
and extensible (i. e., new data types, functions and combining algorithms
can be defined).

In this thesis, we use XACML as technical implementation to demonstrate
the concepts discussed: we have chosen XACML because it is widly known,
open source implementations are available, and we want to demonstrate that
our approach can be implemented with minor effort using an existing policy
language and implementation.

The XACML standard defines the policy language and the query language,
both based on the Extensible Markup Language (XML). In XACML, information contained in the AC request, and about the environment and its state
(i. e., request Q, security state σ_{sec}, and system state σ_{sys}) are modelled as
attributes. The data flow model is rather abstract, as the integration of how
to retrieve attributes depends on the application context and is therefor not
defined. Because of XACML's generic approach it main components such as
PEP and PDP follow the principles discussed in the last subsection 2.2.3.

XACML Policy Language

Central element of an XACML policy is the `<Rule>`. Rules have an effect,
which can either be a PERMIT or a DENY. The `<Target>` and an optional
`<Condition>` define if a rule should be applied, i. e., contribute to the result.
Rules are combined via a rule combining algorithm to a `<Policy>`, policies and
policy sets are combined via a policy combing algorithm to a `<PolicySet>`,
and policy sets again can be combined to a policy set. Policies, policy
sets and, with version 3.0, rules can have `<Obligation>`s. PEPs enforcing
obligations can be PERMIT or DENY biased, i. e., if a PERMIT decision for
which not all obligations can be fulfilled or understood should be handled as
PERMIT or DENY.

Like most languages written in XML, XACML is very chatty, as you
can see along Listing C.1 in Appendix C. This Listing shows an XACML
2.0 policy modeling an aspect of the running example we introduced in
section 1.2: physicians are permitted to read a health record if a patient
gave his consent either to the physician or the physicians department. As
this lengthy notation is hard to read and takes a lot of space, we will use a
reduced representation throughout this thesis as shown in Listing 2.1 and
discuss the sample policy along both representations.

The `<Target>` definition in line 7 in Listing C.1 (line *(2)* in Listing 2.1) defines that the `<PolicySet>` with id `health-record` only contains rules for requests which have a resource-id that starts with `urn:health-record`. The `<ResourceAttributeDesignator>` in line 11 resolves the attribute `urn:oasis:⏎ names:tc:xacml:1.0:resource:resource-id` from the current context, e. g., as defined in the current request or, if not submitted with the request, from the PIP. The flag `MustBePresent` is true, which causes the evaluation result in an error (i. e., the policy will return `Indeterminate` as result) if this attribute cannot be resolved. If the access resource starts with the defined Uniform Resource Identifier (URI), the `<ResourceMatch>` matches to true, and, as no other matches are required, causes the `<Target>` to match. The `<Target>` in line 26 *(5)* defines that the `<Policy>` with id `health-record:physician` only contains rules for the role `physician`. As the role is an attribute of the accessing subject, a `<SubjectAttributeDesignator>` is used to retrieve the corresponding values, and, therefore, is defined within a `<SubjectMatch>`. For the reduced XACML representation in Listing 2.1 we use a simpler target definition: matching a specific resource (line 3), the subject has to have a specific role (line 6), or if a specific action is executed (line 8).

Attribute designators always return a bag of values, e. g., for the `<Subject⏎ AttributeDesignator>` in line 33 all roles of the accessing subject are returned. In subsection 4.1.2 we will present an approach how to manage and store the values for the attributes resolved by attribute designators. The `MatchId` `urn:oasis:names:tc:xacml:1.0:function:string-equal` is executed for every resolved value. The `<SubjectMatch>` evaluates to true, if any execution of the `MatchId` evaluates to true. One can define multiple elements within a `<Target>`, where the direct sub-elements are combined with *and*, i. e., if `<Subjects>`, `<Actions>` and `<Resources>` are defined, all have to match. Sub-elements of those are combined with *or*, e. g., for multiple `<Action>` elements within `<Actions>` only one has to match. Match elements within those (e. g., `<ActionMatch>` within `<Actions>`) are combined with *and*, i. e., all have to match.

The target definition of rules are the same as for policies and policy sets: the `<Rule>` in line 55 *(7)* matches if the action is `read`. Additional to a target definition, rules can have an optional `<Condition>`. Conditions have to contain an expression with a return value of type boolean (`http://www.w3.org/2001/XMLSchema#boolean`), i. e., an attribute designator, an `<Apply>` or a `<VariableReference>` element. An `<Apply>` element executes a function (defined by the `FunctionId` attribute) and may take multiple parameters. Functions should not retrieve any information from the context as this should be done by attribute designators. Thus, a function without parameter

```
   <PolicySet CombiningAlg="permit-overrides">
    <Target><Resource>
3     health-record*</Resource></Target>
    <Policy CombiningAlg="first-applicable">
     <Target><Role>
6      physician</Role></Target>
     <Rule Effect="Permit">
      <Target><Action>read</Action></Target>
9      <Condition FunctionId="or">
       <Apply FunctionId="any-of-any">
        <Function FunctionId="string-equal"/>
12        <SubjAttr>subject-id</SubjAttr>
        <ResrcAttr>treating-physician</ResrcAttr>
        <Apply>
15        <Apply FunctionId="any-of-any">
        <Function FunctionId="string-equal"/>
        <SubjAttr>department</SubjAttr>
18        <ResrcAttr>treating-department</ResrcAttr>
      <Apply></Condition></Rule>
    </Policy>
21    <PolicyRef>health-record:nurse</PolicyRef>
    <Policy CombiningAlg="first-applicable">
     <Rule Effect="Deny"/>
24  </Policy></PolicySet>
```

Listing 2.1: The XACML policy as in Listing C.1 in a reduced representation: physicians are permitted to read a health record if the
patient gave his consent to the physician or the physicians
department.

does not make sense as it could only return a static value, which should be
encoded as attribute value. The XACML standard provides a wide variety of
functions including boolean functions, comparison functions for all supported
data types, mathematical operations, regular expressions, and higher order
functions. Furthermore, custom functions can be defined, e. g., as we did with
the function urn:custom:uri-starts-with used for the target definitions. In
our example, an or function urn:oasis:names:tc:xacml:1.0:function:or in
line 76 *(9)* combines the (boolean) results of a <VariableReference> from line
78 and a higher order function from line 81 *(15)*. A <VariableDefinition>
(line 41) allows to define "variables" once, and reference them – within one
policy – with a <VariableReference> (line 78) several times.

The higher order function `urn:oasis:names:tc:xacml:1.0:function:any-⏎ of-any` takes one `<Function>` and two bags as function parameters. The any-of-any function returns true, if for any of the elements of the first bag any element of the second bag can be found, for which the defined function evaluates to true. The `<Condition>` in our example evaluates to true if either the subject-id is on the list of physicians the patient gave his consent (`<Apply>` on line 42 *(10)* referenced by the `<VariableReference>` on line 78), if the subject is active in a department the patient gave his consent to (`<Apply>` on line 81 *(15)*).

`<PolicyIdReference>` elements, like the one in line 96 *(21)* allow to reference policies which are defined somewhere else. This could be used to, e. g., use one sub policy several times, or to structure and spread policies over multiple files. The final policy on line 97 *(22)* denies all requests which have not been granted so far. An empty `<Target/>` definition, as used for both policy and rule of the final policy, matches every request. For the reduced representation as in Listing 2.1 we do not even write the empty `<Target/>` definition. The decision returned by this policy does not have to be the final AC decision returned by the PDP as this policy set may be combined with other policies or policy sets which may overwrite the result of this policy set.

The `<PolicySet>` in our example uses the *permit-overrides* combining algorithm (line 4 *(1)*): if the policy with Identifier (ID) `health-record:physician` (line 22 *(4)*) denies the request, the policy with ID `health-record:nurse` (line 96 *(21)*) is evaluated and, if returning PERMIT, the `<PolicySet>` returns permit. The `<Policy>` uses the *first-applicable* combining algorithm (23, *4*), i. e., the first element where both target and condition match provides the decision. Other algorithms defined by the XACML standard are *deny-overrides* (ordered and unordered), *permit-overrides* (ordered and unordered), and *only-one-applicable* for both policies and rules. Ordered algorithms have to evaluate the elements as defined in the policy, whereas unordered algorithms can evaluate the elements in any arbitrary order (e. g., for performance reasons). The algorithms for rules (i. e., rule combining algorithms used in policies) and policies (i. e., policy combining algorithms used in policy sets) are very similar and differ mainly in the error handling. One can define custom combining algorithms.

XACML Query Language

The XACML query language allows to formulate AC requests sent to a PDP where attributes describe the request. There are a number of standardized attributes, e. g., `subject-id`, `resource-id`, and `action-id`. Additionally, one can define further attributes as required by application specific policies, e. g., `role` or `patient-id`. As result the PDP may return PERMIT, DENY, NOTAP-PLICABLE (signaling that no decision could be found), or INDETERMINATE (signaling that there was an error during evaluation, some details may be contained in the response). Attached to the result a list of obligations may be returned, where each obligation may have attached a list of attributes.

3 A Generic Break-Glass Model

Our contributions are presented along the life cycle of a Break-Glass access as depicted in Figure 3.1: the Chapters 4-6, where the *pre-*, *at-*, and *post-access* phases of Break-Glass are presented, are based on our Break-Glass model presented in this chapter. In section 3.1, we will discuss the requirements constituting the characteristics of Break-Glass. Throughout the thesis, we will show how those requirements can be implemented. We will introduce our abstract Break-Glass model in section 3.2. The abstract model will be instantiated with two implementations: the core Break-Glass model in section 3.3 is based on our publication [27] and defines privileges only with positive, i. e., PERMIT, permissions; and the constraints Break-Glass model in section 3.4 which also allows to define constraining, i. e., DENY, permissions.

3.1 Requirements of Break-Glass

The here presented requirements are the consolidation of requirements and properties of existing Break-Glass approaches presented in chapter 8, and legal regulations such as Health Insurance Portability and Accountability Act (HIPAA) [82].

The generic idea of Break-Glass is to empower users to decide if a denied access should be overridden, e. g., can be legitimized by an exceptional situation. This approach inherently requires that incorrect behavior can be detected and urged. This gives four fundamental principles for Break-Glass:

1. *Governance:* Persons in charge have to be able to control the range of tolerated empowerment given to end users with Break-Glass.
2. *Accessibility:* The possibility to override Access Control (AC) decisions must be available to end-users whenever needed, i. e., without any complicated procedure that needs to be executed.
3. *Awareness:* End user must be informed that they are overriding a regular AC decision, i. e., that their actions will be subject to further investigations.
4. *Accountability:* It must be possible to hold users responsible for all actions they are executing with exceptional privileges.

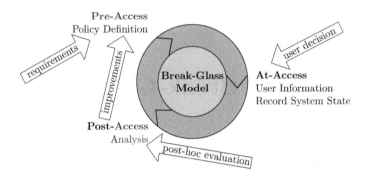

Figure 3.1: The Break-Glass lifecycle: the three phases pre-, at-, and post-access are based on the Break-Glass model.

Governance

The requirement of governance postulates that even in exceptional situation not everything should be permitted. When defining AC policies, there is always a trade off between the risk associated with granting access vs. risk associated with *not* granting access. As argued in the introduction in section 1.1, not all situations can be foreseen, hence, AC policies capturing all possible accesses cannot be defined beforehand. Break-Glass aims to overcome the problem with unpredictable situations, but this does not invalidate the need to define accesses that may or may not occur, e. g., as they do not help in master the exception, or the potential damage is too large. Exceptional privileges are intended to reflect situations where this trade-off cannot be decided at design time: Break-Glass is an exception mechanism for situations where no definite PERMIT or DENY decision can be found. This requires that it has to be possible to separate what is permitted, what could be permitted in an exceptional situation and what should never be permitted.

For defining exceptional privileges, it should be known who is using the exceptional privileges in which context. For example, for a Human Resources (HR) department there will be other exceptional privileges than in an emergency room, or, different persons will have different tasks in exceptional situations. Furthermore, it should be possible to model exceptional privileges without the need to model the exceptional situation.

Break-Glass should enable the person in charge to adopt the tolerated empowerment given to users according to the ongoing situations, without that this person in charge would need either too much time or too deep knowledge of the used technology. This includes that the person in charge may be a regular user who has the power to modify the tolerated empowerment given to themselves and other users – whereas this does not invalidate the need of governance of those special empowerments. For example, the Health Insurance Portability and Accountability Act (HIPAA) [82] requires that a treating physician as health care professionals has the power to decide if exceptional accesses are in the best interest of the patient. Break-Glass has to enable a fine-grained modeling of empowerment, i.e., to increase the tolerated empowerment with a limited scope, e.g., enable exceptional accesses onto a specific patient.

Accessibility

Users should not have to execute complicate mechanisms to use exceptional privileges, e.g., connect to another systems, or understand which AC mechanism would be required to execute a specific task. Exceptional situations are per definition exceptions and hence occur seldom, i.e., users are likely to be nervous in such exceptional or even emergency situations. At best, users should not need education or regular training on using the Break-Glass mechanism. Hence, the interface and the usage of the mechanism should be easy to understand and use. This includes that users should be able to execute exceptional tasks in their usual and custom environment, both to ensure that users are able to handle the exceptional situations and that the workflow is not disrupted.

The Break-Glass mechanism and the required exceptional privileges have to be available (see Definition 3 p.16). While the availability of the mechanism is a non-functional requirement of the implementation and application environment, the availability of exceptional privileges relates to the requirements discussed in the context of governance, i.e., the modification of tolerated empowerment at runtime.

Finally, similar to governance where it is important to separate regular privileges from exceptional privileges, for accessibility, Break-Glass should only be triggered if no regular access can be granted. Exceptional privileges extend regular privileges, but must not influence them. This is required as, first, user have to run their regular tasks with regular privileges without being bothered with any exception mechanisms. Second, only what was exceptional and actually executed at runtime should be required to be handled as exceptional post-access, i.e., a regular access should not require an investigation in the post-access phase.

How those requirements can be fulfilled depends to some degree on the integration of Break-Glass into the application and cannot be fully guaranteed by the chosen Break-Glass approach. However, this integration can be smoother by making Break-Glass an extension of the underlying AC model, which also would allow to reuse existing AC implementations and policies.

Awareness

Using Break-Glass has to be an explicit action by the user as he may be made responsible for it in a later point in time – a user can only be made responsible for what he did if he was aware of what he was doing. Hence, users must receive some warning or have to explicitly request exceptional privileges. Depending on the application, the user may be required to provide a short explanation, e. g., describing the exceptional situation.

User should be enabled to receive some information about the override they are about to execute. This information should give them a feeling how large the override, compared to their regular tasks, is: while the user should understand the actual situation and benefits of the task he is about to execute, he is not required to know which competence is required to execute which task or who could regularly execute the task.

Accountability

The concept of Break-Glass relies on the menace of consequences for incorrect behavior: users have to be made accountable (see Definition 8 p.17) for override accesses. As pointed out by Watzlawick [109], for a menace it is crucial that the menaced is taking the menace seriously, i. e., the user has to be sure that illegitimate accesses will be detected and urged, forcing the user to avoid illegitimate behavior. This requires that, first, incorrect accesses can be separated from legitimate, second, users are authenticated (see Definition 6 p.16) at-access and, third, users are seizable post-access, i. e., the authority granting exceptional privileges has to have some power over users. If those principles cannot be applied, Break-Glass cannot be applied, as the menace of consequences will not be taken seriously by users, breaking the concept of Break-Glass.

The requirement of authenticated and seizable subjects depends on the application context, i. e., defines what is required for authenticated and seizable subjects. This may range from withdrawing some virtual asset from a pseudonym identity up to knowing the real identity of the person to be able to demand for prosecution. A generic Break-Glass approach can only assure that the requirements regarding authentication can be modeled – the rest has to be fulfilled by the integration of Break-Glass into the application.

For the separation of correct from illegitimate accesses, it has to be traceable who was executing which exceptional access. This includes that, first, granted but not executed exceptional privileges should not appear as exceptional access, and, second, only accesses which actually could not be granted with regular privileges need to be investigated. The recording of exceptional accesses has to enable the auditor to decide post-mortem, if an override access was legitimate. Thus, at least information available at-access and used for the AC decision should be available post-access. Furthermore, it should be possible to trigger the recording of additional information which could help the auditor to understand the at-access situation. For post-access investigations, some techniques supporting the auditor in his work, e. g., filter for exceptional accesses or provide fast and easy access to recorded information, should be provided.

Implementing those four fundamental principles of Break-Glass will ensure that the requirements for Break-Glass are fulfilled.

3.2 Abstract Model

Our Break-Glass model contains a set of policies $\mathscr{P}$. Every policy p, $p \in \mathscr{P}$, can be seen as implementing an Access Control Function (ACF) as defined in subsection 2.2.2, i. e., maps a request Q to a result N with $\mathscr{D} \times 2^{\mathscr{O}}$, where the set $\mathscr{D}$ contains at least the two distinctive elements PERMIT and DENY, and the set of obligations $2^{\mathscr{O}}$ is optional or may be empty. Thus, we do not restrict the underlying AC model which is used to define policies $p \in \mathscr{P}$.

Policies are ordered in a *lattice*, e. g., as shown in the example in Figure 3.2. The edges constructing the lattice describe an *extension* (written $p' \sqsupseteq p$) or a *refinement* (written $p \sqsubseteq p'$) relationship, where p is the *smaller* and p' is the *larger* element.

Definition 11. *Extension relationship: a policy p' extends a policy p (p refines p'), written $p' \sqsupseteq p$ ($p \sqsubseteq p'$), if and only if p' returns at least for those access control requests a PERMIT, where p returns a PERMIT.*

Informally, if a policy p' extends a policy p, at least everything permitted under p has to be permitted under p', or, privileges defined in p are inherited by p'. There are two special policies $p^{\perp}$ and $p^{\top}$. $p^{\perp}$ does not permit any request and is the smallest element, i. e., does not grant any privilege. $p^{\top}$

permits every request and is the largest element, i. e., grants every possible privilege.

Definition 12. *The policy lattice is defined as $(\mathscr{P}, \sqsupseteq, p^\perp, p^\top)$, where $\mathscr{P}$ be the set of all policies of the Break-Glass model, $\sqsupseteq$ defines a partial order on all policies p, $p \in \mathscr{P}$, $p^\perp$ is the smallest element which is extended by every policy and $p^\top$ is the largest element which extends every policy.*

The operators $\sqsupseteq$ and $\sqsubseteq$ are transitive, e. g., $p^\perp$ refines all other policies and $p^\top$ extends all other policies. The term *extending policies (refining policies)* of a policy p is used for all those policies with a extending (refining) relationship with policy p towards $p^\top$ ($p^\perp$). Thus, every policy p has at least the conceptual policy $p^\top$ ($p^\perp$) as extending (refining) policy.

Given the lattice, the level ℓ of every policy p can be inferred with the smallest policy $p^\perp$ being always in level ℓ_0.

Definition 13. *The level ℓ of every policy p is defined by the path with the maximum number of non-cyclic edges towards $p^\perp$, with $p^\perp$ being on level ℓ_0.*

Policies $p \in \mathscr{P}$ can have obligations which are applied if the policy is providing a PERMIT decision. Obligations attached to $p \in \mathscr{P}$ have to be distinct from the obligations returned as response N from the underlying ACF. We use obligations as defined for a DENY-biased Policy Enforcement Point (PEP) in XACML [80]: if a PERMIT decision with obligations is returned, all obligations have to be understood and fulfilled. If one of the obligations cannot be fulfilled, the decision has to be treated as DENY. Obligations are used to mark returned AC decisions as exceptional, i. e., avoiding the introduction of an additional AC decision and allowing to return different types of exceptional status to be returned.

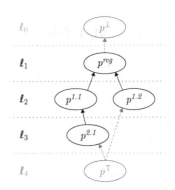

Figure 3.2: A simple policy lattice: the conceptual policy $p^\perp$ on level ℓ_0, the regular policy p^{reg} as solely policy on level ℓ_1.

Policies $p \in \mathscr{P}$ can be active or inactive, i. e., if they are active they contribute to the AC decision, otherwise not. If a policy is activated, all policies which are extended by the activated policy (or, which refine the activated policy) are implicitly activated, as the activated policy per definition inherits all privileges from the policies it extends.

Definition 14. *To activate the privileges granted by a policy $p \in \mathscr{P}$, the policy p has to be active, and the activation of a policy p implicitly activates all refined policies $p', p' \sqsubseteq p$.*

This abstract model (and the instantiations in the following sections) defines Break-Glass independently from the underlying AC model: every AC which implements the ACF from Equation 2.1 (i.e., all AC models we are aware of), can be used within our Break-Glass model. This has two further consequences: first, the underlying AC model does not need to model obligations, nevertheless can obligations be used to mark AC decisions to be exceptional. Second, existing ACF implementations and AC policies can still be used when introducing Break-Glass.

Thus, our Break-Glass model is the first approach which models the characteristics of Break-Glass as orthogonal concept to underlying AC models.

3.3 Core Model

For the core model, one can interpret policies $p \in \mathscr{P}$ as set of positive permissions and read the extension $p \sqsupseteq p'$ and refinement $p \sqsubseteq p'$ operator as set operators which compares the set of permissions: the smaller set of permissions p is a subset of the larger set of permissions p', i.e., $p \subseteq p'$ or $p' \supseteq p$. However, a comparison of permissions depends on the used AC model and can therefor not be used as generic implementation.

To implement the abstract model in a generic way, we introduce a *lattice evaluation algorithm* to evaluate the policy lattice defined with the abstract model. This algorithm follows, as the underlying policies $p \in \mathscr{P}$, the definition of an ACF (see Equation 2.1), i.e., takes a request Q as input, and returns a response N with a decision D and obligations $2^{\mathscr{O}}$. The evaluate() function calls the underlying ACF and provides the corresponding security state σ_{sec} and system state σ_{sys} to the underlying ACF. As part of the security state σ_{sec}, the lattice evaluation algorithm (Listing 3.1) retrieves a list of policies, where the order is derived from the lattice. Policies of level ℓ_1 are evaluated before all others, for policies on the same level the algorithm may choose an order (e.g., from left to right). The algorithm iterates through the policies, starting with the policies on level ℓ_1. Every active policy is evaluated. Whenever a PERMIT is found, the AC decision is enhanced with the obligations defined for this policy and returned as AC decision. The first

```
     //list of policies with derived order from lattice
     Response combAlg(Request requ, List<PolicyId> policies) {
3       Response foundDeny;
        for ( policyId id : policies ) {
          if ( isActive(id) ) {
6           Response res = evaluate(requ, id);
            if ( res.decision == PERMIT ) {
              res.obligations += getObligations(id);
9             return res;
            } else if ( foundDeny == null &&
                        res.decision == DENY ) {
12            foundDeny = res;
            }
          }
15      }
        if ( foundDeny != null )
          return foundDeny;
18    }
     }
```

Listing 3.1: The *lattice evaluation algorithm* for the core model: evaluate
active policies $p \in \mathcal{P}$ and returns the first PERMIT from the
lowest policy level ℓ including the obligations, otherwise return
the first DENY.

DENY decision (and its potentially attached obligations, if the underlying
AC model supports obligations) is stored and returned if no PERMIT can be
found.

The algorithm in Listing 3.1 contains an implementation shortcut to
increase efficiency. Conceptually, for every policy p all refining policies
$p', p' \sqsubseteq p$ have to be evaluated, as positive permissions defined by refining
policies are inherited. As all refining policies are active per definition (see
Definition 14, p.43), we do not need to re-evaluate refining policies: if a
PERMIT would have been found in one of the refining policies, the algorithm
would have terminated and returned this PERMIT. With this, the extension
relationship from Definition 11 holds *per construction*. This is why we do
not need to make any restrictions on the expressiveness or the structure of
the underlying AC model. The policies $p^\perp, p^\top$ from the abstract model are
conceptual polices and do not need to be implemented with the underlying
ACF.

When defining policies, only additional privileges need to be defined
within the extending policies, similar to the inheritance concept of the object
oriented paradigm. However, in contrast to the inheritance concept of the

object oriented paradigm, extending policies cannot overwrite already defined privileges in extended policies, i. e., if there are intersections in the definition of policies, the policy with the lower policy level ℓ_n will *dominate* the policy on a higher level ℓ_{n+x}. This includes that the obligations of the policy with the lower level will be applied.

If the underlying AC model supports further AC decisions, the algorithm in Listing 3.1 has to be adapted to handle those accordingly. Here, the algorithm might be adapted to the meaning of the AC decision and the actual needs, e. g., if the underlying ACF returns an error, this error could be returned whenever detected and aborting the evaluation, or only if no PERMIT with another ACF can be found.

3.4 Constraints Model

In the core model as described in the last section, one cannot define explicit DENY decisions which cannot be overwritten by an exceptional policy: every DENY decision defined by a policy in the lattice can be overwritten by a PERMIT from an extending policy. Such DENY decisions can be used to express *constraints*, i. e., explicitly constraining positive permissions, e. g., Separation of Duty (SoD) or Binding of Duty (BoD), and may be valid only up to a specific level or policy.

To enable the definition of such DENY decisions, we introduce the *constraints model* as extension to the core model[1], which allows to define DENY decisions: extended policies on higher levels may not have to stick to constraints defined by refining policies. Our model allows to define both overridable and non-overridable DENY decisions.

The constraints model is an implementation of the abstract and an extensions to the core model and hence has the same properties, i. e., defines a lattice of policies and guarantee an extension relationship along the lattice. For this, we divide every policy in two parts: while the positive permissions, as defined for the core model, define the PERMIT part p_P, every policy can also define a DENY part p_D. A policy may have a PERMIT, a DENY, or both parts. For example, the regular policy p^{reg} consists out of two parts, p_P^{reg} and p_D^{reg}, represented as P (PERMIT) and as D (DENY) part of a policy in Figure 3.3. The conceptual polices $p^\perp$ and $p^\top$ have only one part: as in the core model, $p^\perp$ denies every request and therefore does not define a

---

[1]The *constraints model* from section 3.4 is in some sense an extension to the *core model* from section 3.3, similar to RBAC where *hierarchical* RBAC is an extension to *core* RBAC.

PERMIT part, and $p^\top$ permits every request and therefore does not define a DENY part.

One characteristic of the extension relationship (Definition 11) and the policy lattice (Definition 12) is that privileges (i. e., effective positive permissions) have to increase towards $p^\top$: in $p^\top$ everything is permitted, in $p^\perp$ everything is denied. Consequently, positive (PERMIT) permissions are inherited towards $p^\top$ and negative (DENY) permissions are inherited towards $p^\perp$. Thus, every policy inherits the PERMIT permissions of its refining policies (i. e., all policies towards $p^\perp$) and the DENY permissions of its extending policies (i. e., all policies towards $p^\top$). Consider, for example, the lattice in Figure 3.3: $p^{1.1}$ inherits the

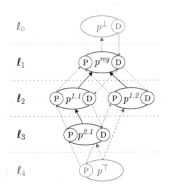

Figure 3.3: Policy lattice with DENY policies.

PERMIT policy of p^{reg} (as p^{reg} is refining $p^{1.1}$) and the DENY policy of $p^{2.1}$ (as $p^{2.1}$ is extending $p^{1.1}$). p^{reg} is extended by all other policies and hence will inherit the DENY policies of $p^{1.1}$, $p^{1.2}$, and $p^{2.1}$.

Definition 15. *Implementing the extension relationship from Definition 11 for a policy lattice from Definition 12 with positive (PERMIT) and negative (DENY) permissions, every policy $p \in \mathscr{P}$ inherits all PERMIT permissions from its refining policies $p' \sqsubseteq p$, and all DENY permissions from its extending policies $p' \sqsupseteq p$.*

Definition 15 is a conclusion of Definition 11 and Definition 12, i. e., describes the implementation of PERMIT and DENY permissions within the abstract model from section 3.2. Following this definition, there are some non-obvious consequences. First, Definition 15 is independent of the activation of policies (Definition 14), i. e., DENY permissions are always inherited from extending policies, independently which polices are active. This is also true for PERMIT permissions, i. e., PERMIT permissions are always inherited from refining policies, however, following Definition 14, this direction is different as the activation of a policy activates all refining policies. Thus, PERMIT permissions are only inherited if the policy defining them is activated, whereas DENY permissions are always "active." This is a consequence of the properties defined for the abstract model.

```
   //list of policies with derived order from lattice
 2 Response combAlg(Request requ, PolicyLattice lattice) {
   Response foundDeny;
   for ( policyId id : lattice.getPoliciesOrdered() ) {
 5   if ( isActive(id) ) {
       Response permit, deny;
       // check refining policies for (inherited) permit
 8     for ( policyId refining : getRefPolicies(id) ) {
         Response res = evaluate(requ, refining);
         if ( res.decision == PERMIT ) {
11          permit = res;
            break; // found inherited permit
         } else if ( foundDeny == null &&
14                     res.decision == DENY ) {
           foundDeny = res;
         }
17     }
       // check extending policies for (inherited) deny
       for ( policyId extending : getExtPolicies(id) ) {
20       Response res = evaluate(requ, extending);
         if ( res.decision == DENY ) {
           deny = res;
23          if ( foundDeny == null ) {
              foundDeny = res;
            }
26          break;
         }
       }
29     // if we found a permit but no deny
       if ( permit != null && deny == null ) {
         // return permit with obligations of current policy
32        permit.obligations += getObligations(id);
          return permit;
       } else if ( deny != null && foundDeny == null ) {
35        foundDeny = deny;
       }
     }
38 }
   if ( foundDeny != null )
     return foundDeny;
41 }
   }
```

Listing 3.2: Naive lattice evaluation algorithm for the constraints model, i.e., with support for DENY policies.

Second, a request may be granted by another policy than defining the corresponding PERMIT permission: if a request is permitted from a policy p_P^a on ℓ_x (e. g., p_P^{reg} on ℓ_1) but denied by an extending policy p_D^b on level 1_{x+n} (e. g., $p_D^{1.1}$ on ℓ_2), the request may still be granted by another policy. Either by a policy p^c on $\ell_{x+i}, i \geq 1$, if p^c (e. g., $p^{1.2}$) is extending p^a but not refining p^b. Or, by a policy p^d on ℓ_{x+n+m} (e. g., $p^{2.1}$) extending both p^a and p^b. Such a policy has to be active to actually permit the request. The Break-Glass obligations from the policy effectively permitting the request (and not the one defining the PERMIT permission in the first place) are attached to the AC result. For example, if p_P^{reg} permits the request, but $p_D^{1.1}$ denies the request, and $p^{1.2}$ is not active but $p^{2.1}$ is, the PERMIT from p_P^{reg} with the obligations of $p^{2.1}$ will be returned.

DENY policies in our model are overridable, i. e., a policy not refining the policy defining DENY permissions may grant the request, and hence can dominate the DENY policy. However, a policy engineer is free to define non-overridable DENY permissions by making every other policy refining the policy which contains the non-overridable DENY permissions. Such a policy does not have to contain PERMIT permissions.

To handle DENY policies, the algorithm from Listing 3.1 for the core model has to be extended. We will first present a naive implementation in Listing 3.2 and then a more enhanced algorithm in Listing 3.3 which implements some shortcuts for policies following the default deny principle. In contrast to the initial algorithm, the algorithms for the constraints model require the whole lattice as input (and not only an ordered list), as the list of extending (getExtPolicies(id), line 34 in Listing 3.2) and refining (getRefPolicies(id), line 48) policies for a specific policy need to be retrieved. The function getPoliciesOrdered() returns the list of policies, ordered according to the order defined by the lattice. getExtPolicies(), getRefPolicies(), and getPoliciesOrdered() have to return all policies within the lattice, i. e., despite if active or not. All three functions have to return the policies ordered according to the lattice, starting with policies on lower levels. The lists returned by the two functions getExtPolicies(id) and getRefPolicies(id) also contain the policy for which the list is requested, i. e., as first (extending) and last (refining) element.

```
   // store (all) DENY results
   Map<PolicyId, Response> denyCache;
3  // store found PERMITs in cache
   Map<PolicyId, Response> permitCache;

6  //list of policies with derived order from lattice
   Response combAlg(Request requ, PolicyLattice lattice) {
```

```
     Response foundDeny;
 9   for ( PolicyId id : lattice.getPoliciesOrdered() ) {
       if ( isActive(id) ) {
         PolicyId permitted = isPermitInh(id);
12       if ( permitted == null  ) {
           // no inherited permit found
           Response res = evaluateP(requ, id);
15         if ( res.decision == PERMIT ) {
             permitCache.put(id, res);
             permitted = id;
18         } else if ( foundDeny == null &&
                       res.decision == DENY ) {
             foundDeny = res;
21         }
         }
         if ( permitted != null && ! isDenyInh(requ, id) )
24         return ( permitCache.get(id) + getOblg(id) );
       }
     }
27   if ( foundDeny != null ) {
       return foundDeny;
     } else {
30     return DENY;
     }
   }
33 boolean isDenyInh(Request requ, PolicyId id) {
     for ( PolicyId extId : getExtPolicies(id) ) {
       Response res;
36     if ( denyCache.contains(extId) ) {
         res = denyCache.get(id);
       } else {
39       res = evaluateD(requ, id);
         denyCache.put(id, res);
       }
42     if ( res.decision == DENY )
         return true;
     return false;
45 }
   PolicyId isPermitInh(PolicyId id) {
     if ( permitCache.size() > 0 ) {
48     for ( PolicyId refId : getRefPolicies(id) ) {
         if ( permitCache.contains(refId) )
           return refId;
51     }
     }
     return null;
54 }
```

Listing 3.3: Lattice evaluation algorithm for the constraints model, optimized for default deny based policies.

The naive algorithm in Listing 3.2 directly implements what was defined for the constraints model. For every active policy, it has to be checked if a PERMIT decision can be found in one of the refining policies, and if a DENY decision can be found in an extending policy. If a PERMIT but no DENY can be found, the found PERMIT, attached with the obligations of the current policy, can be returned. This algorithm is also the naive implementation of the algorithm shown in Listing 3.1.

A more efficient algorithm for the constraints model has to consider two things. First, a found PERMIT does not mean a request can be permitted as it may be denied by an extending DENY policy, i.e., before a found PERMIT can be returned, it has to be checked if a DENY is inherited. Thus, the function isDenyInh() in Listing 3.3 iterates over all extending policies to find an inherited DENY. For this, a denyCache is used where the results of once evaluated DENY policies are stored. Second, a PERMIT may not be returned by the policy that defined the PERMIT, but by a policy which inherits a PERMIT but does not inherit or define a DENY. Hence, the function isPermitInh() iterates over all refining policies to find an inherited PERMIT, and uses a permitCache where PERMIT results of PERMIT policies are stored. We only need to cache found PERMIT decisions returned by PERMIT policies, whereas we have to cache all decisions returned by DENY policies. This implements a similar shortcut as for the core model.

The algorithm in Listing 3.3 iterates over all active policies. If for the given policy no inherited PERMIT can be found, the PERMIT part of the current policy is evaluated. If the result is permitted (either inherited or with the current policy) and no inherited DENY can be found, the found PERMIT attached with the obligations of the current policy is returned. As for the algorithms in Listing 3.1 and Listing 3.2, if no PERMIT can be found, the first found DENY is returned. A full implementation in Java as eXtensible Access Control Markup Language (XACML) policy combining algorithm can be found in Listing C.2 in Appendix C.

4 Policy Definition: Pre-Access

In the previous chapter 3 we presented a generic Break-Glass model, which uses the Access Control Function (ACF) as abstraction of underlying Access Control (AC) models. We will now introduce the differentiation between *policy permissions* and *policy state*, representing a more concrete abstraction of AC models. Based on this, we will show how our Break-Glass model can be used to define Break-Glass policies for the running example. But first of all, we will present an authorization infrastructure which allows to implement the (regular) privileges needed in the running example.

4.1 Authorization Infrastructure

4.1.1 Break-Glass Architecture

Figure 4.1 shows a Break-Glass architecture based on the architecture presented in Figure 2.3. The (Break-Glass) Policy Decision Point (PDP) has to be able to support the Break-Glass model defined in the previous chapter 3, which includes the implementation of the lattice evaluation algorithm and support for obligations used by this algorithm. Similar to the reuse and adoption of existing policies, existing implementations of the PDP can be adopted for the Break-Glass PDP. This can be done by, either, enhancing the existing implementation with support for the lattice evaluation algorithm and obligations, or, as indicated in Figure 4.1, by encapsulating existing PDPs and adding the required support in a Break-Glass PDP. The existing PDP implementations (i. e., existing implementations of the ACF) are encapsulated, the Break-Glass PDP acts as a wrapper which implements the lattice evaluation algorithm and provides support for obligations. The evaluation of every single policy $p \in \mathscr{P}$ can be done by separate instances of the given PDP and ACF implementation . However, this is an optional property which allows to reuse and integrate existing technologies. Implementations which provide obligation support and allow to implement the lattice evaluations algorithm (e. g., XACML as we will use it in subsection 4.1.4) can directly use existing implementations and policies.

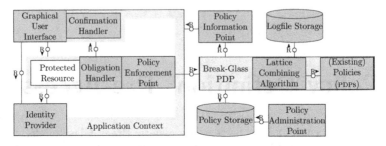

Figure 4.1: Extending the basic architecture from Figure 2.3 with support for Break-Glass.

   The security infrastructure has to support the fulfillment of the obligations returned by the PDP, in particular a *user confirmation obligation*, i. e., the requirement that users confirm the usage of Break-Glass privileges. This affects several components. The communication channel between PDP and Policy Enforcement Point (PEP) has to support obligations, i. e., they have to be part of the returned AC decision. Furthermore, the PEP has to be able to enforce the obligations returned by the PDP, e. g., with the help of an *Obligation Handler* attached to the PEP. The base for this consideration is an architecture with no support for obligations, i. e., for systems which already support obligations, those requirements are standard requirements and already fulfilled by standard implementations. Finally, a *Confirmation Handler* has to reside on the Graphical User Interface (GUI) and be able to request the confirmation from the user.

   The flows for a PERMIT or DENY decision do not differ from a standard model as discussed in subsection 2.2.3. Figure 4.2 shows a sequence diagram with an AC decision granting Break-Glass privileges which get executed by the user. As in the standard flow, the user accesses a resource via the GUI. The resource is protected by the PEP, which queries the PDP for an AC decision, providing all the required information to the PDP in the AC request. The PDP evaluates the AC request. If the request is not permitted by regular privileges (e. g., p^{reg}) but by an exceptional policy, the AC decision is PERMIT with a user confirmation obligation, i. e., granting exceptional privileges. The PEP calls the obligation handler to fulfill this obligation. For this the user has to confirm the Break-Glass access, e. g., a message box is shown to the user where the user who can decide if the exceptional privilege should be used or not. In case the user confirms the Break-Glass access and the access can be successfully logged (e. g., to a

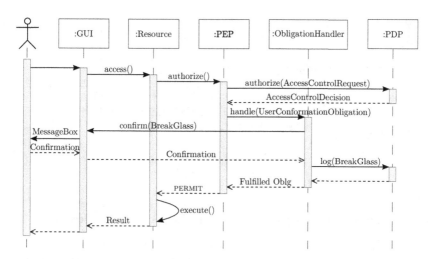

Figure 4.2: Sequence Diagram of a user confirmed Break-Glass access.

log store maintained by the PDP), the obligation handler can report all obligations to be fulfilled back to the PEP. In this case, the PEP can return PERMIT as AC decision, i.e., the resource can execute the action requested by the user as under a regular PERMIT.

In case the user does not confirm the Break-Glass access (Figure 4.3), the obligation handler does not have to send the log notification to the PDP, and cannot report the fulfillment of the obligation. If not all obligations can be fulfilled, the authorization has to be treated as DENY, i.e., the PEP returns DENY to the resource as AC decision, resulting in an abortion of the requested access.

4.1.2 Policy Permissions and Policy State

As refinement to the techniques discussed in subsection 2.2.3, we need a notion for managing the security relevant system state, i.e., the security state σ_{sec} passed to an ACF. For this, we introduce the distinction of policy permissions versus policy state.

In a security architecture as sketched in subsection 2.2.3, the Policy Decision Point (PDP) implementing the ACF (and the ACF_a), is the one central point where AC decisions are made. The PDP can be split into several components. The core PDP retrieves the security state σ_{sec} (i.e., the AC configuration such as AC policies) from the policy storage, while

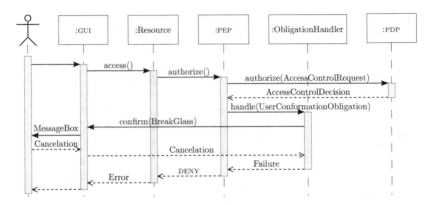

Figure 4.3: Sequence diagram of a user canceled a Break-Glass access.

this security state is managed via the Policy Administration Point (PAP). Information which is passed to the PDP and not part of the security state has to be treated as system state σ_{sys}, which can be retrieved by the PDP from the application context via the Policy Information Point (PIP).

Conceptually, it is not always clear what should to be modeled as security state σ_{sec} and what is defined by the context and hence retrieved as system state σ_{sys} via the PIP. For example, while most approaches agree that permissions (PRMS) of a Role Based Access Control (RBAC) model are part of the security state, this is not so clear for the user assignments (UA). While ANSI RBAC [2] defines administrative controls for all relations in RBAC and hence makes it a part of the security state, user assignments could also be derived from some information maintained by the Human Resources (HR) department, e. g., as described by Schaad et al. [100]. In a health care scenario (as we introduced it in our running example), one may choose to retrieve the information about Treatment Relationship (TR) between physicians and patients from the application context (as the application could be made responsible for managing this information), or make it part of the policy (e. g., as done by Becker [14]).

From an information security point of view, administrative controls (see Definition 10) have to control the access to the security state, i. e., the PAP is implementing such controls for the policy store: the security state has to fulfill the integrity property (see Definition 2) as otherwise, subjects would be allowed to modify the security state in a way so that they could achieve higher privileges (*privilege escalation*). Such administrative controls are also a legal requirement: regulations such as Sarbanes-Oxley Act (SOX)

[99] require that AC decisions are reproducible, which includes that, first, it has to be reproducible which subject assigned the required privilege to the accessing subject, and, second, privilege assignments have to be authorized, i. e., implementing an administrative control. Thus, all changes to the system which influence AC decisions have to be protected by an administrative control.

For the security state, one can differentiate between permissions which are independent of the system state, and permissions which are changed due to changes in the application or environmental context, i. e., reflecting the *state* of the system and its environment. To account for those considerations we propose to explicitly divide the security state (or AC configuration or AC policy) in two parts.

Policy permissions are the more static part and consist of, e. g., in the case of RBAC, the permissions (PRMS) and their assignment to roles (PA). Policy permission are likely to be only defined by experts which know the policy language and the tools to define and modify permissions.

The *policy state* is the more dynamic part, and changes more frequent (e. g., user assignments (UA) or TRS between physicians and patients) and depends on the state of the protected resources, the application, and the environment. Two hospital may have the same policy permissions when using the same software, but will never have the same policy state. The policy state can also be defined by non-security experts (e. g., roles can be assigned by the HR department) or even dynamically at runtime out of the context of the application (e. g., creating a relationship between a physician and a patient). As the policy state influences the AC decisions, we consider the policy state to be part of the security state and therefore that it has to be protected by administrative controls enforced by the PAP.

Applied to the running example, policy permissions are the "static rules" (e. g., nurses can view general information of patients with a valid TR), whereas the policy state is represented by actual assignments (e. g., subjects assigned to roles, a TR created when a patient comes to the hospital, or qualifications of physicians). The policy permissions are maintained and approved by security experts, whereas the policy state can be maintained by non-security experts. For example, the role assignments or qualification of physicians could be done by the HR department, TRs could be updated according to actions executed within the application. Both, policy permissions and policy state are modifiable and protected by an administrative policy, i. e., can be changed only via the PAP. Applying this concept, there are three types of information which can be retrieved by the PDP – policy permission and policy state (giving the security state σ_{sec}) and context information defining the system state σ_{sec}. In more detail:

1. Policy permissions are expected to change seldom, the PDP retrieves the current version from the policy storage, e. g., when loading policies at startup. Those changes are done only by security experts and will in most cases need some test and verification phase. If a new policy has to be applied, the PDP has to reload the policy permissions from the policy storage.

2. The policy state is retrieved from the policy storage at runtime. The policy state is expected to change frequently. Changes can be triggered by non-security experts or even be automatically derived from events within the application.

3. Context information is resolved from the PIP at runtime, which connects to the right system to get the required information. The authorization infrastructure does not have control how and when the required information changes and, therefore, has to query the required information every time it is needed.

Policy permissions are or can be defined in a text based format (or can at least be exported to such a format), whereas the used policy language defines how to structure those permissions. The policy state and the context information are defined by assignments. For example, in RBAC roles are assigned to subjects, in Bell-La Padula subjects and resources are assigned to labels, or, for a TR in our running example, the department of a hospital is assigned to subjects and patients.

The security σ_{sec} can hence be divided into policy permissions $\sigma_{\text{sec}}^{perm}$ and the policy state $\sigma_{\text{sec}}^{state}$, i. e., $\Sigma_{\text{sec}} = \Sigma_{\text{sec}}^{perm} \times \Sigma_{\text{sec}}^{state}$. While the ACF requires both as input, the ACF_a can be refined if the policy permissions $\Sigma_{\text{sec}}^{perm}$ or the policy state $\Sigma_{\text{sec}}^{state}$ can be changed by the administrative control. Hence, we refine Equation 2.2 with

$$\text{ACF}_a^{perm} : \mathscr{Q} \times \Sigma_{\text{sec}}^{perm} \times \Sigma_{\text{sec}}^{state} \times \Sigma_{\text{sys}} \to \mathscr{D} \times 2^{\mathscr{O}} \times \Sigma_{\text{sec}}^{perm} \qquad (4.1)$$

$$\text{ACF}_a^{state} : \mathscr{Q} \times \Sigma_{\text{sec}}^{perm} \times \Sigma_{\text{sec}}^{state} \times \Sigma_{\text{sys}} \to \mathscr{D} \times 2^{\mathscr{O}} \times \Sigma_{\text{sec}}^{state} \qquad (4.2)$$

The administrative ACF for policy permissions ACF_a^{perm} in Equation 4.1 controls changes to the policy permissions $\sigma_{\text{sec}}^{perm}$, the administrative ACF for the policy state ACF_a^{state} in Equation 4.2 controls changes to the policy state $\sigma_{\text{sec}}^{state}$.

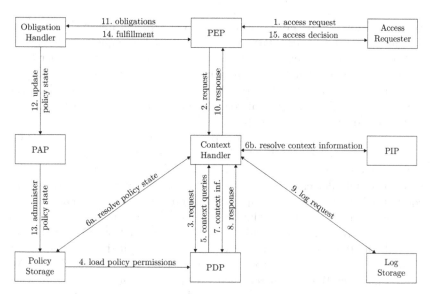

Figure 4.4: Data-flow in an authorization infrastructure, based on [80].

Data Flow

To demonstrate how policy permissions and policy state integrates into the Break-Glass architecture of subsection 4.1.1, we will disscuss the data-flow between the components along Figure 4.4. We furthermore introduce a context handler as mediator between PEP, PIP, PDP, policy storage and log storage. Figure 4.4 and the data flow are based on and compatible to the eXtensible Access Control Markup Language (XACML) [80].

The requester sends an AC request to the PEP in step 1. The PEP is embedded into the protected resource and provides an interface which is consumable by the access requester and independent from the used protocol between PEP and PDP. The PEP translates the AC request into a language which is understandable by the PDP, eventually collecting some further information on client side. The PEP is responsible for sending the created request to the central PDP, which includes the configuration how the PDP can be connected and how the trust relationship is established. The context handler receives the request (step 2), eventually enhancing the request with some context information, and sending it to the actual PDP (step 3).

The PDP loads the policy permissions from the policy storage in step 4. The PDP may cache the policy permissions and be triggered by the PAP to execute a reload if the policy permissions change. During evaluation, the PDP may require further information to evaluate the request, for which he sends one or more context information queries to the context handler (step 5). Here, the context handler is responsible for two things. First, resolve reliant information to be able to retrieve the information required by the PDP. For example, the relevant roles for the current AC request can only be determined in reliance on the accessing subject. Second, the context handler is responsible for connecting to the correct component which is able to resolve the required information. This can either be the policy storage, which is able to resolve information regarding the policy state (step 6a). Or, the context handler can contact the PIP (step 6b) which will retrieve the required information from the application context or the environment, e. g., an Identity Provider (IDP). The resolved context information is sent back to the PDP (step 7). If the required information cannot or only partially be resolved, the PDP has to decide how to proceed, i. e., if the AC request can be answered without this information or if an error has to be raised. The AC decision made by the PDP is returned via the context handler (step 8). The context handler stores the AC request to the log storage (step 9), assigning an "evaluation-Identifier (ID)" to every entry, allowing to unambiguously reference every AC request. In step 10, the decision is returned to the PEP.

If the returned AC result contains obligations, those are sent to an obligations handler (step 11). The obligations handler has to understand and fulfill all obligations, otherwise the AC result has to be treated as DENY. Some actions executed in the application may require the modification of the policy state. As only the PEP is aware if an action is actually executed, the update of the policy state can be modeled as obligation. Thus, one of the obligations which can be sent to the obligation handler is an obligation to update the policy state. For this, the obligation handler has to send an according request to the PAP (step 12), where the PAP has to check if the update is permitted, and make the update in the policy storage (step 13). Step 12 and 13 are outlined as calls without response, as only a success message is expected as response. Here, an error would indicate an inconsistency, e. g., between the administrative policy enforced by the PAP and the policy enforced by the PEP. The obligation service returns a message to the PEP if all obligations have been fulfilled (step 14). Finally, the PEP returns the AC decision to the access requester (step 15).

Following this architecture, the PDP itself remains stateless, all the state is saved in the policy storage, or, retrieved at runtime via the PIP and, e. g., stored in the protected application itself. The security state is retrieved in "real time" from the policy storage, i. e., there is no delay after updates to the policy state. Both, the policy permissions and the policy state are managed through a PAP. The PAP provides several interfaces to modify both the policy permissions and the policy state, while the PAP itself is protected by a PEP. While the policy permissions will only be modifiable by a set of users (e. g., administrators or security engineers), the policy state will be modifiable by more users, e. g., HR staff assigning roles or qualifications, or even automatically out of the application context. For example, a PEP which enforces the policy on managing patient to physician relationships will receive an obligation to notify the PAP of such a newly created or terminated relationship.

This is a rather generic architecture and data flow, nevertheless, it is compatible to and based on to the XACML architecture and data flow [80]. This is due to the fact that what is described by the XACML standard is a rather generic architecture, i. e., it is intended to be generic to allow XACML to be implemented in a wide range of settings. Thus, XACML integrated some best practices which evolved over time into the standard. Steps 5 to 7 (querying context attributes) are optional both in the sense of a specific AC request (i. e., some requests may be decidable for the PDP without the need to retrieve context information) or in the sense of the architecture, i. e., a special case of this architecture is where the steps 6a and / or 6b are not required and therefore not supported. As we use XACML in this thesis for the prototypic implementation, we decided to use the XACML terminology.

4.1.3 Policy State Administration

The policy state σ_{sec}^{state} as part of the security state σ_{sec} has to be protected by administrative controls, i. e., implementing an ACF_a^{state}. For changes to the security state σ_{sec}, a client (explicitly) calls the PAP, e. g., assigning a role to a user. However, for changes to the policy state σ_{sec}^{state}, there may be changes in the application which cause an implicit change in the policy state, e. g., a new Treatment Relationship (TR) is created when a patient registers at the hospital. For such implicit changes to the policy state σ_{sec}^{state}, we have to solve two problems: first, the application has to be aware that the policy state has to be changed and has to notify the PAP about this state change, and second, the action must only be executed if both the action in the application and the policy state change are permitted.

For this, we will introduce *policy state assignments*, which associate a state change in the application to a change of the policy state. We will show how policy state assignments allow to write a single policy defining triggers for the update of the policy state, instead of writing AC policies for the application and administrative policies for the PAP, keeping those two policies in a consistent state, and writing additional application logic for the client when to notify the PAP.

Regardless if a policy state changes is triggered explicitly or implicitly out of the application context, it has to be authorized by the ACF_a^{state}, i.e., an administrative control has to permit the change, and the PAP has to persist the change in the policy storage. The client has to be aware if a request changes the security state and hence the PAP for evaluating a ACF_a^{state} has to be called, or if the action will not trigger a security state change and hence the PEP for evaluating a ACF has to be called. This can cause problems as it may depend on the AC policy, if a change in the application context implicitly causes a change in the policy state. It depends on the AC policy if the client (PEP) has to call the PDP for a ACF or the PAP for a ACF_a^{state}. Furthermore, the client may need to change if the policy changes.

As a first step towards a solution, we make the PDP the only decision point, regardless if an access will trigger an implicit policy state change or not: looking at our definition of the ACF (Equation 2.1) and the ACF_a (Equation 2.2), the ACF_a extends the ACF with the notion of a security state change, whereas an ACF_a with an unchanged security state σ_{sec} is equivalent to an ACF. Hence, the PDP can implement the ACF_a and therewith the ACF. If a request implicitly changes the security state σ_{sec}, the PDP has to notify the PAP to update the change in the policy storage. As the PDP is implementing the ACF_a, the PDP is the authority to decide if a security state change is permitted. Hence, if the PAP receives a trustworthy notification from the PDP to update the security state, no separate AC request has to be executed. This eliminates the problem that an action must only be executed if both the action in the application and the policy state change are permitted, by simply eliminating a duplicate evaluation.

The ACF_a only decides if a request is permitted and what would have to be done, i.e., which set of obligations $2^{\mathcal{O}}$ have to be fulfilled and how the security state σ_{sec} changes. However, only the PEP knows if an action is actually executed: an AC request does not mean that the requested action is actually executed. For example, the obligation service may not be able to fulfill an obligation attached to the AC decision (e.g., the user may decide to not break the glass and hence the system must not reach a state as if the glass would have been broken), or requests could be made only to decide if elements should be depicted in the GUI.

To solve this, as the second step in our solution, the PDP notifies the PEP that the PAP has to be notified if the access is executed. This can be implemented with an obligation containing a token, e.g., a reference to the

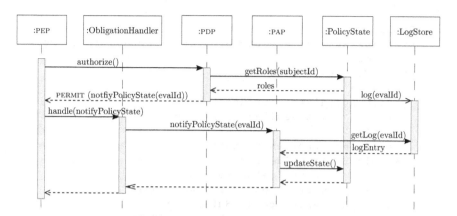

Figure 4.5: Usage of the policy state concept: create a role assignment.

(permitted) AC request. Once the PEP knows that the access is executed, it passes the token to the PAP which updates the policy storage accordingly. This finally eliminates the problem that the application has to be aware if an access implicitly changes the policy state, by simply moving all the required logic into the central components PDP and PAP. The PEP does not need to posses any further information, but only to fulfill obligations.

Figure 4.5 shows the sequence diagram for a policy state change along the example of a role assignment. For the evaluation of a AC request, the PDP retrieves the roles assigned to the accessing subject from the policy state. As the request causes a policy state change, a *notify-policy-state* obligation (which we will encode in the eXtensible Access Control Markup Language (XACML) as `urn:oblg:notifyPolicyState`) is returned to the PEP, containing the evaluation-ID as token. The PEP executes the access, and hence sends a notification to the PAP which triggers the update in the policy state. DENY-biased PEPs as we are using them, need to understand and fulfill all obligations, otherwise the AC decision has to be treated as DENY.

Modeling Policy State Assignments with Dependency Definitions

As noted in subsection 4.1.2, the policy state is defined by assignments. We will now model such assignments as "dependency definitions." First, we introduce the notion of a "policy state variable," whereas every policy state variable depends on a number of variables. For example, in RBAC ROLES are *assigned* to USERS; at runtime, the ROLES used for evaluation

```
    <Policy>
    <Target><Resource>resource:roleAssignments</Resource>
3   </Target>
    <Rule Effect="Permit">
     <Target>
6    <Role>administrator</Role>
     <Action>deleteAssignment</Action>
     </Target>
9    <Condition FunctionId="not">
      <Apply FunctionId="and">
       <Apply FunctionId="any-of-any">
12      <Function FunctionId="string-equal"/>
        <SubjAttr>subjectId</SubjAttr>
        <ResrcAttr>resource:subjectId</ResrcAttr>
15      </Apply>
        <Apply FunctionId="any-of" FulfillOn="Permit">
         <Function FunctionId="string-equal"/>
18       <Attribute>administrator</Attribute>
         <ResrcAttr>resource:role</ResrcAttr>
        </Apply></Apply>
21   </Condition></Rule>
     <Obligations><Obligation
                   ObligationId="urn:oblg:notifyPolicyState">
24    <Attribute Id="dependency">roleAssignment</Attribute>
      <!-- optional parameter not applied in this example
      <Attribute Id="duration">3600</Attribute> -->
27   </Obligation></Obligations>
     </Policy>
```

Listing 4.1: Using a policy state assignment in a policy: an administrator must not remove his own administrator role.

depend on the USERS, i. e., the system needs to know the accessing subject to retrieve the roles to be applied. Or, for a TR, the accessing subject and the patient are *assigned* to a TR; at runtime, if a TR exists *depends* on the accessing subject and the patient, i. e., the system needs to know the subject and the patient to decide if a TR exists. Thus, the policy state variable role depends on one variable subjectId, the policy state variable treatmentRelationship on the variables subjectId and patientId. Variables with no dependency may exist and are hence applicable for all AC requests, e. g., the set of active policies in our policy lattice.

Consider as example administrative controls for role assignments, defining which subjects are allowed to assign and remove which roles to and from which subjects. Listing 4.1 exemplarily describes the permission for removing roles, requiring the role `administrator` to be assigned to the accessing subject (line 6), i. e., only administrators are allowed to remove roles. To make sure that an administrator cannot remove his own administrator role, the `<Condition>` makes two checks: the `<Apply>` in line 11 checks if the accessing subject (`subjectId`) is the one which is affected (`resource:subjectId`) by the `deleteAssignment` action. The `<Apply>` in line 16 checks if the role `administrator` is part of the roles to be removed. If both apply, the condition returns `false` and hence does not permit the action.

In this example, there are two types of "role identifiers" and "subject-IDs." The AC request is executed for the subject s_1 (e. g., $s_1 = admin$), the policy store will resolve a set of roles R_1 (e. g., $R_1 = \{administrator, root\}$) assigned to s_1. Thus, using the attribute `subjectId` ($admin$), the attribute values for `role` ($\{administrator, root\}$) get resolved. Additionally, the request also has to contain the information from which subject s_2 (e. g., $s_2 = john$) which set of roles R_2 (e. g., $R_2 = \{employee\}$) should be removed, i. e., using the attributes `resource:subjectId` ($john$) and `resource:role` ($\{employee\}$).

To be able to update the policy state, i. e., remove the roles as defined by the AC request, we introduce a policy state assignment (Listing 4.2) which consists out of two parts. First, the definition on which other attributes a policy state variable depends, or, to which other attributes a policy state variable is assigned to. For the example introduced above, the policy state variable `role` depends on the attribute `subjectId`, and the policy state variable `treatment` depends on the attributes `subjectId` and `patientId`. This information is required during evaluation of the policy to resolve a policy state variable: the `subject-id` (`subjectId` and `patientId`) is retrieved from the context to resolve the assigned `role` (`treatment`) attribute values. The second part of the policy state assignment is the administrative part and defines which elements from the AC request should be assigned to which element in the dependency definition. In our example, the roles defined by `resource:role` (R_2) shall be removed from the policy state variable `role` (R_1), while `resource:subjectId` (s_2) describes the `subjectId` (s_1) for which the assignment shall be removed.

Listing 4.2 depicts such dependency definitions. The first policy state assignment `roleAssignemt` is the definition of the assignment used in the policy in Listing 4.1, i. e., roles depend on (or are assigned to) the accessing subject (line 2). The following administrative part defines that the values of the attributes `resource:role` and `resource:subjectId` from the AC request should

be used for the policy state update of the attributes `role` and `subjectId`
(lines 3 and 4). The lines with `add:` and `remove:` define which action should
be mapped to an "add assignment" or "remove assignment" action, while
either `add:` or `remove:` may define a wildcard * to match all actions except
the one which is defined for the converse operation. Thus, if the policy
from Listing 4.1 returns PERMIT and the PEP executes the obligations, the
policy state will retrieve the evaluation-ID and retrieve the corresponding
AC request from the log store. It will find the `notifyPolicyState` obligation
and retrieve, according to the `roleAssignment` dependency definition, the
values for `resource:role` ($\{employee\}$) and `resource:subjectId` ($john$) from
the request. The action `deleteAssignment` defines a remove action, i. e., the
roles defined by `resource:role` will be removed from the subject defined by
`resource:subjectId`.

The `notifyPolicyState` obligation (e. g., Listing 4.1 line 16) defines if and
which dependencies have to be updated. The obligation may also have
a `duration` attribute attached (line 26), defining for how long the add or
remove operation should remain valid. For our example in Listing 4.1, it is
commented out as the removal of roles should be permanent.

The second assignment `treatmentAssignment` in Listing 4.2 defines a
`treatment` attribute (line 9) as depending on the accessing subject (`subjectId`)
and the accessed patient (`patientId`). If a TR is created, the boolean value
`true` should be assigned instead of an attribute from the AC request (line
10). As for the `roleAssignemt` dependency, the `resource:subjectId` from the
AC request is mapped to the policy state attribute `subjectId`. This does not
forestall that `subjectId` and `resource:subjectId` have the same value, i. e.,
a subject may assign a TR to himself (if this is permitted defines the administrative policy, not the dependency definition). Finally, for the attribute
`patientId`, the attribute from the AC request can directly be assigned to
the policy state attribute `patientId` (line 12).

When resolving a policy state assignment, the result is an attribute which
may be assigned to another policy state assignment. Thus, it is possible to
build policy state assignment chains.

Policy State in XACML

The XACML standard is intentionally does not define technical details of how
and where policies are stored and also how and where information which we
categorize as policy state is stored, and how it can be retrieved at runtime.
For example, how and where user-role assignments are stored is neither
defined by the XACML standard nor by the XACML RBAC profile [79].

```
  dependency:roleAssignment
  role -> subjectId
3 role -> resource:role
  subjectId -> resource:subjectId
  add:createAssignment
6 remove:deleteAssignment

  dependency:treatmentAssignment
9 treatment -> subjectId, patientId
  treatment -> [true]
  subjectId -> resource:subjectId
12 patientId -> patientId
  add:create
  remove:drop
```

Listing 4.2: Dependency definition modeling a policy state assignment.

This is by intention, as XACML as standard defines a policy language and a query language thereon, but does not dictate how the implementation has to be done, i.e., leaving the required options for the architecture and effective implementation. Consequently, there is no definition of a policy storage: conceptually, the policy is maintained by the PAP and provided to the PDP – how the communication between PAP and PDP has to be implemented is not defined.

The basic AC model used for XACML can be seen as attribute based AC, i.e., everything is modeled as attribute, including the policy state. In subsection 2.2.4 we introduced an exemplary XACML policy (Listing C.1), using, for example, the role attribute `urn:custom:subject:role` without defining how and where the values of such an attribute are maintained and how they are retrieved. We will now discuss how the distinction of policy permissions and policy state can help in deciding such questions.

The standard defines the context handler as the one component responsible for querying the correct information source to retrieve attributes at runtime. In the standard there is no direct information flow between the context handler and the PAP maintaining the policy, although the context handler is the component responsible for resolving the information which is managed by the PAP. Also, there is no definition how the PAP has to provide the defined policies to the PDP. For the implementation of an XACML based authorization infrastructure, one needs to close those gaps. The proposed policy storage and the distinction between policy permissions and policy state

allow for a quite general solution of this problem. The policy storage becomes
a central component between PAP, context handler and PDP. The PAP
stores the policy (policy permissions and policy state) to the policy storage,
which is the trusted source for the PDP to retrieve the policy permissions,
and it is the trusted source for the context handler to retrieve the policy state.
XACML policies itself are categorized as policy permissions. To load a new
policy version, the PDP has to re-load the XACML policies from the policy
storage. Attributes which are resolved by the context handler are defined
with `<AttribtueDesignator>`s in the XACML policy (see subsection 2.2.4 for
details). At runtime, the context handler can decide, along the required
type of the attribute, if the attribute has to be resolved from the policy
storage (i. e., the attribute is part of the policy state $\sigma_{\text{sec}}^{state}$), or if the PIP
has to be contacted to resolve the attribute from the application context
(i. e., the attribute is part of the system state σ_{sys}). Thus, the introduction
of the policy storage is rather a way to implement the XACML and therefore
a natural extension than a modification to the proposed concepts in the
XACML standard.

We have now presented the distinction of policy permission and policy state
and the hereof derived concept of policy state assignments. The presented
techniques allow to model the ACF and the administrative ACF (ACF_a)
centrally in one place, i. e., the PDP. With this, two problems are solved.
First, if changes in the application context are considered to cause implicit
changes in the policy state, the application does not need to posses any
knowledge about it, but only has to follow the obligations returned by the
PDP to trigger the change in the PAP. Second, a change to the application
state is only permitted if the corresponding change in the policy state is
permitted, without the need to keep the policies for the PAP and PDP in
a consistent state. We will apply this concept for implementing a stateful
Break-Glass approach, i. e., where a Break-Glass should have an effect on
following (Break-Glass) accesses, in subsection 4.2.3.

4.1.4 Policy Language

In this section we will introduce a policy language based on XACML, i. e.,
we will present some best practices how to define and structure policies and
make use of the presented concepts. For a general introduction to XACML
see subsection 2.2.4.

In XACML everything is treated as attribute. Attribute designators allow
to load attribute values into the evaluation context, where a bag of size zero
means that an attribute could not be resolved. Thus, attributes can either

be defined with the policy, having a static value, or can be retrieved from the context with attribute designators. PEPs have to be implemented as DENY-biased, i.e., have to fulfill all obligations and treat a result as DENY if not all obligations can be fulfilled. Beside PERMIT and DENY, two further results can be returned by the PDP: INDETERMINATE marks an error during evaluation, NOTAPPLICABLE defines that no matching policy could be found. In such cases, the PEP should deny the request. There are three standard attributes which have to be included in every request:

- `urn:oasis:names:tc:xacml:1.0:subject:subject-id` of type `string` in the subject category defining the accessing user, e.g., `admin⌐ @hospital.com`.
- `urn:oasis:names:tc:xacml:1.0:resource:resource-id` of type `anyURI` in the resource category defining the accessed resource, e.g., `urn:healthrecord:patient:medication`.
- `urn:oasis:names:tc:xacml:1.0:action:action-id` of type `string` in the action defining the executed action , e.g., `read`, `add`, `update`.

We structure the policies along resources, i.e., defining a category tree of resources. The function `start-with` is used to traverse the resource and the thereof derived policy tree. For example, a `<PolicySet>` may define a `<Target>` definition for the `resource-id` matching `urn:healthrecord` with `anyURI-starts-with`. The sub-`<Policy>` defines, e.g., a `<Target>` definition for the `resource-id` matching `urn:healthrecord:patient`.

Expressing Assignments

In our policy language, we use policy state assignments to express concepts such as RBAC, i.e., assigning subjects to roles, or model Treatment Relationships (TRS) between physicians and patients. For example, a subject may only access a patients health record, if both being assigned to the role `physician` *and* if there is a TR between physician and patient.

One can comprehend assignments beyond role assignments as constraints of the permission assignment (PA) defined by RBAC, e.g., as done by SecureUML [13]. We follow this understanding to some extent, as we will use RBAC assignments in the `<Target>` definition and other assignments in the `<Condition>` definition. Assignments in XACML are, as almost everything in XACML, modeled with attributes. There are two types of assignments

- **1:n**: given a single value and a bag[1] of values, a comparison function checks if a match between the single value and one item of the bag

---

[1] In XACML, a "bag" is "an unordered collection of values, in which there may be duplicate values" [80]

can be found. This can be done using the higher-order function `urn:`⏎
`oasis:names:tc:xacml:1.0:function:any-of` or using a `Match` element
in the `<Target>` definitions (which is, basically, an `any-of` function
where the value has to be defined as `<AttributeValue>` and may not
be resolved with an attribute designator). A 1:n assignment is for
example used for checking if a user with a bag of roles is assigned to
a specific role, e. g., line 29 in Listing C.1.

- **m:n**: providing two bags, a comparison function checks if a match between one element out of each bag can be found. This can be done using
  the higher-order function `urn:oasis:names:tc:xacml:1.0:function:`⏎
  `any-of-any`. A m:n assignment is for example used for checking if a
  physician is in a working group for which the patient gave his consent,
  e. g., line 81 in Listing C.1.

The values for the comparison can either be part of the policy (e. g., as
`<AtttributeValue>` in `Match` elements), or be resolved at runtime by an
attribute designator. As an attribute designator always returns a bag, one
has to, when implementing a 1:n assignment with runtime resolved values,
use the $type$-`one-and-only` function, which assures that only one value is
contained in the bag, and returns this value.

The values returned by the attribute designator can, as for every attribute,
either be resolved from the AC request, a PIP, or the policy state. Resolved
attributes may depend on the AC request. For example, to resolve the value
for `treating-physician` or `treating-department` from our running example
in Listing C.1, the resolving component (i. e., the context handler) has to
know for which patient this request is made. Thus, the `patient-id` has to
be resolvable during evaluation, e. g., be part of the request.

4.1.5 Expressing Regular Privileges for Healthcare

In the context of the British National Health Service (NHS) program, Becker
[14] presented a formal language for expressing health care policies. With
this section, we show that using the concept of policy state assignments
the same policies can be expressed in XACML. The here presented policies
express regular privileges, i. e., are not related to Break-Glass. Later, we
will use the here defined privileges as p^{reg}. This should demonstrate that
Break-Glass can be extended based on existing policies.

As for the most kind of source code, a clear structure helps in avoiding
redundancy in policies. The policy state concept allows to model security
relevant aspects as policy state variables, which are protected by an ACF_a^{state}.
Rules defining changes to those policy state variables and rules using those

variables for their AC decisions can be defined independently. Our policy state approach allows to express domain specific variables along which the AC policies can be structured.

For example, there are multiple ways how a TR can be created: a patient coming with or without a referral from his General Practitioner (GP), an agent confirming the relationship for a patient, a referral within the hospital, et cetera. Hence, a condition such as "a TR has to exist" can be very complex, and it should be avoided to model it as condition in a rule (which would be possible in XACML). Furthermore, if and with whom a TR exists is relevant for different aspects within the hospital. Thus, a TR can be defined as policy state variable: rules how a TR can be establish is defined once, and all other parts of the AC policy can use the policy state variable instead of having to define their own rules when a patient has a TR with a physician. Similar, when checking if a subject is in a specific role, it is not checked if all conditions are met so that the subject can get into this role. To implement policies, the following steps have to be executed:

1. The initial step for implementing policies is to collect the requirements, i. e., define what should be permitted by the system and what should be prohibited. This should result in a requirement definition similar to our running example in section 1.2 exists.
2. Next, all attributes required by the rules are modelled, i. e., the attributes which are required for the evaluation of AC requests are defined.
3. It has to be defined if attributes are part of the system state σ_{sys} or the policy state $\sigma_{\text{sec}}^{state}$, whereas one can follow the guidance at the end of subsection 4.1.2. Attributes being in the system state have either to be part of the AC request or being resolvable from a PIP. For example, all requests have to contain the triple subject, resource, action, i. e., the standard attributes defined in subsection 4.1.4.
4. For attributes in the policy state the policy state assignments as discussed in the previous section 4.1.4 have to be defined.
5. XACML a `<VariableDefinition>` can be used to structure attributes and policy state assignments into variables.
6. Finally, the policies can be defined, including the administrative policies required to protect the policy state $\sigma_{\text{sec}}^{state}$.

Modeling Attributes, Policy State Assignments and Variables

For the first step, collecting the requirements, see our running example. Step two reveals the following attributes:

- `role` defines a role as defined for RBAC, e. g., nurse or physician.
- `qualification` is used to identify the qualification of the accessing subject, e. g., gynecologist or oculist.
- `subject-department` defines the department the accessing subject is currently working on. It should allow to uniquely identify departments across hospitals.
- `treating-department` defines to which departments a patient is (currently) assigned, i. e., where he is receiving treatment.
- `treating-subject` defines a physician in person providing treatment. This can either be a permanent assignment, e. g., a General Practitioner (GP), or a temporary, e. g., as for a referral.
- `patientId` identifies a patient or an agent.
- `agent` identified an agent assigned to a patient
- `healthRecord:Id` defines the instance of an health record.
- `healthRecord:label` defines labels of a health record identifying the content of the health record.
- `healthRecored:sealed` defines if a health record is sealed, either by the attending physician, or the patient itself.
- `unsealed-department` defines all departments for which a – in general – sealed health record is unsealed.
- `unsealed-subject` defines all subjects for which a – in general – sealed health record is unsealed.

Given those attributes, the following policy state assignments can be modeled:

- `role`, `qualification` and `subject-department` as dependency to `subjectId`.
- `patient-id`, `healthRecored:sealed`, `unsealed-department`, and `unsealed-subject` as dependency to `healthRecord-id`
- `treating-department`, `treating-subject`, and `agent` as dependency to `patientId`

When accessing the health record of a patient, additionally to the three standard attributes (`subject-id`, `resource-id`, `action-id`) the health┘ `Record-id` has to be contained in the request. Note that the `healthRecord-id` can be used to retrieve the `patient-id` from the policy state.

Based on the attributes and heron defined policy state assignments, XACML variables (`<VariableDefinition>`) are expressing conditions combined over several attributes. For example, a TR can be defined as shown in Listing 4.3: it is checked if either the patient is directly assigned to the accessing subject, or if the patient is treated on a department to which the accessing subject is assigned to. At runtime, for resolving the `treating-subject` and

```
  <VariableDefinition
      VariableId="runEx:treatment_relationship">
3   <Apply FunctionId="or">
    <Apply Function="any-of-any">
     <Function Function="string-equal">
6     <SubjAttr>subject-id</SubjectAttr>
      <ResrcAttr>treating-subject</ResrcAttr>
     </Apply>    <Apply Function="any-of-any">
9     <Function Function="string-equal">
      <SubjAttr>subject-department</SubjectAttr>
      <ResrcAttr>treating-department</ResrcAttr>
12  </Apply> </Apply> </VariableDefinition>
```

Listing 4.3: Variable definitions for the running example in XACML: boolean expression if there is a treatment relationship between the current `subject-id` and the `patient-id`.

the `treating-department` assignment, following the dependency definition, the `patient-id` has to resolved from the context. Either, the `patient-id` is contained in the request, or it is resolved following the dependency definition from the `healthRecord-id`. For the `subject-department` the `subject-id` has to be resolved from the request. Also, references to a `<VariableDefinition>` can be used for the definition of a `<VariableDefinition>`.

Modeling Access Control Policies

When modeling AC policies, it has to be identified which kind of information has to be protected. Resources to be protected are identified along the standard XACML Uniform Resource Identifier (URI) attribute `urn:oasis:⏌ names:tc:xacml:1.0:resource:resource-id`. In our running example, we are focused on the policies for accessing health records, where we will later demonstrate how to override those with Break-Glass. Hence, we will discuss only permissions directly related to such accesses and leave other aspects out of scope, e. g., how the assignment of roles is managed.

For our running example, we structure all patient data with the URI prefix `urn:runEx:patient` and four sub elements `masterdata`, `agent`, `healthcord`, and `treatment`. The `masterdata` contain information such as name and birth date, the `agent` a list of persons who can act as agent for the patient. The `healthrecord` contains the sub elements `header`, `content`, `creator`, `sealed`, `unsealed-subject`, and `unsealed-department`, i. e., containing the health infor-

mation. The `treatment` contains, below administrative data such assignments
with URI `administrative` and the current medication with `medication` the
treatment information `treating-subject` and `treating-department`.

```
   <Policy PolicyId="runEx:patient:nurse:permits"
      CombiningAlg="first-applicable">
 3 <Target><Role>nurse</Role></Target>
   <Rule Effect="Permit"
      RuleId="runEx:patient:nurse:permits:01">
 6  <Target>
    <Action>read</Action><Resource>
       urn:runEx:patient:treatment:medication</Resource>
 9  <Target>
    <Condition FunctionId="time-in-range">
    <EnvAttr>current-time</EnvAttr>
12  <AttrValue>06:00:00Z</AttrValue>
    <AttrValue>12:00:00Z</AttrValue>
   </Condition></Rule>
15  <Rule Effect="Permit"
      RuleId="runEx:patient:nurse:permits:01">
    <Target><Resource>
18     urn:runEx:patient:treatment:administrative
    </Resource></Target>
   </Rule></Policy>
21
   <PolicySet PolicyId="runEx:patient:physician:permits"
      CombiningAlg="first-applicable">
24 <Target><Role>physician</Role></Target>
   <Policy PolicyId="runEx:patient:physician:stateChange"
      CombiningAlg="first-applicable">
27  <Rule Effect="Permit"
      RuleId="runEx:patient:physician:stateChange:01">
    <Target><Resource>
30     patient:healthrecord</Resource>
    <Action>create</Action></Target>
   </Rule>
33  <Obligation ObligationId="notifyPolicyState">
    <Attr AttrId="dependency">resource:creator</Attr>
    <Attr AttrId="dependency">resource:patient-id</Attr>
36 </Policy></Obligation>
   <Policy PolicyId="runEx:patient:physician:stateless"
      CombiningAlg="first-applicable">
39  <Rule RuleId="runEx:patient:physician:stateless:01"
         Effect="Permit">
```

```
      <Target><Resource>patient:healthrecord:entry
42    </Resource><Action>read</Action></Target>
      <Condition FunctionId="or">
       <Apply FunctionId="and">
45      <VarRef VarId="runEx:healthRecored_SealOK"/>
        <VarRef VarId="runEx:healthRecord_labelMatch"/>
       <Apply>
48      <VarRef VarId="runEx:resource-creator"></Condition>
      </Rule>
      <!-- further permissions for physicians -->
51  </PolicySet></Policy>
```

Listing 4.4: Positive permissions for nurse and physician.

Following the running example, health care professional shall have access to resources with the URI `healthcord`, and `treatment` only if there is valid treatment relationship. We structure positive permissions for nurses and physicians into a policy without taking the TR into consideration in the first place. The policy `runEx:patient:nurse:permits` permits subjects with role `nurse` `read` access to the medication of patients druing 6 p.m. and 12 p.m., and full access on the administrative data. The policy `runEx:patient:⌐physician:permits` defines permissions for the role `physician` and contains two sub-policies. The first allows for the creation of a new health record entry and updates the policy state with the according information. This is done by adding a `notifyPolicyState` obligation: the referenced dependency `resource:creator` assigns the accessing `subject-id` as creator to the new created `healthrecord-id`, and the dependency `resource:patient-id` assigns the `patient-id` to the `healthrecord-id`. As exemplary rule in the second policy (Listing 4.4 does not show all rules) allows `read` access to a health record entry, if the seal is allows for it (i. e., the entry is either not sealed or unsealed for the accessing subject), or, if the accessing subject is the creator of the resource.

However, before evaluating the positive permissions in the regular policy (Listing 4.5), it is first checked if the access can be granted for a patient accessing his own data, e. g., sealing one of his health record entries. If this is not the case, it is checked if there is a regular TR. If not, the request will be denied. Otherwise, the positive permissions as described before are evaluated.

This section should give an understanding of how health care policies can be defined and structured with the help of our policy state assignments concept. Due to space reasons we are more focusing on the definition of Break-Glass policies in the next section 4.2.

```
   <PolicySet PolicyId="runEx:patient"
     CombiningAlg="first-applicable"><Target>
3    <Resource>urn:runEx:patient</Resource></Target>
   <!-- permissions for patients -->
   <PolicyRef>runEx:patient:patient</PolicyRef>
6  <Policy PolicyId="runEx:patient:nonTreat"><Target/>
   <Rule RuleId="runEx:patient:nonTreat:01"
          Effect="Deny"><Target/>
9   <Condition FunctionId="not">
      <VarRef VarId="runEx:treatment_relationship"/>
    </Condition></Rule>
12 </Policy>
   <PolicyRef>runEx:patient:nurse:permits</PolicyRef>
   <PolicyRef>runEx:patient:physician:permits</PolicyRef>
15 </PolicySet>
```

Listing 4.5: The regular policy for patient data first checks if access can
be granted for the patient. If no no treatment relationship
can be found, a DENY is returned. Only after that, positive
permissions (**permits** policies for nurses and physicians) are
evaluated.

4.2 Break-Glass Policies

In this section we are putting the so far presented building blocks together
and demonstrate how to define Break-Glass policies following our Break-
Glass model and exploiting the policy state concept. In subsection 4.2.1 we
will show how the policies of our Break-Glass core model (section 3.3) are
structured within XACML. subsection 4.2.2 will show how the policy state
is used for the activation of policies and how the lattice obligations can be
used to model Break-Glass aspects such as the required user confirmation
of logging Break-Glass accesses. In subsection 4.2.3 we will introduce the
notion of "stateful Break-Glass," i.e., how to let some specific "area" remain
broken for a defined time-frame, again exploiting the policy lattice and policy
state concepts.

In subsection 4.2.4 will present a dedicated XACML policy combining
algorithm for implementing the lattice evaluation algorithm for both the
Break-Glass core and constraints model from chapter 3.

4.2.1 Policy Structure

With the policy structure, we have to solve two problems. First, in XACML, policies are an already existing concept, i. e., we need to integrate our concept of lattice policies into XACML. Second, we need to implementing the lattice evaluation algorithm with a policy combining algorithm.

Lattice Policies vs. XACML Policies

XACML policies and policy sets (using policies as synonym for both) are conceptually different from *lattice policies* (with lattice policies we refer to policies in our Break-Glass lattice). While XACML policies are used to structure permissions, lattice policies are in a refinement relationship with other lattice policies. In general, a lattice policy consists our a set of XACML policies. Furthermore, our Break-Glass model requires that obligations used as lattice obligations are not used within XACML policies, e. g., a `userConfirmation` obligation must not be used by an XACML policy.

When structuring policies in XACML, all policies defined as top element in a file are assumed to be a main policy, i. e., functioning as entry point for the evaluation. As for such main policies no combining algorithm is defined, a common solution is to implicitly apply an `only-one-applicable` combining algorithm for all main policies.[2] This requires all main policies to define a disjunct `<Target>` definition and circumvent ambiguous situations where two policies provide a result without a definition how to combine them. However, this will cause problems if policies are referenced as sub policy but not defined within the same file as the super policy, or if exceptional lattice policies extend privileges what has to be done by defining another XACML policy. To avoid this, we introduce the notion of an explicit main policy.

A *main policy* is the entry point into a policy lattice, i. e., contains (references) to the lattice policies. A main policy is a `<PolicySet>` and has to define a `PolicyId` or `PolicySetId` ending with `main` (e. g., see line 2 in Listing 4.6). Still, the `<Target>` definitions of all main policies have to be disjunct. If, at runtime, two main policies claim to be responsible (i. e., the `<Target>` matches), an `Indeterminate` decision will be returned, indicating an error in the policy (as done for the `only-one-applicable` combining algorithm). If no policy matches, a `NotApplicable` decision will be returned. Thus, when defining a policy lattice following our Break-Glass model, best practice would be to define one main policy. Defining several main policies

---

[2]See http://lists.oasis-open.org/archives/xacml-dev/201107/threads.html#00007 for a discussion on the OASIS mailing list.

```
    <PolicySet CombiningAlg="ordered-permit-overrides"
       PolicySetId="healthrecord:main">
 3  <Target>
    <!-- disjunct target for all main policies -->
    </Target>
 6  <PolicySet PolicySetId="healthrecord:preg">
      <Target>
        <Environments><Environment>
 9        <EnvironmentMatch MatchId="string-equal">
          <EnvAttrDesignator AttrId="activePolicies"/>
          <AttributeValue>preg</AttributeValue>
12        </EnvironmentMatch>
      </Environment></Environments></Target>
      <!-- place for policies and sets, policy references
15           and rules for health records in preg -->
      <Obligations>
      <!-- obligations as defined for the lattice -->
18    </Obligations>
    </PolicySet>
    <!-- place for further policy sets, policies and
21         policy references as defined by the lattice -->
    </PolicySet>
```

Listing 4.6: XACML policy structure.

means defining several policy lattices having disjunct targets (following the requirements of XACML). This is an additional method to structure policies. When defining one lattice, the only main policy can define a `<Target/>` matching every request.

Lattice Evaluation Algorithm

As sub-elements of the main policy, policies are structured as defined by the policy lattice. Using an `ordered-permit-overrides` policy combining algorithm (line 1 in Listing 4.6), policies are ordered along levels ℓ, i.e., starting with the policies on ℓ_1 towards higher levels. This algorithm can be used to implement our lattice evaluation algorithm as it searches for a PERMIT and terminates when the first PERMIT in the ordered list of policies was found.

Every lattice policy defines a `<Target>` definition which defines an environment target with an attribute designator for `activePolicies` (line 10 in

Listing 4.6) and an attribute value containing the policy ID. The attribute `activePolicies` is a policy state assignment as shown in Listing 4.7. Furthermore, every such policy has attached the obligations as defined for the lattice. Listing 4.6 shows the required structure.

4.2.2 Modeling Break Glass

Our Break-Glass model (implemented with the policy structure presented in the previous subsection 4.2.1) allows us to separate regular from exceptional permissions, the policy language presented in subsection 4.1.4 allows to express both regular and exceptional privileges. Thus, for implementing Break-Glass, we only need to describe how the activation of policies can be done using the policy state concept, and how the user confirmation and the logging of a Break-Glass access can be implemented using lattice obligations attached to our lattice policies.

Activation of Policies

The activation of policies is modeled using the attribute `activePolicies`. Using the policy state concept, the set of active policies is modeled as policy state assignment. The dependency `activePolicies` (Listing 4.7) does not depend on any other attribute and is hence valid for all requests. Polices are activated and deactivated by adding an according value in the policy state for the attribute `activePolicies`, e. g., adding an assignment with value `preg`. For policy state assignments, one can define fine-grained administrative policies who is allowed under which circumstances to activate and deactivate which policy. Those policies imposes great power and should be defined carefully, as all kinds of administrative controls. For example, it should not be possible to disable any access to the system as it would also exclude the possibility to reactivate any policy again.

At runtime, the `<EnvironmentMatch>` (line 9 in Listing 4.6), resolves the currently active policies (line 10) and, consequently, only matches if the policy is in the list of currently active policies.

The implicit activation of extended policies can either be modeled as obligations attached to the administrative controls, or be implemented with separate logic as part of the PAP. In subsection 4.2.4 we will present a dedicated XACML lattice evaluation algorithm which will handle the implicit activation of policies and furthermore implement the Break-Glass constraints model as discussed in section 3.4.

```
  dependency:activePolicies
  policyId -> null
3 policyId -> resource:policyId
  add:activate
  remove:deactivate
```

Listing 4.7: Modeling the activation of policies as policy state dependency.

User Confirmation and Logging Break-Glass Accesses

The central idea of Break-Glass is to let the user decide if an exceptional situation can justify the usage of exceptional privileges. To declare permissions as exceptional, we attach a `userConfirmation` obligation, which requires the PEP to show some information to the user. Depending on the scenario, users may be required to provide a text message which has to be stored in conjunction with the log of the Break-Glass access. Depending on the implementation, the `userConfirmation` obligation may have different semantics, i. e., requirements which go beyond only requesting a confirmation for the user. For example, the logging of the Break-Glass access or the requirement to leave a message may be implicit or modeled as additional parameter or obligation.

Also, the logging of Break-Glass accesses for post-access investigations can be done in several ways. We will discuss our approach in more detail in a dedicated section 5.2. We will argue that the logging should be done centrally within the authorization infrastructure. As the PDP cannot know if an access is actually executed, the PEP will notify the PDP – similar as for policy state changes – about an actually executed Break-Glass access. To ease the required protocol between PEP and PDP (as for the policy state management described in subsection 4.1.3), we assign a unique ID – the evaluation-ID – to every request. Thus, only this ID has to be sent to the PDP. See section 5.2 for a detailed discussion about which information will be required and how it is stored for post-access analysis.

4.2.3 Stateful Break-Glass

Two types of Break-Glass accesses can be distinguished:

- *Stateless Break-Glass* accesses which do not influence the security state, i. e.,. Break-Glass is only "active" for single actions.

- *Stateful Break-Glass* accesses influencing the security state, i. e., the PDP "remembers" past Break-Glass access, influencing the behavior for follow-up accesses.

What we discussed so far is stateless Break-Glass, i. e., permissions structured into exceptional policies and attached with obligations can be defined for exceptional situations. When such an exceptional policy is active, the exceptional permissions can be used to execute single actions, requiring the user to confirm the exceptional situation for every request. In the examples 1 and 3 of our running example, Carol and Dave are executing stateless Break-Glass accesses. The PDP or the policy state do not have to remember such Break-Glass accesses, i. e., the security state is not modified. Using such a stateless Break-Glass approach removes complexity from the PDP, as no state has to be stored. However, using a stateless approach, our example 2 cannot be implemented: once an exceptional situation was confirmed by a subject, for following accesses no further confirmation is required, i. e., once the glass is broken, exceptional privileges can be used just as regular privileges.

Stateful Break-Glass allows to model the state of an "already broken frame of glass." As this mechanisms potentially activates exceptional privileges for other subjects, it has to be modeled very carefully which privileges are unlocked under which conditions (and obligations) for which subjects. Here, the question arises who should be made responsible once an access using such exceptional privileges turns out to be illegal: the user who breaks the glass in the first place cannot foresee and influence all possible following accesses executed by other users, and hence can hardly be made accountable for those. On the other hand, the user who executed such a follow-up request may not have known that the request could be illegal, as he did not receive any warning. Such a situation would be a contradiction to the Break-Glass requirement that users can be made responsible for their actions.

As such questions cannot be decided in general, our approach of stateful Break-Glass allow to define exactly which "frame of glass" should be broken, and to define in a fine-grained way which following accesses should be permitted, and if and how users are warned or required to confirm the exceptional access.

Example 2 from our running example sketches our solution for those kind of questions. First, a physician (Alice) is able to create an exceptional TR, which will activate some (exceptional) privileges both for her and for other subjects. However, those privileges are not granted transparently to other subjects. Instead, second, every subject which can access the patients data only with an exceptional TR, has to confirm that the exceptional TR shall be used to access those data. Thus, every subject using such exceptional privileges has to break the glass to confirm the usage of exceptional privileges, and can hence be made responsible if those accesses turn out to be not legitimate. We will now demonstrate how the policy lattice and the policy state can be exploited to achieve such a behavior. We will assume there is a policy state assignment modeling the exceptional TR, and focus on the stateful Break-Glass, i.e., users have to confirm the usage of the exceptional TR only once for several accesses.

When introducing a state for Break-Glass accesses, one has to answer four questions (additionally to the question with which privileges the glass can be broken in the first place):

- Frame: Which parts of the "glass" should be broken?
- Privileges: Which privileges should be granted once a specific frame is broken?
- Obligations: If such privileges are granted, how should users be informed and/or confirm that they are using exceptional privileges?
- Duration: For how long should the glass remain broken, i.e., for how long should the exceptional privileges remain active?

As there are no general answers to those questions, they have to be modeled as part of the AC policies. Our framework is general in the sense that it allows a flexible modeling of all those questions. We will discuss the following concepts along XACML, however, they may be adopted to other policy languages as well.

Defining Break-Glass Frames

First of all, it has to be defined which types of frames can be broken. This can be modeled as *frame type*, which can be seen as n-dimensional area, having n "axes". Every such frame type gets assigned an identifier. The n axes are defined by attributes. To instantiate an frame type, for every axis a "point" has to be defined, i.e., assigning a value to the attribute. The more "dimensions" a frame has, the more fine-grained it can be. For example,

- 0-dimensional: no axis is defined; there is only one overall "glass" which can be broken.
- 1-dimensional: one axis is defined, e.g., `resource-id`, `patient-id`, or `healthrecord-id`. Values for those examples could be, e.g., `urn:healthrecord`, `Bob`, and `42`. In the first case, the glass for all health records would be broken, in the second case the glass for the patient Bob, and in the third case the glass for health recorded with ID 42 would be broken.

```
  dependency:confirmedBG:subject-patient
  confirmedBG:subject-patient -> patientId, subjectId
3 confirmedBG:subject-patient -> [true]
  patientId -> patientId
  subjectId -> subjectId
6 add:*
  remove:reconstituirGlass
```

Listing 4.8: Stateful Break-Glass policy state dependency.

- 2-dimensional: two axis are defined, e.g., `resource-id` and `healthrecord-id`, or `patient-id` and `subject-department`. Here, the glass is only broken for a frame defined by two according values, e.g., `urn:healthrecord` and `Bob`, or 42 and `gynaecology`.

There are no restrictions in the number of dimensions, however, attributes defining the axes have to be resolvable from the context, i.e., have to be contained in the AC request or be resolvable with an attribute designator from the policy state or PIP. This only defines the frame for which the glass is broken, but not what is actually accessible for whom if the glass is broken. For example, if the 1-dimensional `patient-id` frame with value `Bob` is broken does not mean everybody can access all data of Bob.

A frame is modeled as policy state assignment, while the axes correspond to depending attributes, and a boolean value is assigned to the policy state variable. Thus, the context handler can query the policy state if a specific frame is broken by resolving the policy state variable as for any other policy state variable.

For our running example, once a subject confirms the usage of an exceptional TR for a specific patient, no further confirmation should be required, as long as an exceptional TR to the same patient exists. For this, we define a 2-dimensional frame type (see the dependency definition in Listing 4.8) with two axes defined by `patientId` and `subjectId`, assigning the identifier `confirmedBG:subject-patient` to it (this identifier is used for both updating the policy state and retrieving a value from the policy state). Next, we will show how to use this "frame of glass."

```
  <!-- policy p^broken: confirmedExcp -->
2 <Policy CombiningAlg="first-applicable"
    PolicySetId="healthrecord:confirmedExcp">
    <Target> <Resource>urn:healthrecord</Resource>
5   <Environment>confirmedExcp</Environment> </Target>
```

```
   <Rule Effect="Deny">
    <Target/>
 8  <Condition FunctionId="not">
     <Apply FunctionId="and">
      <EnvAttr>confirmedBG:subject-patient</EnvAttr>
11    <VarRef>exceptionalTreatment</VarRef>
     </Apply>
    </Condition>
14  </Rule>
   <!-- rules granting permissions for pᵇʳᵒᵏᵉⁿ -->
   <Obligations>
17    <!-- obligations for pᵇʳᵒᵏᵉⁿ defined here, e.g.,
            set the background color of the GUI to red -->
   </Obligations>
20 </Policy>
   <!-- policy pᵇʳᵉᵃᵏ: confirmExcp -->
   <Policy CombiningAlg="first-applicable"
23   PolicySetId="healthrecord:confirmExcp">
   <Target> <Resource>urn:healthrecord</Resource>
   <Environment>confirmExcp</Environment> </Target>
26 <Rule Effect="Deny">
    <Target/>
    <Condition FunctionId="not">
29   <VarRef>exceptionalTreatment</VarRef>
    </Condition>
   </Rule>
32 <!-- rules granting permissions for pᵇʳᵉᵃᵏ;
        those may be the same as for pᵇʳᵒᵏᵉⁿ -->
   <Obligations>
35  <userConfirmation FulfillOn="Permit"/>
    <notifyPolicyState FulfillOn="Permit">
     <Dependency>confirmedBG:subject-patient
38        </Dependency>
     <Duration>10min</Duration>
    </notifyPDPState>
41 <!-- further obligations for pᵇʳᵉᵃᵏ defined here -->
   </Obligations>
   </Policy>
```

Listing 4.9: Stateful Break-Glass policy.

Stateful Break-Glass Privileges

How the glass can be broken and what this means for further accesses is defined by two policies $p^{broken} \sqsubseteq p^{break}$, i.e., p^{break} extends p^{broken}. The policy p^{broken} defines who has access to which part of the data under which obligations once the glass is *broken*. Thus, p^{broken} retrieves the broken frame state (which is a policy state assignment as, e.g., depicted in Listing 4.8) from the policy state. The second policy p^{break} defines who can *break* the glass on which frame type. To update the broken frame state, the mechanism to update a policy state assignment is used, i.e., a `notifyPDPState` obligation. This obligation also contains the definition for how long the glass should remain broken. The policy p^{break} has to extend the policy p^{broken}, $p^{break} \sqsupseteq p^{broken}$, as it should first be checked if the glass is already broken, before checking if it could be broken. Thus, p^{break} defines how the glass can be broken in the first place, which part of the glass should be broken (i.e., defining the frame), and for how long the glass should remain broken (i.e., defining the duration). p^{broken} defines the permissions and obligations once a specific frame is broken. p^{break} may grant the same permissions, or request the PEP to re-execute the AC request once the glass has been broken.

Listing 4.9 shows the policy `confirmedExcp` as p^{broken} and the policy `confirmExcp` as p^{break}: `confirmedExcp` defines privileges and obligations if the exception is confirmed, `confirmExcp` defines privileges and obligations to confirm an exception. The policies are ordered according to the refinement relationship and check if they are active (line 5 for p^{broken} and line 25 for p^{break}). For our running example, assume we defined a `<VariableDefinition>` `exceptionalTreatment` (used within a variable reference in lines 11 and 29) which returns `true` if there is an exceptional TR.

Policy p^{broken} (`confirmedExcp`) shall only define exceptional privileges if the glass is already broken, hence, in line 10 it is checked if the glass is already broken, i.e., the environment attribute `confirmedBrokenGlass:⏎` `subject-patient` evaluates to true. Furthermore an exceptional TR has to exist, which is checked in line 11. If not both of those conditions evaluate to true, the privileges granted by this policy shall not be applied and hence the rule and the policy return DENY. After this DENY rule, permissions granted by p^{broken} have to be defined. The obligations of p^{break} could, e.g., define that the background of the user should be colored red, to make him aware of ongoing Break-Glass accesses.

Policy p^{break} (line 22) has a similar DENY rule, however, it is only checked if there is an exceptional TR (line 29). The obligations of this policy should contain a `userConfirmation` obligation and a `notifyPDPState` obligation to

update the policy state with the broken glass frame `confirmedBG:subject-⏎`
`patient`. For this, the PAP will retrieve a notification about the state change,
retrieve the defined duration and frame type (i. e., dependency), and the
herewith assigned "axes" (i. e., attributes) and retrieve the associated values
as defined in the AC request. Using this information the PAP can update
the policy state accordingly. In our running example, the privileges granted
by p^{break} and p^{broken} are, with the exception of the obligations and the
DENY rule, the same.[3]

Let us assume there is a request which is not permitted by another
policy on a lower level but matches the targets of p^{break} and p^{broken}. Also
assume an exceptional TR was already created, i. e., the variable reference
`exceptionalTreatment` evaluates to true. When a user the first time tries to
access the health record of a patient for whom an exceptional TR exists, the
environment attribute `confirmedBG:subject-patient` in p^{broken} will evaluate
to false (i. e., the user did not confirm the usage of the exceptional TR
for this patient within the last ten minutes). The condition DENY rule of
p^{break} will not match, as there is already an exceptional TR. If there is a
rule in p^{break} granting access, the `userConfirmation` obligation will allow the
user to decide if the glass should be broken. If the user decides to do so,
the `notifyPDPState` obligation will be executed, updating the policy state
accordingly. A follow up access of this user to a health record of the same
patient within the defined duration of ten minutes will not match the DENY
rule of p^{broken} and can be permitted by a following rule. Hence the user will
not have to confirm the exceptional situation again.

The privileges granted by p^{break} and p^{broken} are the same in our running
example. Depending on the modeled scenario, one may define more complex
privileges here. For example, p^{break} could allow physicians to break the glass
for the whole department for a specific patient. p^{broken} could grant nurses
additional exceptional privileges only in case a physician broke the glass
already, however, still having to fulfill the obligations attached to p^{broken},
which could be a `userConfirmation` obligation, hence, requiring a Break-Glass
confirmation from the nurse. In such a scenario the nurse would not be
permitted to execute a Break-Glass access without a physician confirming
an exceptional situation.

Overall, stateful Break-Glass modifies the policy state and hence the
security state and hence the behavior of the PDP for a predefined area

---

[3]XACML allows to "re-use" such once defined permissions by using policy references,
i. e., in our prototyping implementation we define the permissions a physician has
with a regular TR in a separate policy, allowing us to reference those permissions in
multiple policies.

in a predefined extent, i.e., changes the security state and is hence an administrative control as defined by ACF$_a$ (Equation 2.2). While, in a similar way, Break-Glass could be used to activate another exceptional policy, using the definition of a frame type allows to define a fine-grained subset of permissions which should be "unlocked" in case of an exceptional situation.

4.2.4 Constraints Model in XACML

In subsection 4.2.1 we presented how to implement the Break-Glass core model (section 3.3) with the toolset available in XACML. For this, the lattice evaluation algorithm is implemented by ordered-permit-overrides combining algorithm, and the policies are ordered as defined by the lattice. Now, we will show how the policy lattice evaluation algorithm can be explicitly implemented in XACML by implementing a policy evaluation algorithm. The constraints algorithm (`getExtPolicies(id)` and Listing 3.3) is an extension to the core algorithm (Listing 3.1): if no DENY policies are defined, the constraints algorithm is equivalent to the core algorithm, i.e., the here presented policy combining algorithm implements both the core and the constraints models.

Our XACML policy combining algorithm `urn:policy-combining-⌐algorithm:policy-lattice` takes, as every policy combining algorithm, a number of policies and policy sets as argument, representing the policies of the policy lattice. To define the lattice for the combining algorithm the following `<CombinerParameters>` for policies of the lattice can be used:

- `urn:policyLattice:identifier` (required): identifies the policy within the lattice. Here, the same value as for the `<EnvironmentMatch>` on `urn:activePolicies` (line 11 in Listing 4.6) have to be used.
- `urn:policyLattice:type` (optional): defines if the policy is a PERMIT or a DENY policy (default is PERMIT). The value pairs of `urn:⌐policyLattice:identifier` and `urn:policyLattice:type` have to be unique, i.e., for every policy at most one PERMIT and DENY policy may exist.
- `urn:policyLattice:extends` (optional, multiple values possible): defines which policies in the lattice are extended, i.e., referencing a set of `urn:policyLattice:identifier`. If the extending policy defines both a PERMIT and a DENY policy, only one needs to define an `urn:⌐policyLattice:extends` parameters.

When loading the policy using this algorithm, the combining algorithm creates a representation of the defined lattice which allows to iterate over

all refining and extending policies and therefore implement the functions
`getPoliciesOrdered()`, `getExtPolicies(id)` and `getRefPolicies(id)` as they
are used by the lattice evaluation algorithm (Listing 3.2 and Listing 3.3). If
the optional attribute `urn:policyLattice:latticeIdentifier` (as in line 3 in
Listing 4.10) is defined, the created lattice can be cached as all information
required to create the lattice remains static at runtime. An implementation
has to ensure that the cache is erased if a new policy version is loaded.

Listing 4.10 shows how a policy lattice with DENY policies can be defined.
The defined policy is a `main` policy (line 2) and is therefore an entry point for
the evaluation. As it defines an all matching `<Target/>` (line 4), it has to be
the only main policy. The `latticeId` combining parameter in line 3 allows the
combining algorithm to cache the constructed lattice. The regular policy p^{reg}
is defined as `PolicyIdReference` to the policy with the ID `runex:preg` in line
8. The `<PolicyCombinerParameters>` from line 5 are assigned to `runex:preg`
and define only the identifier as `preg` (line 6). Thus, `preg` is, defined per
default, a PERMIT policy on ℓ_1. On ℓ_2, the policy `excp1` extends `preg` (line 11)
and has both a PERMIT (implicit defined per default from parameters on line
9) and a DENY (line 16) policy. Finally, on ℓ_3, `excp2` extends `excp1` with a
PERMIT policy. So, for example, if an access is permitted by `preg`, but denied
by the DENY policy of `excp1`, i. e., the policy `runEx:deny1` returns DENY for
this request, and if `excp2` is not active, the request will be denied. If policy
`excp2` is active, the access will be granted with obligations attached to `excp2`.
The definition of DENY policies is not required for the definition and usage of
the `urn:policy-combining-algorithm:policy-lattice` combining algorithm.
Thus, one can also use this combining algorithm also for the core model,
i. e., to explicitly define the lattice within the policy instead of the proposed
structuring described in subsection 4.2.1.

The activation of policies is, as presented in subsection 4.2.2, done using
an environment attribute `activePolicies`. However, the implicit activation
of policies along the hierarchy can be implemented within the function
`isActive(id)`, i. e., iterating over all extending policies and check if one of
them is active. Thus, policies do not need to define an environment match
as it is required in line 9 in Listing 4.6.

When implementing the combining algorithm defined in Listing 3.1 or
Listing 3.3 for XACML, one has not only PERMIT and DENY as AC decisions,
but also INDETERMINATE and NOTAPPLICABLE. Following a similar behavior
as the standard XACML `ordered-permit-overrides` combining algorithm, if
a policy evaluates to NOTAPPLICABLE the corresponding policy does not
provide anything to the AC decision and is therefore "ignored." For an INDE-
TERMINATE decision things are a little bit more complicated, as this signals

```
   <PolicySet CombiningAlg="policy-lattice"
     PolicyId="runEx:main">
 3   <CombParam Id="latticeId">runEx</CombParam>
     <Target/>
     <PolicyCombParams PolicyIdRef="runEx:preg">
 6     <CombParam Id="identifier">preg</CombParam>
     </PolicyCombParams>
     <PolicyIdReference>runEx:preg</PolicyIdReference>
 9   <PolicyCombParams PolicyIdRef="runEx:excp1">
       <CombParam Id="identifier">excp1</CombParam>
       <CombParam Id="extends">preg</CombParam>
12   </PolicyCombParams>
     <PolicyIdReference>runEx:excp1</PolicyIdReference>
     <PolicyCombParams PolicyIdRef="runEx:deny1">
15     <CombParam Id="identifier">excp1</CombParam>
       <CombParam Id="type">deny</CombParam>
     </PolicyCombParams>
18   <PolicyIdReference>runEx:deny1</PolicyIdReference>
     <PolicyCombParams PolicyIdRef="runEx:excp2">
       <CombParam Id="identifier">excp2</CombParam>
21     <CombParam Id="extends">excp1</CombParam>
     </PolicyCombParams>
     <PolicyIdReference>runEx:excp2</PolicyIdReference>
24 </PolicySet>
```

Listing 4.10: Policy lattice with DENY policies.

an processing error which prevents the PDP from providing an accurate AC decision. While one could, when a policy returns an INDETERMINATE decision, abort the evaluation and let the INDETERMINATE decision be the result of the combining algorithm, we decided to continue the evaluation and further search for a PERMIT, out of two reasons:

- The policy lattice evaluation algorithm may be used as explicit error handling mechanism, i.e., if a complex regular policy results in an error, define a policy on a higher level to grant exceptional privileges. Here exceptional does not mean the real-world situation but the fact, that the regular policy "throws an exception."
- The XACML `ordered-permit-overrides` policy combining algorithm also searches for another permit in case of a INDETERMINATE.

Implementing the lattice evaluation algorithm in XACML, the evaluated policy is responsible for attaching obligations to a result. Thus, in case of an inherited PERMIT, we have to remove the lattice obligations from the original permit and attach the obligations by the effectively permitting obligation. As stated in subsection 4.2.1, we assume that obligations used as lattice obligations are distinct from obligations used by the underlying XACML policies, thus, obligations can be removed from the result without having to know which policy contributed it to the result.

4.3 Expressing Exceptional Privileges

As argued in the introduction, it is impossible to write policies capable of detecting all possible exceptional situations. As consequence, privileges granted in exceptional situations cannot not define *why* exceptional privileges are granted, but only *what* should be granted in exceptional situations. Defining exceptional privileges follows the same rules as defining regular privileges, e. g., the policy state concept is used to model exceptional situations in the security state, e. g., an exceptional TR.

The concept of exceptional policies allows to structure exceptional privileges. First, exceptional privileges can herewith be activated and deactivated as needed, without that the person in charge would need to be a security expert. Second, meaningful messages for the users what they are about to override can be defined, hence, allow users to make a more informed decision if the glass should be broken.

Hence, for the definition of exceptional privileges we do not need to introduce new concepts. We will demonstrate how the presented concepts can be used to implement our running example using our policy lattice and policy state concepts, and how the definition of exceptional policies can support the user in his decision.

Exceptional Privileges for the Running Example

In example 1, physician Carol gets the warning that she is not a treating physician of the patient, however, it is known that the patient is currently treated within the hospital. Hence, for exceptional privileges the constraint that a direct TR has to exist is relaxed: if there is any TR, exceptional access can be granted. To define such an exceptional privileges, no further information about the system or security state is needed: instead of checking if the patient is assigned to the same department as the accessing subject, it is checked if the patient is assigned to any department or physician and hence if there is an ongoing treatment within the hospital. Having the policy state for regular privileges in place, this can simply be done by adapting the variable definition from Listing 4.3 by checking if the list of treating-department of the patient is non-empty. All other permissions are not effected.

In example 2, an exceptional situation is explicitly modeled, i. e., if a patient cannot give his consent, a health care professional is able to create an exceptional TR. One can define administrative controls of who and how such an exceptional TR can be created, e. g., implement a four-eyes principle. In terms of exceptional privileges, two concepts can be separated. First, the exceptional TR is introduced as an additional type of TR, modeled as additional policy state assignment. This exceptional TR is only used by exceptional privileges and does not affect the regular privileges. Such an exceptional TR may be taken into account when checking if there is a TR within the hospital, i. e., for example 1. Second, the stateful Break-Glass approach as discussed in subsection 4.2.3 is applied: to "remember" which subject already confirmed the usage of an exceptional TR and hence should not be required to confirm the usage of the same exceptional relationship within a restricted period. Here, confirmExcp as p^{break} is used to require a confirmation from the user and change the policy state, while confirmedExcp as p^{broken} will grant exceptional privileges if both an exceptional TR is available and the user confirmed its usage. How the broken area can be defined using a policy state assignments and how those permissions can be expressed for the running example has been discussed in subsection 4.2.3 and is shown in Listing 4.9.

For the so far discussed examples 1 and 2, the exceptional permissions are modeled by relaxing the constraint that a TR is required, leaving further permissions untouched. However, for example 3, nurse Dave executes a task which is for usual only permitted to physician. For this, privileges usually assigned to physicians can be assigned as exceptional privileges to nurses. Physicians can break seals by relaxing the constraints defined for seals.

Exceptional Policies

The exceptional privileges are now grouped into policies. The regular privileges are part of preg (p^{reg}) on level ℓ_1. The stateful Break-Glass policies confirmedExcp (p^{broken}) and confirmExcp (p^{break}) as presented in subsection 4.2.3 extend p^{reg}, i. e., preg ⊑ confirmedExcp ⊑ confirmExcp. To confirmExcp, additionally to the notifyPolicyState obligation, a user⏋ Confirmation obligation with the message as shown to Carol in example 2 is attached. To `confirmedExcp`, obligations to log the access as Break-Glass access, and to color the background of the subject red are attached. Except for the relaxed TR, the permissions are the same as for the regular case.

The policy `excpRelationship` defines how exceptional TRS can be entered into the system: health care professionals have to request such an exceptional TR explicitly and provide a note, why no regular TR could be created. A PERMIT granted by `excpRelationship` has three obligations attached: First, `userConfirmation` lattice obligation, attached with a message as shown to Alice in example 2. Second, defined by the underlying XACML policy, a `notifyPolicyState` obligation to create an exceptional TR (e. g., for 24 hours) between the department of the subject and the patient. Third, another `notifyPolicyState` obligation to update the `confirmedBrokenGlass⏎ :subject-patient` dependency as in `confirmExcp`, i. e., the subject creating an exceptional TR also implicitly confirms the usage of it. As the creation of an exceptional TR only makes sense if the according permissions can be used (i. e., `confirmedExcp` and `confirmExcp` are active), `excpRelationship` extends `confirmExcp`, i. e., `confirmExcp ⊑ excpRelationship`. Thus, if `excp⏎ Relationship` is activated (i. e., the creation of exceptional TR is possible), `confirmedExcp` and `confirmExcp` are activated automatically.

The policy `relaxedTR` allows, on a per action basis, to break the glass, if there is a known regular or exceptional TR within the hospital. However, as for `confirmedExcp` and `confirmExcp`, only the constraints for the TR are relaxed, the privileges granted by the policy are the same as for `preg`. As we want those permissions only to be applied if no regular or exceptional TR for the accessing subject can be found, `relaxedTR` extends `confirmExcp`, i. e., `relaxedTR ⊑ extRelationship`. This policy implements example 1 and hence has an obligation attached with a message as defined in example 1.

Finally, the policy `fullExtended` further extends the so far presented policies. This policy gives subjects the possibility to execute tasks beyond their regular responsibility, e. g., nurse Dave in example 3, as long as some kind of TR of the patient within the hospital exists. Here, the subject gets an explicit warning that he is leaving his regular responsibilities and both the patient and the supervisor of the subject will be notified about this override. This is the highest Break-Glass policy and shall only be applied if no permission can be found in all other policies, i. e., `relaxedTR ⊑ fullExtended`.

This are only examples how Break-Glass policies could be modeled, and are designed to implement our running example. An actual implementation of Break-Glass may choose other approaches how to override privileges. The examples chosen here should not be understood as suggestion how to model polices in general and Break-Glass policies in particular in health care scenarios, but only demonstrate the flexibility of the here presented approaches.

In this chapter we have introduced the policy state concept and shown how policy state assignments can be used to define administrative controls for regular policies, implement a stateful Break-Glass approach and the activation of policies in our policy lattice. Along those concepts, we have shown how the Break-Glass models from chapter 3 can be used to define Break-Glass policies.

5 User Information: At-Access

Users are made responsible when using exceptional privileges in an illegitimate way. Thus, users have to make a decision if they want to break the glass, or if the situation does not justify such an override. Hence, the user needs to know which regular privileges have been extended and has to put this information into the context of the current access.

In the previous section 4.3, we demonstrated how the policy lattice can be exploited to define messages attached to obligations, i.e., describing the type of override the user is about to execute. In section 5.1, we will present, based on our publication [32], an approach which allows the system to inform the user who actually has the required permission to execute the current request.

In section 5.2, we will discuss the concepts and techniques of how to record the system state at-access. This is required to ensure the non-repudiation of Break-Glass accesses, and to make it available for post-access investigations.

5.1 Override Measurement

When talking about amount of override, a number as quantification of override seems to be a natural choice. One could base such an analysis on existing work, i.e., measuring the similarity of policies, e.g., Bryans [36], Fisler et al. [54], Lin et al. [71], Warner et al. [107]. However, a number is rather abstract information which does not help to estimate the override in respect to the current situation. Also, a number would suggest that there is a precise measurement of the override, but what can be provided to the user is always an imprecise assessment and can never be a precise advice. If the system would be able to make precise decisions, no Break-Glass would be needed.

We propose to inform the user which other users would be permitted to execute the request. Those users have to be "close" to the accessing user so that he can estimate what kind of qualification and job profile is required to executed the requested action. This raises two question. First, what is the definition of "close," and, second, how to define the set of permitted subjects.

We now present an approach which allows to determine a set of subjects which are, first, permitted to execute a specific access, and, second, close in respect to the searching user. Access Control (AC) frameworks are designed to decide efficiently if a specific subject has access to a resource. The inverse problem, i. e., which subjects have access to a specific resource, is for usually not supported. Due to the complexity and expressiveness of most modern policy specification languages (including arbitrary and complex constraints), such implementations may only be able to approximate the result.

As a consequence, we suggest to over-approximate the AC policy by converting it (statically) into an information graph. This information graph should provide (in combination with other information graphs) an efficient way for determining the set of users that potentially have access to a given resource. Assuming that this over-approximation is not too coarse, we can use the existing Policy Decision Point (PDP) for testing that a user can in fact access the given resource.

To find close users, the general idea is to use multiple – preferable existing – information sources and compute them to an ordered list of users, ordered along the closeness to the requesting user. This list of "best candidates" is reduced using an over approximation of the policy, i. e., removing all users which are, under no circumstances, permitted to execute the task. For the rest of the users it is tested if, under the current policy at the current point in time, a request is permitted.

Note we have published some techniques presented here under the term *delegation assistance* [32], where users are assisted in finding a mentor who can execute a specific task for them (or, in systems supporting delegation, find a mentor who is permitted to delegate a specific task). Here, we will present the core techniques to find such a mentor, however, we will use this information to give the user a better understanding of what he is doing. With delegation assistance, for some situations it might also be possible to circumvent the need of Break-Glass and execute the denied access with what delegation assistance can provide. However, we agree with Rissanen [89], delegation cannot handle all kinds of exceptional situations and hence cannot eliminate the need for Break-Glass. Although we will not discuss the delegation aspects of the techniques presented in [32], we will use the term delegation assistance to reference to this core technique and use mentor as name for the person which would be permitted.

5.1.1 Information Sources

When speaking of close, one needs to define what close means. The overall goal is that the user knows the "close" user, its qualification and job profile. Here, one can consider multiple categories of how users can be close to each other. We model those multiple categories as multiple *information sources*, e. g., user can be

- close with respect to the organizational hierarchy,
- close with respect to their office or department location,
- close with respect to their current location, or
- close with respect to their qualification

These information sources can be represented as directed weighted graphs, called information graphs. Subjects are represented as vertices, the edges represent how close subjects are. More formally, an *Information Graph* is a directed weighted graph $G = (\mathcal{V}, \mathcal{E}, \omega, \omega_m)$ where $\mathcal{V}$ is a set of vertices (representing the subjects), $\mathcal{E}$ is a set of edges (representing the relations between the subjects), and $\omega : \mathcal{V} \to \mathbf{N}_0$, where for all $v \in \mathcal{V}$. $0 \le \omega(v) \le \omega_m$, is a function assigning a weight, i. e., a numeric label, to each edge which has to be smaller than ω_m.

The edge weight represents the (degree of) familiarity, on scale from 0 (very familiar) to ω_m (not familiar), between two subjects. We use directed graphs for representing asymmetric relations. Finally, we denote the set of information graphs (with maximum weight ω_m) with $\mathcal{G}_{\omega_m}$. All information sources which should be used for the delegation assistance have to be represented as information graph.

Modeling Information sources

To model information graphs, given information sources can and should be reused, i. e., the expert has to define a transformation which creates, given the current state of the information defined by the information source, an information graph. While deriving information graphs requires, usually, expert knowledge, there is a general rule: subjects that are close to each other should be connected with an edge having a (relatively) small weight. In subsection 5.1.2 we will show how several information graphs can be merged into one information graph. We discuss several information sources as possible examples:

Role hierarchy: For systems using hierarchical role-based access control, we propose the similarity of assigned roles as distance function, where the estimation algorithm should especially consider the role hierarchy.

Using this information source as distance function prefers the delegation of sub-task to users with the least additional access rights needed for executing the given task.

Security labels: In systems using an access control systems based on labeling (e. g., Bell-LaPadulla [17]), we propose to use the hierarchy of security labels, which prefers resolution strategies that minimize the declassification distance of data.

Organizational structure: By using information about the organizational structure of a company (membership of users to divisions, administrative areas of accountability), assisted delegation can prefer subjects that are, somehow, responsible for the user. For example, this strategy would prefer a mentor within the same department and is therefore more likely to be known by the user.

Management hierarchy: Similar to the organizational structure, the management hierarchy can be exploited: this would prefer mentors within the same level or sub-tree of the hierarchy.

Process model: In systems driven by business processes, the process models are another information source. Here, one would prefer to delegate sub-tasks to subjects that are already involved in the overall process.

Office location: Subjects that know the user personally should be preferred. This sorting can be done by using the office location as a measurement and preferring users that work close to each other.

This list of information sources is not meant to be exhaustive, other information sources can be integrated.

Policy Over-Approximation

The so far discussed information sources are only meant as examples and may only be partially be implemented or be extended by other information sources – depending on the given infrastructure and scenario. However, one special information graph is required for a resource-sparing implementation: the over-approximation of the policy.

As already noted, the policy over-approximation is used to reduce the list of close users, derived from the combination of several information graphs, to a set of users which could be permitted. The remaining users are ordered along the closeness, and the existing PDP is used to test which user can in fact access the given resource.

Thus, the goal of the policy over-approximation is to remove a large amount of those users which cannot be permitted for a given access, while assuring that no users are removed which could have access. Thus, the corresponding information graph should contain as few as possible users without defining edges between those users, i. e., the policy information graph $G_p = (\mathcal{V}_p, \varnothing, \omega_m, \omega_m)$ only defines a set of vertices $\mathcal{V}_p$.

As for other information graphs, this over-approximation depends on the given infrastructure and the chosen AC model. Given our example, one could over-approximate the policy by taking all PERMIT permissions into account, and ignoring all constraints attached to those permissions, i. e., doing the over-approximation based on resource, role and action. A more complex approach could also take the concept of Treatment Relationships (TRS) into account when modeling the over-approximation of the policies for health records.

5.1.2 Merging Algorithms

To achieve a better order of closeness along several information sources, we allow to merge several information graphs and therefore combine the information represented by those information graphs. Here, two information graphs are combined to a new information graph, which can be combined with another information graph.

Assume two information graphs $G_1, G_2 \in \mathcal{G}_{\omega_m}$ with $G_1 = (\mathcal{V}_1, \mathcal{E}_1, \omega_1, \omega_m)$ and $G_2 = (\mathcal{V}_2, \mathcal{E}_2, \omega_2, \omega_m)$. Conceptually, we merge G_1 and G_2 into a new information graph $G = (\mathcal{V}, \mathcal{E}, \omega, \omega_m) \in \mathcal{G}_{\omega_m}$ using a three-folded algorithm:

1. we merge the set of vertices:

$$\mathcal{V} = \mathcal{V}_1 \odot \mathcal{V}_2, \text{ where } \odot \in \{\cup, \cap, \setminus, \ominus\}. \tag{5.1}$$

2. we merge the set of edges:

$$\mathcal{E} = \{e \in \mathcal{E}_1 \cup \mathcal{E}_2 \mid \text{src}(e) \in \mathcal{V} \wedge \text{dest}(e) \in \mathcal{V}\} \tag{5.2}$$

where $\text{src}(e)$ denotes the source vertex and $\text{dest}(e)$ the destination vertex of the edge e.

3. we update edge weights for all edges $e \in \mathcal{E}$:

$$\omega(e) = \begin{cases} \omega_1(e) & \text{if } e \in \mathcal{E} \cap \mathcal{E}_1 \setminus \mathcal{E}_2 \\ \omega_2(e) & \text{if } e \in \mathcal{E} \cap \mathcal{E}_2 \setminus \mathcal{E}_1 \\ f(\omega_1(e), \omega_2(e)) & \text{otherwise.} \end{cases} \tag{5.3}$$

where $f : \{0, \ldots, \omega_m\}^2 \to \{0, \ldots, \omega_m\}$ is a user-defined function merging the weights of edges that are part of both input graphs.

Thus, our algorithm is not only parametrized over the two input graphs, but also over the functions for merging vertices $(\_ \odot \_)$ and edges $(f(\_, \_))$. In the following, we discuss different choices for these functions.

Vertices

The join and disjoin are, in our experience, the most often used methods for merging vertices. On the one hand, joining all vertices, i.e., $\mathcal{V} = \mathcal{V}_1 \cup \mathcal{V}_2$, guarantees the maximal set of solutions, i.e., is used to combine the information of two information graphs. On the other hand, disjoining the vertices, i.e., $\mathcal{V} = \mathcal{V}_1 \cap \mathcal{V}_2$, allows for a quick reduction of the solution set, i.e., is used when information in both information graphs has to exist to be valid. Hence, the disjoining can be used to remove vertices which would not contribute to the solution.

The selection of the vertices merge function depends on the information contained by the graph, where two main types can be distinguished: information graphs enhancing the quality of the edge weights are for usual combined with $\_ \cup \_$ (e.g., combining the organizational information graph and the policy information graph), information graphs enhancing the quality of the vertices are for usual combined with $\_ \cap \_$ (e.g., only consider users logged in or from the same location) or $\_ \setminus \_$ (e.g., remove users that are currently not available).

Edges

The merging of edges is defined by (5.2) and does not need any adoption.

Edge weights

Choosing a good strategy for merging edge weights is more difficult than choosing a strategy for merging vertices. Overall, the class $\mathcal{G}_{\omega_m}$ should be closed under the application of this function, i.e., we require for a merge function f and a given ω_m that

$$\forall w_1, w_2 \in \mathbf{N}_0. \ (0 \le w_1 \le \omega_m) \wedge (0 \le w_2 \le \omega_m) \qquad (5.4)$$
$$\implies (0 \le f(w_1, w_2) \le \omega_m)$$

holds. Recall that a small edge weight represents a strong connection between the two subjects (vertices). Therefore, an intuitive (but not formal) requirement is

$$\forall w_1, w_2 \in \mathbf{N}_0. \ f(w_1, w_2) \le w_1 \wedge f(w_1, w_2) \le w_2, \qquad (5.5)$$

i. e., the merged edge weight is smaller or equal the minimum of the two input weights. Thus, an obvious choice, satisfying both requirements, for f is the minimum function:

$$f(w_1, w_2) = \begin{cases} w_1 & \text{if } w_1 \leq w_2, \\ w_2 & \text{otherwise.} \end{cases} \tag{5.6}$$

As an alternative, we will use the function

$$f(w_1, w_2) = \frac{w_1 \cdot (\omega_m - w_2)}{\omega_m} \tag{5.7}$$

which also satisfies our requirements and, moreover, guarantees for all $0 < w_1, w_2 < \omega_m$ that the weight $f(w_1, w_2)$ is strictly smaller than the minimum of both input weights. Intuitively, we interpret w_2 as the percentage to be subtracted from w_1.

Further, we present a variant allowing to influence the reduction of merged edges by a factor $c \in \mathbf{R}$ ($c \geq 1$). Without loss of generality, we assume $w_1 \leq w_2$ and define:

$$f(w_1, w_2, c) = \frac{w_1 + \frac{w_1 \cdot w_2}{\omega_m} \cdot (c-1)}{c} \tag{5.8}$$

Informally, c describes the gradient used for decreasing edge weights. This function has the following properties:

- If $c = 1$ then $f(w_1, w_2, c) = w_1$ holds.
- If $c_1 \geq c_2$ then $f(w_1, w_2, c_1) \leq f(w_1, w_2, c_2)$ holds.
- If $w_2 = \omega_m$ then $f(w_1, w_2, c) = w_1$ holds. Thus, if one of the input weights is equal to ω_m, the other weight remains unchanged.

Summarizing, choosing the appropriate methods for merging information graphs requires domain knowledge, i. e., an understanding about the information represented in the graphs.

5.1.3 Identifying Mentors

In the last step, one has to identify those users which are effectively permitted and can therefore function as *mentors*. For finding a set of close mentors, for several information sources a transformation to a information graph should be implemented and an according merging strategy for the given information graphs has to be chosen. This gives an combined information graph $G_n = (\mathcal{V}_n, \mathcal{E}_n, \omega_n, \omega_m)$. From G_n, all users which cannot be permitted have to be removed, i.e., combining G_n with the policy over-approximation information graph $G_p = (\mathscr{V}_p, \varnothing, \omega_m, \omega_m)$, i.e., merging the vertices (5.1) with $\mathscr{V}_n \cap \mathscr{V}_p$. As G_p does not define any edges, the mering of edges (5.2) and update of edge weights (5.3) leaves the edge weights as defined by G_n as long as the user is contained in G_p.

From the resulting information graph, all users with a direct connection to the accessing user are ordered along the increasing edge weight, i.e., the user having the smallest weighted connection to the user is chosen first. One may also include users with indirect connections, i.e., applying an all-pairs shortest path search algorithm to construct the ordered list of users.

Starting with the first user, AC requests are evaluated on the PDP, replacing only the `subject-id` in every request. The search for a mentor terminates if, first, a given number of mentors, e.g., three, is found, or, second, there are no more users in the list. The found mentors are returned.

It may be the case that no mentor could be found, i.e., no user close to the accessing user would be permitted to execute the request. However, also such an information is valuable to the user. For example, if the user is sure that the access has to be done (i.e., is justifiable), but no other (close) user would be permitted to do so, someone has to use Break-Glass to execute the required action. On the other side, if the user is, e.g., working on the advice of someone close, or, if the user is not sure what the consequences of a Break-Glass access are, he might reject to take the risk of using Break-Glass, as no one in his surroundings is permitted to execute requested action.

Overall, we are aware of the fact that this approach does not give the user precise information or advice. However, Break-Glass is needed as the system is not able to have precise information and therefore not able to give a precise advice. Requiring the system to give precise advice in case of Break-Glass would therefore be contradiction. Also, when using Break-Glass the user is likely to be in a stressful situation and more complex information he is not used to understand (such as "you are breaking a separation of duty constraint") would barely help him to come to a more substantiates decision.

5.2 Recording the System State

For post-access investigation, information which is available at-access has to be recorded to be available in the post-access phase. We will show how to record the information which is available for the PDP at-access in subsection 5.2.1, and how to record further information which cannot be interpreted by the PDP in subsection 5.2.3. In subsection 5.2.2 we will show how to ensure non-repudiation of Break-Glass accesses.

5.2.1 Versioning System State and Security State

To record the system and security state at-access, the theoretical complete approach would be to either always save the complete system state (e. g., dump the memory and the persistent state of all applications and the authorization infrastructure to a persistent store such as a hard disk) and preserve it for a post-access analysis, or log every single state transition executed in the system. This would guarantee that all information about the system state and its history is known in the post-access phase. However, there are some practical drawbacks, e. g., the time and persistent memory needed to make such a dump, the effort during the analysis to determine which kind of information is required, where it is located and in which format it is saved. Analogical, it is not possible to create a full recording of the environment, out of technical and legal constraints.

As such a solution, we collect and store the information which is acquired by the PDP for AC request evaluation. By this the auditor has at least the information which has been available and known at-access by the PDP. As this is information is already available at-access, this approach causes only minor overhead. By consequently capturing all information, regardless if there is a regular or a Break-Glass access, the auditor will be able to see all security relevant changes before and after the access. The concepts to do this are discussed in this section. Second, we will discuss in subsection 5.2.3 how to collect information beyond what is resolved by the PDP at-access.

As described in subsection 4.1.2, the information acquired for the PDP, being an implementation of the Access Control Function (ACF) from Equation 2.1, can be divided in four parts: AC request Q, policy permissions σ_{sec}^{perm} and policy state σ_{sec}^{state} (i. e., the security state σ_{sec}) and context information retrieved from Policy Information Point (PIP) (i. e., the system state σ_{sys}). Policy permissions and policy state are managed by the authorization infrastructure, thus, we have full control over this information and changes executed thereon. Instead of saving the policy and the policy state for every request, we introduce the third main concept within this thesis: the notion of *versioning*.

Versioning allows to determine the security state for every point in time. For the policy permissions, which are defined in a text based form, one can use a Subversion (SVN) like system (subversion.apache.org), where all permissions are stored in their textual form. For the policy state, which are attributes assigned to some identifying entity, the versioning is done on the assignment level, i. e., every assignment has a temporal validity from when until when this assignment was, is, or will be valid. On an abstract level, for every assignment a start and an end date have to be provided when creating an assignment. To query the security state a date for when assignments are requested has to be provided. Practically, the creation, deletion, and query of an assignment will have the same Application Programming Interface (API) and the versioning logic will take care of the correct dates, e. g., start "now" and end "infinite" for the creation of an assignment. Further details will be discussed with the implementation section 7.1.

For the context information σ_{sys} a similar concept as for the policy state $\sigma_{\text{sec}}^{state}$ is applied, with two differences. First, in contrast to the policy state, the authorization infrastructure does not have control over the context information, i. e., there may be changes without that the authorization infrastructure will recognize it. Therefore, no time range can be defined for the validity of the assignment, but only the point in time when the context information was retrieved. Second, while for policy state assignments an identifying entity is defined, context information is associated to the specific request the information was requested for.

By logging the context information σ_{sys} associated to the request Q and versioning policy permissions $\sigma_{\text{sec}}^{perm}$ and policy state $\sigma_{\text{sec}}^{state}$, all parameters for the ACF can be restored post-access. Thus, for a post-access investigation, the security relevant state of the IT system can be reproduced. We will discuss in subsection 6.2.1 how this concept is integrated in our analysis infrastructure.

5.2.2 Logging Break-Glass Accesses

Logging of Break-Glass accesses is required to ensure the non-repudiation (see Definition 8) of Break-Glass accesses, i. e., subjects must not be able to dispute to have executed a Break-Glass accesses. Given the concept of a central PDP and the versioning of at-access information at the central PDP, we envision the logging of actual usage of exceptional permissions by the user, by a notification sent from the Policy Enforcement Point (PEP) to the PDP. The PDP then marks granted exceptional privileges as actually executed. This, however, is just one approach, others may implement a distributed logging mechanisms which can ensure non-repudiation with, e.g., with cryptographic means.

While the versioning of the security state σ_{sec} (i.e., policy permissions $\sigma_{\text{sec}}^{perm}$ and policy state $\sigma_{\text{sec}}^{state}$) will be implemented by the *versioning policy storage* (see subsection 6.2.1), the versioning of the AC request Q and the system state σ_{sys} (i.e., context information) will be done in a *versioning log storage*. Thus, for every AC request, the versioning log storage will store

- An evaluation-ID uniquely identifying every request.
- The point in time when the request was executed and, hence, which timestamp was used to resolve information from the versioning policy storage.
- The information contained in the request, i.e., subject, resource, action, and possible further information such as, e.g., the health record ID.
- Further context information as resolved by the PIP, i.e., implementing the assignment of context information to the AC request.
- The result as returned to the PEP and required by the Policy Administration Point (PAP) for the policy state management.

Given this, the logging of Break-Glass accesses can be implementing by enforcing the PEP to notify the central log storage about an actual exploited exceptional privileges. This is a natural choice, as, first, this way all information required for post-access is in one place, and, second, the central authorization infrastructure with its security relevant components has to provide an environment where the integrity of the logs and hence the non-repudiation of Break-Glass accesses can be ensured.

A `userConfirmation` obligation implicitly includes that the obligation handler shall, if the user confirms the usage of exceptional privileges, notify the log storage about the execution of a Break-Glass access by submitting the evaluation-ID. The PDP may provide an interface to the log storage to ease the implementation.

5.2.3 Recording At-Access Information

There are two further types of information which can be collected at-access for later evaluation. First, information which can be resolved and understood by the PDP, but is not needed for the evaluation. Second, information which can be resolved (or recorded), but is not interpretable by the PDP, e.g., a video.

```
   <Policy>
    <Rule Effect="Permit">
 3    <Target> <!-- some target definition --> </Target>
    <Condition FunctionId="and">
     <!-- place for regular conditions -->
 6    <Apply FunctionId="or">
      <Apply FunctionId="value-is-in">
       <AttributeValue>pseudoValue</AttributeValue>
 9     <!-- first pseudo attribtue -->
       <AttributeDesignator
            AttrId="healthRecord:label"/>
12     </Apply>
       <AttributeValue>true</AttributeValue>
       <!-- place for further pseudo attributes -->
15    </Apply>
     </Condition>
    </Rule>
18   <Obligations>
     <UserConformationObligation/>
     <StartVideoRecordingObligation>
21    <Duration>5min</Duration>
     </StartVideoRecordingObligation>
    </Obligations>
24 </Policy>
```

Listing 5.1: XACML policy shows how to record information using pseudo
attributes and triggering a video recording.

Information which can be resolved and understood by the PDP can be
recorded by adding "pseudo attributes" to exceptional permissions, i.e.,
attributes which are not required for the evaluation. Such attributes can
be queried when exceptional permissions are about to get granted and –
just as regular attributes – recorded and therefore available post-access.
For example, XACML allows to resolve attributes without letting them
influence the actual AC decision, as shown in Listing 5.1. Here, the value for
healthRecord:label shall be resolved, but the availability and content shall
not influence the result. For this, we use the bag function value-is-in (line
7) which checks if a specific value is contained in the bag returned by the
attribute designator (line 10). As we are only interested in the resolution
of the attribute, we can place an arbitrary value (line 8) for the check. An
or (line 6) combined with a true value assures that, to whatever result the
value-is-in function evaluates, only the attributes are resolved but do not

influence the result of the condition. In particular, those additional attributes are only resolved and cause additional effort, if the <Target> and the regular part of the <Condition> evaluated to true. If several such attributes should be resolved, they can be sequentially defined in the same fashion, e. g., starting in line 14.

For recording information not interpretable by the PDP, one can use obligations attached to exceptional permissions which trigger, e. g., a video recording of the environment. Here, especially legal constraints have to be taken into account. Information which is captured this way has still to be interpreted by the auditor. And, the auditor will also use other information sources independent from the Information Technology (IT) system such as witness's statement. In this thesis, we focus on the IT system state and history, as the implementation of techniques to capture some environment information always depends on the actual environment. However, information which is captured this way should also be stored attached close to the ofter information, i. e., allow to assign it to an AC request. Listing 5.1 shows an obligation that additional information is recorded by the PEP, i. e., the <StartVideoRecordingObligation> in line 20 requests the PEP to trigger a recording of five minutes.

6 Analysis: Post-Access

An integral part of Break-Glass is the need to separate legitimate from illegitimate accesses, i. e., analyze Break-Glass accesses in the post-access phase. Only if users know that misuse of Break-Glass will be punished, they will use Break-Glass the way it is intended: as exception mechanism for exceptional situations. However, making a post-access decision is a non-trivial task, as a lot of information is required to make a well-founded decision. Furthermore, it requires a human person – or an auditor as we will refer to them – to make the decision. As manual work is expensive, auditors should be supported in their work by the system, thus increasing the efficiency and reducing the need for investigations and therefore reducing the costs of the Break-Glass system.

In this chapter, we will show how auditors can be supported in their work. For this, we will first discuss in section 6.1 what has to be done for a post-access analysis. We will identify two challenges where the authorization infrastructure can support the auditor and discuss them in Sections 6.2 (based on our publication [29]) and 6.3. The core proposition will be that investigations of a Break-Glass accesses do not end in itself, but should be used to increase the quality of policies, both regular and exceptional. Once acquired knowledge can thus be preserved for future use. We will present a policy-driven approach for post-access analysis, which allows for an automated evaluation of some Break-Glass accesses, and allows to define guidance for other Break-Glass accesses. Altogether, the techniques presented in this chapter are intended to reduce the effort and costs of Break-Glass.

6.1 Post-Access Break-Glass Analysis

Deferring the Access Control (AC) decision to the post-access phase does not solve the question if the access was correct or not, i. e., the decision is postponed but not omitted. Post-access control decisions have to be made to separate the legitimate from illegitimate accesses – Break-Glass can only work if illegitimate accesses are detected and dishonest users are punished. As motivated in section 1.1, deferring an AC decision to the post-access phase is more than just moving a problem to a later point in time. In contrast to the pre-access phase, where machine readable policies for making decisions at the at-access phase have to be defined, making a decision in the post-access phase has some advantages.

Decision maker: A human can make the decision. He can use his human mind to use more information for the decision than a machine could, i. e., use both hard to encode (i. e., in a machine-readable form) rules and hard to formalize information.

Concrete situation: In the post-access phase, no likelihoods, or unforeseeable situations have to be considered; the access is concrete and specific.

Temporally constraints: The decision is not time-critical which allows, for example, to execute operations which would not terminate within the allowed time-frame at-access.

Information: Other and under certain circumstances more (machine interpretable) information is available: information which is available at-access can be recorded, information which has not been available at-access might have become available.

Break-Glass does not mean that the AC decision is omitted, but just postponed. Also, Break-Glass is not intended to annul the corporate policy, i. e., the regular policy to which all accesses have to stick to. AC policies are the technical representation of the corporate policy which has to be fulfilled. Consequently, we see one of the main tasks of the auditor to understand how, where, and why the regular AC policy was violated. Although a Break-Glass access violated the regular (and hence the corporate policy), Break-Glass access can still be legitimate. This apparent contradiction can have two reasons:

- The regular, technical policy is not (fully) correct. This can be caused by several reasons, e. g., a clean translation from the corporate policy to the technical policy is not possible or was incorrect. Or, as we argued in the motivation, the policy is too strict or is incomplete, caused by, e. g., hard to encode rules, missing information, or unconsidered scenarios.

- The access violates the corporate policy, but can be legitimated post-hoc by a human. This can be caused, e. g., by inaccuracy in the corporate policy – in which case the corporate policy should be rectified. It may also be the case that it has to be decided on a case to case basis by an authorized person, e. g., by the patient who's health record has been accessed with Break-Glass, or a superior recognizing the benefit of the access over the damage caused by the policy violation. Finally, there can be situations where the policy has to be hurt the one or the other way to avoid a deadlock. [1]

A deferred post-access control decisions must not be decoupled from the requirements which lead to the regular policy, i. e., at-access and post-access decision have to comply to the same corporate policy (being implemented by the regular policy p^{reg}). The requirements identified in the pre-access phase are used to define the policies which are enforced at-access. Break-Glass allows to defer some decision which are "unclear" at-access to the post-access phase, however, just because they are decided and enforced in another way does not mean that other requirements can be applied. To comply to the same requirements, an auditor, when making a post-access decision, will have to understand how and where the regular policy was violated. Furthermore, he has to understand both the benefit of the access and the environment of the accessing user, i. e., why the achievement of the benefit in another way was not or hardly possible.

To comply to the same requirements, an auditor, when making a post-access decision, will run through a similar decision process as the security engineer in the pre-access phase. While the security engineer has to find a trade-off between risks and likelihoods (i. e., for potential damage and benefit of an access) for possible future scenarios, the auditor has only to deal with one concrete situation, the damage and the benefit should be known post-access. Also, the auditor can rely on the knowledge which is formulated in the regular policy and does not have to run through the whole requirements analysis as it is required for the definition of the policies pre-access. Thus, an auditor has to understand three questions:

1. Why did the regular policy not permit the request. Examples could be that a Separation of Duty (SoD) or legal constraint was violated, the user was missing some specific qualification or privilege, or in the policy this specific scenario was not considered. This allows to determine the amount of override done by the user or the inadequacy of the regular policy.
2. What was the benefit or goal of the executed request, e. g., saving a patients life or releasing the system from a deadlock.
3. To put the first two into context and judge if the trade-off of the user was right, the auditor has to understand the situation at-access.

---

[1]On some level this is a contradiction, if both the policy and the violation of the policy are "correct." However, such contradictions can also be found in the "real world," e. g., the Austrian "Military Order of Maria Theresia," having been the highest order in the Habsburg monarchy, was given, among other, for successful military acts achieved by consciously acting against an explicit order.

Regarding the first question, our framework can support the auditor in two ways. First, we will discuss some techniques in section 6.2 which support the auditor in determining how and where the regular policy was hurt. To save such acquired knowledge we will, second, introduce post-access policies in section 6.3.

The answer to the second question is needed to put the amount of override in ratio to the benefit. Only a large benefit may justify a large override. Even a clear validation of the corporate policy can be justified if some other major damage could be avoided this way. For example, if the Break-Glass access was the only way to save a patients life, this Break-Glass access will most likely be ratified.

Finally, the auditor needs to understand why it was not or hardly possible for the user to achieve the benefit in another way without using Break-Glass.

The result of such an investigation is not only if the user behave correctly, but also if the AC policies, both regular and exceptional, are correct and implement the corporate policy in an appropriate way.

Only information which has been foreseen as relevant in the pre-access phase can be captured and used for the AC decision at-access. Similar, the auditor relies on information which is available post-access: one cannot go back to the past and collect additional information. Although an auditor has the possibility to use information sources outside of the Information Technology (IT) system (e. g., ask people involved in the exceptional situation), information which can be foreseen to be relevant should be collected at-access. We discussed how this can be done in section 5.2. Post-access, one can differentiate three types of information:

IT system state: information regarding the state of the IT system the access was executed in, i. e., the information available in both the authorization infrastructure and the application context.

IT system history: information regarding how the system came to the actual state, and what happened after the actual access within the system, e. g., following accesses or policy changes.

Environment: information regarding the state of the real world which is unknown by the system but can only be interpreted by a human. We do not make a separation into state and history, as the human mind combines both and does interpret a situation as a sequence of states with state transitions.

At-access, the Policy Decision Point (PDP) has only a subset of the IT system state information. The past history may be accessible for the PDP, but can be interpreted as part of the current state and information accessible therein. Post-access, an IT system can provide access to system state and history information if it was recorded accordingly.

An IT system can trigger the gathering of information of the environment at-access and support the auditor in finding those recordings post-access. However, an IT system cannot help in interpreting the environment information – if it could do so, this could be used at-access to make a more accurate decision. Thus, an IT system supporting the investigation will have to focus on the preparation of the information where it knows the semantic, and leave the interpretation of the environment information to the auditor.

6.2 Analysis Infrastructure

6.2.1 Authorization Infrastructure

We will now discuss how the versioning concept described in subsection 5.2.1 integrates into an authorization infrastructure which can be extended with analysis capabilities. Based on this, we will discuss how this can be used to construct an analysis workbench, which allows for both using the given concepts but also integrate further analysis capabilities by using existing or implementing new tools.

Versioning

To implement the versioning concept presented in subsection 5.2.1, the components of the authorization infrastructure as discussed in subsection 4.1.1 have to be adopted:

Versioning Policy Storage provides a storage for the AC policy, i. e., policy permissions $\sigma_{\text{sec}}^{perm}$ and policy state $\sigma_{\text{sec}}^{state}$, and keeps track of all changes of the AC policy. In general, policy permissions will only be accessible by some administration and management cockpit, while changes to the policy state are possible from from both the administration cockpit or from the application context.

Versioning Log Storage stores both the AC requests Q and the context information σ_{sys}. As discussed in subsection 5.2.1, the context information is bound to the AC request and are therefore stored with the request log. Also the result the AC decision including obligations are stored. The policy and log storage provide an interface to search for and load elements by multiple selection criteria.

Policy Decision Point loads the currently active policy permissions $\sigma_{\text{sec}}^{perm}$ from the versioning policy storage and logs accesses to the versioning

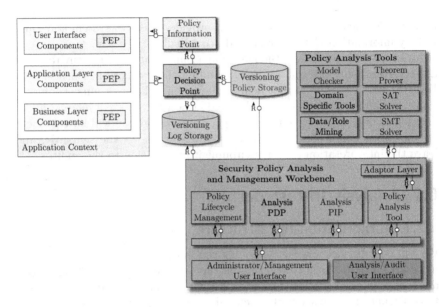

Figure 6.1: Analysis Workbench Architecture.

log storage. As part of the PDP, the context handler is aware which information to resolve from the versioning policy storage (retrieving the $\sigma_{\text{sec}}^{state}$), and which information to resolve via the Policy Information Point (PIP) from the application context (retrieving the σ_{sys}).
The other components, i. e., Policy Enforcement Points (PEPS), PIP and the resource implementation remain untouched.

Analysis and Management Workbench

The *Analysis and Management Workbench* can be divided into two parts. The policy life-cycle management allows to administer the policy storage, i. e., is functioning as Policy Administration Point (PAP). All the other components are for analysis and have only read access to versioning policy and log storage, i. e., it is neither possible to access the productively running applications nor to modify information in the log or policy storage.

Policy Lifecycle Management consists out of back-end services and a User Interface (UI) (the administrator and management user interface) which allows for the administration of policies. For example, policies can be modified (i. e., new versions of policies can be created) and activated (i. e., the version of the active policy can be defined) whereon the productive PDP is triggered to reload the currently active policy.

Analysis PDP operates in a simulated environment, i. e., it is not not connected to productive application context. Instead, it is using the analysis PIP to resolve attributes from the "virtual system state." The Analysis PDP can be used with different policy configurations, i. e., can load different versions of policy permissions and policy state from the versioning policy storage.

Analysis PIP acts as context information service for the Analysis PDP. During analysis, no application context is available, hence, the Analysis PIP either retrieves context information from the log storage (i. e., use attributes as they have been available at-access) or from the policy analysis tool.

Analysis Tools consisting out of a set of Policy Analysis Tools and a dedicated UI which allows to analyze policies together with the corresponding log entries. For example, they allow to load information from the versioning storage, load Analysis PDPs, execute (recorded) requests against those Analysis PDPs, and modify the context information with the help of the analysis PIP.

Moreover, various external analysis tools can be integrated, ranging from generic to domain specific tools and algorithms. Generic tools such as model checkers, Boolean Satisfiability Problem (SAT) solvers, theorem provers, or data mining tools may be used to solve complex tasks needed for an analysis method implemented by the policy analysis tools. Such external tools may accept a set of policies, a set of AC requests, a set of log entries, and an analysis query (such as "compute the difference between two given policy versions" or "compute all users that, under a certain policy, are allowed to access a specific resource") as input. An Adapter Layer may provide a uniform interface to the analysis tool and for abstracting from the concrete data formats of the different externals tools.

The Analysis PIP does not (and is not allowed to) access the productive application context, but can simulate the environment as it has been at-access: versioning log and policy storage can be accessed with read access.

Based on this, several analysis scenarios can be implemented, e. g., AC requests can be *replayed*. All input parameters as needed for the Access Control Function (ACF) can be "reconstructed." Requests Q are stored in the versioned log storage, the Analysis PIP provides the system state σ_{sys} as it has been at-access based on the versioned log storage, policy permissions $\sigma_{\text{sec}}^{perm}$ and policy state $\sigma_{\text{sec}}^{state}$ is retrieved from the versioned policy storage.

The analysis PIP also allows to simulate a different environment, i. e., the availability and values of attributes defining the environment can be "injected" into an analysis evaluation. This allows the auditor to run through what-if scenarios, e. g., would the access have been permitted if the patient had been assigned to the department of the nurse. Furthermore, the Analysis PDP can be loaded with any policy version; a request can be replayed with a policy as it was active, e. g., one week before or after the actual AC request was made, while the auditor can change the used version of the policy permissions and the policy state. The analysis workbench can also be enhanced with the capability to access further at-access information, i. e., as it has been recorded described in subsection 5.2.3.

6.2.2 PDP Analysis Extension

With the so far presented architecture a wide range of analysis scenarios can be implemented. To implement more analysis techniques, we enhance the PDP with further analysis capabilities. For the description and the implementation of the here shown concepts, we will use eXtensible Access Control Markup Language (XACML) as concrete example, however, the shown concepts could also be adapted for other languages.

First, we keep track of runtime information during the evaluation and of the order of evaluation of elements of the policy language to, e. g., be able to access the "call stack" and the value of resolved attributes. Second, the Analysis PDP generates *evaluation events* before and after the evaluation of every policy element, and provide those evaluation events to the analysis workbench.

This can be used for a variety of tools, e. g., a debugger where "break-points" can be defined before and after an language element is executed (or evaluated). When replaying an AC request the auditor can easily figure out which rules of the policy contributed to the AC decision. Such an analysis could either be done by an interactive debugger, or, the workbench also allows to implement this as an analysis tool. Such a tool could print all rules and their effects contributing to the AC decision, i. e., print the unique identifier of the rule, the encapsulating policies and policy sets including their rule and policy combining algorithms, if `<Target>` and `<Condition>` of the element matched. This gives a quick overview which rules contributed to the result.

As example, consider the policies from Listing 4.5 and the referenced policies as defined in Listing 4.4, modeling the regular privileges of nurses and physicians for health records. Assume, a physician tried to read the

```
   PolicySet :: runEx : patient ( first - applicable ) {
   Policy :: runEx : patient : nonTreat ( first - applicable ) {
 3 }
   Policy :: runEx : patient : nurse : permits ( first - applicable ) {
   }
 6 PolicySet :: runEx : patient : physician : permits (
                                          first.-applicable ) {
   Policy :: runEx : patient : physician : stateChange (
 9                                        first - applicable ) {
   }
   Policy :: runEx : patient : physician : stateless (
12                                        first - applicable ) {
   Rule :: runEx : patient : physician : stateless :01  →  permit
   }
15 }
   }
```

Listing 6.1: Reducing the policies from Listing 4.5 and Listing 4.4 by means of a concrete request, using our analysis tool.

entry of a health record and the auditor needs to know which rule contributed to the AC decision. Listing 6.1 shows what the tool could have provided as output. All matching XACML elements are printed, thus, the policy runEx:patient:patient did not match the request. The policies runEx:patient:nurse:permits, runEx:patient:physician:stateChange, and runEx:patient:nonTreat matched, however, did not contain any matching rule. The rule runEx:patient:physician:stateless:01 matches returns PER-MIT. Please be aware that an example with multiple encapsulated policy sets using different combining algorithms would make the example more interesting as not only one rule would match and hence the combination would not be that obvious. However, the example policies presented so far are intended to be simple and hence we lack such an complex policy.

Abstract Evaluation

Another PDP extensions for the Analysis PDP is *abstract evaluation*. Here, instead of using values for resolving attributes, the Analysis PDP allows to uses "abstract attributes," i. e., an attribute which is not instantiated (with a concrete value). The goal of abstract evaluation is not to find an AC decision, as this is not possible with missing information. Instead, using abstract evaluation allows to evaluate all those parts of a policy which would be evaluated if the abstract attribute would take an arbitrary value. With abstract evaluation a partial evaluation is done, whereas the evaluation is "concrete" as far as the attributes are not abstract. If all information would be considered as abstract, i. e., including `subject-id`, `resource-id`, and `action-id`, the whole policy would be evaluated.

Abstract evaluation allows for evaluating AC requests without the need of resolving all attributes, e. g., from the Analysis PIP or the versioning policy storage. This is of special interest if a request is replayed on another version of the policy permissions $\sigma_{\text{sec}}^{perm}$ or policy state $\sigma_{\text{sec}}^{state}$ and some attributes are missing, i. e., the attribute can neither be resolved from the policy state $\sigma_{\text{sec}}^{state}$ nor from the security state σ_{sec}. This can be the case if, e. g., attributes have not been resolved at-access and are therefore not available in the versioned log storage.

Conceptually, whenever an abstract attribute is used during evaluation, the result of this evaluation has also to be treated as abstract: using abstract values, all possible evaluation paths have to be evaluated. For example, in most policy languages an *or* statement of the form $stmt_1 \vee stmt_2$ will be implemented "lazy," i. e., if the first statement $stmt_1$ evaluates to true, the second statement $stmt_2$ will not be evaluated as the whole statement will evaluate to true anyhow. For abstract evaluation, if $stmt_1$ is abstract, the *or* cannot be implemented lazy, i. e., $stmt_2$ has to be evaluated. However, if $stmt_2$ evaluates to true, the result of $stmt_1 \vee stmt_2$ is not abstract as, independent of $stmt_1$, the overall statement will evaluate to true. Hence, for abstract evaluation, those parts of the language implementation have to be modified where lazy evaluation is applied. For example, in XACML, this are combining algorithms and the logical functions *or* and *and*. For policy combining algorithms, obligations have to be considered, i. e., the result of $stmt_1 \vee stmt_2$ with $stmt_2$ could only be then be considered as non-abstract, if $stmt_1$ and $stmt_2$ (which have to be policies) have the same (e. g., no) obligations attached.

As example, consider we extend our tool with support for abstract evaluation. Using the same example, assume that for the attributes `treating-⏎ subject` and `treating-department` (see Listing 4.3) abstract values are injected. Let us furthermore assume that Carol is working on the `casualty` department and requests read access to a health reord entry. When evaluating the `<Condition>` of rule `runEx:patient:nonTreat:01` (Listing 4.5) using the variable `runEx:treatment_relationship` (Listing 4.3), the rule cannot be evaluated, as for the two attributes abstract values are injected. However, the rest of the policy can evaluated in the same way as for Listing 6.1 and resulting in the same output (Listing 6.2). One can see that injecting those abstract values, with this request only the rule `runEx:patient:nonTreat:01`

```
     PolicySet::runEx:patient(first-applicable) {
       Policy::runEx:patient:nonTreat(first-applicable) {
 3     Rule::runEx:patient:nonTreat:01( not( or(
         any-of-any(string-equal(), "carol",
                                   $treating-subject),
 6         any-of-any(string-equal(), "casualty",
                                   $treating-department)
       )))  → deny
 9     }
       Policy::runEx:patient:nurse:permits(first-applicable) {
       }
12     PolicySet::runEx:patient:physician:permits(
                                   first-applicable) {
       Policy::runEx:patient:physician:stateChange(
15                                 first-applicable) {
       }
       Policy::runEx:patient:physician:stateless(
18                                 first-applicable) {
       Rule::runEx:patient:physician:stateless:01 → permit
       }
21   }
     }
```

Listing 6.2: Reducing the policy as for Listing 6.1, but using abstract evaluation for two missing attributes **treating-subject** and **treating-department**.

is effected. Furthermore, one can see that either **treating-subject** has to contain the string **carol** or **treating-department** has to contain the string **casualty**, otherwise rule **runEx:patient:nonTreat:01** would match, return DENY and hence DENY the request as the first matching result is returned by the encapusulating policy and policy set.

Policy Animation

Abstract evaluation can also be used for symbolic input-partitioning [30, 46] (i. e., the computation of equivalence classes), which we call *policy animations*. We use HOL-TESTGEN [31] as an external analysis tool for implementing the policy animation. The formalization of security policies in HOL-TESTGEN (see [34] for details) allows for handling a large set of attribute types and functions defined over them – without the need of converting those data types into bit-vectors. We integrate the input partitioning of HOL-TESTGEN into our analysis workbench by writing a tool which does the abstract evaluation and prints the not evaluable part of the policy as *test specification* for HOL-TESTGEN.

For policy animation we need to restrict the used policy language. In more detail, we need to restrict attributes and functions. Attributes have to be restricted to those which can be represented as boolean, number, or string. This includes attributes such as `urn:oasis:names:tc:xacml:2.0:data-type:⏎ ipAddress` or `http://www.w3.org/2001/XMLSchema#dateTime`, as long as it can be mapped to a number or `http://www.w3.org/2001/XMLSchema#anyURI` as long as it can be mapped to a string.

Functions are typed, for example, the `type`-equal function takes two parameters of `type` where `type` could be, e. g., `string`. Based the three basic types, we allow the following "primitives" for functions

- Logical function `and` ($\wedge$), `or` ($\vee$), and `not` ($\neg$) for boolean attributes.
- Arithmetic functions for numbers which are based on plus (+), minus (−), multiplication (∗), and division (÷)
- Compare functions for numbers based on <, ≤, =, >, and ≥
- Compare functions for strings which are based on `type`-equals or `type`-starts-with (checking if one of the strings is equal to the beginning of the other; `starts-with` is a function defined by us and used to structure the policies).
- Bag functions to handle bags of values, e. g., as returned by attribute designators
  - `type`-one-and-only returns the first value of the bag if the size of the bag is one, and raises an error otherwise
  - `type`-bag-size returns the size of the bag
  - `type`-bag returns a bag created by a number of values
  - `type`-is-in returns true, if, for the provided attribute, the function `type`-equal returns true for any value of the provided bag.
- Higher order functions which take a function and attributes (either one value or a bag of values) as input

Functions which can be defined with those primitives are allowed. For example, the `time-in-range` function, can be mapped to the here presented functions as shown in section 6.2.2. Furthermore note that the XACML code presented in this thesis follows those restrictions.

In case of XACML, the test specification needs to consider the different rule and policy combining algorithms, XACML functions and data types have to be translated a format understandable by HOL-TESTGEN. This puts some restrictions on this analysis technique, as, first, not all function defined in the XACML standard can be translated for HOL-TESTGEN, e. g., regular expressions. Second, XACML explicitly allows the definition of customized

```
   definition
     timeInRange :: int → int  → int →  bool
3    where
     timeInRange x m n =
       (({x, m, n} ⊆ {0 .. 24})
6          ∧ (if m < n
          then (m ≤ x) ∧ (x ≤ n)
          else ((m ≤ x) ∧ (x ≤ 86400000)
9               ∨ (0 ≤ x) ∧ (x ≤ n)))))
```

Listing 6.3: Time-in-range function for HOL-TESTGEN.

functions as we, for example, use it with *type*-starts-with to structure policies. Given those restriction, all data types and 192 out of 212 functions listed in the XACML standard can be used for policy animation. Functions which have to be excluded are string manipulation and compare functions, regular expressions, and XPath functions.

For example, consider the function time-in-range which takes three input parameters of type time[2], and "shall return true if the first argument falls in the range defined inclusively by the second and third arguments" [80], while the third argument has to be interpreted as equal or later than the second, i. e., time ranges may span over midnight. For example, if the second argument is "18:00:00Z", the third is "06:00:00Z", a time-frame over midnight is defined. Time can be encoded as integer, e. g., as milliseconds from 0:00 a.m. as 0 to 12:00 p.m. as 86400000. The time-in-range function can be expressed as logical function, taking x as first value and m and n as second and third value, i. e., testing if $m \leq x \leq n$. As the function allows to test time-frames over midnight, one has to distinc two cases:

- $m \leq n : x \geq m \wedge x \leq n$
- $m > n : (x \geq m \wedge x \leq 86400000) \vee (x \geq 0h \wedge x \leq n)$

In most cases m and n will be known at runtime as they are most likely defined as attribute values and not as attribute designators. In this case, the two cases can be differentiated by the tool at runtime. However, if this is not the case, one can also express the whole function as boolean expression, i. e., $((m \leq n) \wedge (x \geq m \wedge x \leq n)) \vee ((m > n) \wedge ((x \geq m \wedge x \leq 86400000) \vee (x \geq 0h \wedge x \leq n)))$. As HOL-TESTGEN is extensible using higher-order logic, which is quite similar to a functional programming language, also the translation into a

---

[2]Omitting the lengthy prefix for both urn:oasis:names:tc:xacml:2.0:function:⏎ time-in-range and http://www.w3.org/2001/XMLSchema#time

test-specification is possible. The time-in-range function can be defined as shown in Listing 6.3.

6.3 Policy-Driven Analysis

In the previous section we have shown how an authorization infrastructure can be enhanced to support the auditor in evaluating an Break-Glass access. The goal is to determine how and where the regular policy was violated. One result can be that the quality of the regular or exceptional policy can be enhanced, i. e., future similar accesses are handled in a more proper way. However, as motivated in the introduction, policies cannot be defined fully correct, hence, at some stage policies may be as correct as they can be, and Break-Glass is the only way to handle exceptional situations. If it has to be assumed that a similar Break-Glass access will occur in the future, one may want to preserve the once acquired knowledge which factors could justify or disprove the Break-Glass access. Such knowledge could help during future investigations to determine how and where the regular policy was violated in a faster way.

In the introduction we stated that the regular policy may not be able to make a definite decision as information is missing, but this information may get available post-access, possibly in machine-readable form. One may want to use such information in an automated way before having to investigate every Break-Glass access in a manual way.

To enable both, preserving once acquired knowledge and use information which is only available post-access, we introduce the notion of *post-access policies* p_F, which are used to encode the post-access knowledge. The techniques behind post-access policies are the replay facility of our analysis workbench in conjunction with the versioning of the policies and the policy state in particular. They are evaluated in the system state of the actual Break-Glass access, i. e., replay the access with the system and security state as it has been when the actual AC request was executed.

Conceptually, a post-access policy p_F is a direct extension of the post-access policy, i. e., $p^{reg} \sqsubseteq p_F$. Practically, only the post-access policy needs to be evaluated post-access, as the regular and exceptional policies will provide the same result as at-access: if p^{reg} would have returned a PERMIT, the user would have been able to access the resource without the need of Break-Glass. In alignment to the two goals of post-access policies, there are two conceptually types of post-access polices:

- p_F^f policies allow for a fully automated investigation by using information which is only available post-access,
- p_F^k policies allow to preserve once acquired knowledge, i. e., guide the auditor to those factors which were identified in past investigations to be relevant for the decision if a Break-Glass access was legitimate or not.

Obviously, results from the fully automated post-access policy are preferred, hence, $p_F^f \sqsubseteq p_F^k$.

6.3.1 Automated Analysis with Post-Access Information

The post-access policy p_F^f allows for an automated investigation with information available only post-access, i. e., using information which has not been available at-access (e. g., during the evaluation of p^{reg}):

- Information which does not exist at runtime, e. g., a Treatment Relationship (TR) which was entered into the system with some delay, or an inquiry result. Such information may become available post-access. This includes information which is prospective from at-access point of view, e. g., events happening after the access.
- Information which cannot be accessed (as fast as needed) for evaluating an AC request, e. g., information which is generated every day or once a week, e. g., as report. This type of information is available "somewhere" in the system, but hard and expensive to get within the short time-frame the request has to be answered at-access.

Thus, one can see p_F^f as the "better informed" version of the regular policy p^{reg} which can only be evaluated in a post-hoc fashion. Consequently, the definition of p_F^f might be done in together with p^{reg}.

For the evaluation of p_F^f no manual effort is needed, as only automatically retrievable information is used. For this, one may need to introduce *post-access attributes* and implement the required attribute resolvers. Those attributes resolvers could be required able to access, e. g., log files of the system, the versioning log storage, or data which originated after the actual access (which is obviously not possible at-access). Also, the versioning feature of the policy state can be exploited, e. g., to resolve TRS not only valid at-access, but within a certain time-frame after the access.

For example, suppose for a patient an exceptional TR was created because, e. g., as the patient was unconscious and no agent was available which could have confirmed the TR. In the following some Break-Glass accesses were executed, and an auditor has to determine if all of them have been legitimate.

Within the next 24 hours after the exceptional TR was created, either the patient or one of his agents could confirm a (regular) TR.

For an post-access analysis, the policy engineer defines that Break-Glass accesses, which would have been legitimate if a TR would have been existent at-access, and a TR was created within the next 24 hours, should automatically be marked as legitimate. For this, an attribute resolver for the attributes `treating:department+24h` and `treating:subject+24h` are implemented, which return all known treating departments and subjects of the patient within the point in time of the access and the next 24 hours, exploiting the versioning feature of the policy storage (i. e., policy state). Those attributes are used to implement the post-access policy as shown in Listing 6.4. This post-access policy is similar to the regular policy as defined in Listing 4.5 and Listing 4.3 and also makes usage of the same permits for nurses and physicians, but only defines the TR in another way, i. e., taking TRS established after the actual access into account.

Note, that this enables the auditor to quickly justify all accesses which would have been permitted if the relationship would have been established in a regular way. This can be done in a fully automated way without that an auditor has to explicitly start the process. For example, an automated analysis process could be started once a day to mark all Break-Glass accesses as justified which can be approved with a p_F^f policy.

Furthermore note, that this does not sort out those accesses which have been done during an exceptional situation, but cannot be justified this way. For example, a user may use privileges granted by `extRelationship` or `fullExtended` which cannot be justified this way. As those accesses may be illegitimate, they have to be investigated separately. However, the more access can be justified in an automated way, the more time for a detailed investigation of the remaining accesses is saved.

6.3.2 Preserving Analysis Knowledge

Policies of type p_F^k also use information which is not available at-access, but requires the human sanity to resolve this information. Thus, the evaluation of p_F^k policies in an interactive, access-specific questionnaire, which guides the auditor to the relevant factors which adjudicate if an access was legitimate. The questions are modeled as *post-access attributes* which can only be "resolved" by the understanding of a human, e. g., `was:physician:reachable` or `is:patient:a:celebrity`.

Post-access attributes are used and treated as regular attributes in the analysis workbench. When evaluating a p_F^k policy in the analysis workbench,

```
   <PolicySet PolicyId="runEx:analysis:patient"
     CombiningAlg="first-applicable"><Target>
3     <Resource>urn:runEx:patient</Resource></Target>
   <Policy PolicyId="runEx:analysis:patient:nonTreat">
     <Target/> <VariableDefinition
6            VariableId="runEx:treatment_relationship+24">
     <Apply FunctionId="or">
      <Apply Function="any-of-any">
9        <Function Function="string-equal">
        <SubjAttr>subject-id</SubjectAttr>
        <ResrcAttr>treating-subject+24</ResrcAttr>
12      </Apply>    <Apply Function="any-of-any">
        <Function Function="string-equal">
        <SubjAttr>subject-department</SubjectAttr>
15        <ResrcAttr>treating-department+24</ResrcAttr>
     </Apply> </Apply> </VariableDefinition>
     <Rule RuleId="runEx:patient:analysis:nonTreat:01"
18                         Effect="Deny">   <Target/>
      <Condition FunctionId="not">
      <VarRef VarId="runEx:treatment_relationship+24"/>
21    </Condition></Rule>
   </Policy>
   <PolicyRef>runEx:patient:nurse:permits</PolicyRef>
24 <PolicyRef>runEx:patient:physician:permits</PolicyRef>
   </PolicySet>
```

Listing 6.4: Post-access policy for automated analysis.

regular attributes should be resolvable from the log storage or the policy state, while the resolution of post-access attributes will fail. Thus, the analysis workbench will ask the auditor to either provide a value for the attribute or choose an analysis technique. While the auditor can, as with every missing attribute during an analysis replay, start analysis techniques such as abstract evaluation, the intended behavior is to answer the "question."

Technically, p_F^f and p_F^k differ only in the usage of post-access and post-access attributes. While there is a conceptual differentiation between those two types of attributes, on a technical level both attribute types can be used within one policy. Post-access attributes for p_F^f require some effort when introduced to implement the attribute designators. However, this allows to retrieve the required information in an automated manner once the required attribute designators are implemented. Not all kind of attributes can be made a post-access attribute, e. g., if human sanity is required. Post-access attributes for p_F^k, on the other hand, are easy to introduce, however cause some overhead as they have to be answered manually specific for every investigated access. Thus, if an attribute is modeled as post-access or as post-access attribute will depend on the effort to implement an attribute designator vs. the effort to resolve the value manually, and how often the attribute will be needed to be resolved.

Post-access policies, e. g., p_F^f and p_F^k, are, as every policy, ordered in a policy lattice. During an investigation, we do not need to evaluate the regular or exceptional policies. Hence, post-access policies form a distinct lattice, with all post-access policies being active. Policies causing minor manual overhead, e. g., a p_F^f policy only using post-access attributes, will be on a low level. This allows to find a result with least possible effort. Policies requiring human work, e. g., a p_F^k policy requiring a human to provide some information, are on a higher level.

For post-access policies, it is also possible to define DENY rules, i. e., allowing to define a suggestion to the auditor that the Break-Glass access was illegitimate. If the post-access policy comes to a result (PERMIT or DENY) this can be seen as suggestion to the auditor how to assess the Break-Glass access. The auditor should evaluate the post-access policies in debug mode and halt on every matching rule. By this, the auditor will see the rule and therefore the condition which contribute to the result. Rules in the post-access policies should be documented, i. e., using the <Description> element, to allow auditors understand for which situations the rule is intended for. Depending on the implementation of the debug infrastructure, the auditor may be able to set the result from PERMIT to NOT_APPLICABLE, i. e., search for another matching rule if the currently matching rule is, in the opinion of the auditor, not applicable. If there is no suggestion (i. e., the post-access policy does not have a rule for the corresponding access and returns a NOT_APPLICABLE decision), or the auditor does not accept the suggestion, the auditor has to "fall back" to a manual investigation. Overall, post-access policies will be similar to the regular policy, but using other and further attributes and conditions.

In this chapter we have shown how our analysis infrastructure with a replay facility can support auditors during analysis, and how a policy-driven analysis approach can automate the post-access evaluation of Break-Glass accesses and hence decrease the costs of Break-Glass.

7 Implementation

We use the XACML implementation of SUN (sunxacml.sourceforge.net) with a patch which enhances both the code quality and already contains some XACML 3.0 features[1]. Altough the Sun Microsystems (SUN) project is not maintained anymore (the last update on the project website dates back to June 2006), it was the most accurate open source implementation available at the time we started our prototypic implementation (2008). This implementation turned out to be a well-designed implementation, almost bug free, supporting the full XACML 2.0 standard, and allows for an easy adoption and modification (as discussed in section 7.2). Thus, we had no motive to switch to another implementation.

Nonetheless, we introduced some changes to the source code. First, we raised the code from Java 1.4 to Java 5, i. e., introduced Java generics. By doing this, the code can be compiled on an up to date compiler without warnings and it is easier to make changes (the implementation makes heavy use of typed collections – knowing which type a collection contains helps to understand the code). Second, we enhanced the configuration capabilities, as the given implementation is primary the XACML engine itself without a sophisticated connectivity to its environment. The implementation efforts can be divided into two parts: first, the implementation of the landscape where Break-Glass accesses can be executed in, i. e., the productive landscape (section 7.1). Second, the analysis workbench, where Break-Glass accesses can be analyzed (section 7.2).

7.1 Break-Glass Landscape

SUN XACML Implementation

As the description of our implementation will in major parts rely on the SUN implementation of XACML, we will sketch the architecture of the given implementation to make our explanations more understandable.

---

[1] The patch was provided by sics.se but is not publicly available anymore.

Every XACML element is represented as Java object. The unmarshaling (i. e., read from Extensible Markup Language (XML) and generate Java objects) is based on a Document Object Model (DOM) parser, thus, every type of input (e. g., text files, databases, Simple Object Access Protocol (SOAP) or Representational State Transfer (REST) messages etc.) which can be provided to a DOM parser can be used to load and interpret XACML policies and requests. For marshaling, objects write "itself" to an output stream. To evaluate policies with the Policy Decision Point (PDP), a `PolicyFinderModule` has to be implemented. Depending on the implementation, varying input sources can be used and it can be decided if policies are loaded for every evaluation or if they are cached. To resolve attributes during evaluation, an `AttributeFinderModule` has to be implemented. Those finder modules resolve, depending on the order they are defined in the PDP configuration, specific attributes. An `EvaluationCtx` (evaluation context) keeps track of the current context of the evaluation, i. e., being the implementation of the context handler from Figure 4.4. The default evaluation context reads the attributes provided with the request and makes them available during evaluation, i. e., without the need to implement an `AttributeFinderModule`.

Policy State

For the policy state concept as presented in subsection 4.1.2 and subsection 4.1.3 we implemented a generic component which is also capable of the versioning concept presented in subsection 5.2.1. The policy state implementation can be partitioned into three parts. First, a component which stores the data (dependency definition, assignments) and provides an Application Programming Interface (API) to manage and retrieve the policy state. Second, an `AttributeFinderModule` which is used by the XACML PDP as context handler to retrieve attributes. Depending on the context, this module retrieves either the currently valid attributes for the productive PDP or the attributes valid at some specific point in time for the analysis PDP. Third, a management component which is able to retrieve an evaluation-ID (from the Policy Enforcement Point (PEP)), load the Access Control (AC) request from the log server (described later) and update the policy state according to the contained `notifyPolicyState` obligations.

The core of the policy state configuration are the dependency definitions, e. g., as shown in Listing 4.2, Listing 4.7, and Listing 4.8. Our implementation supports the format of dependency definitions as shown in those Listings. To identify XACML attributes, attributes are defined with `category`, `attribute⌐`

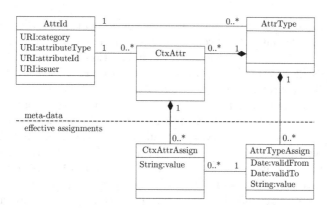

Figure 7.1: Class diagram: policy state implementation.

Type, `attributeId`, and `issuer`. The name of the attribute definition can then be used within the dependency definitions.

Based on this configuration, the policy state persists dependencies as attribute type (`AttrType`) and instances of dependencies as attribute assignments (`AttrTypeAssign`) to a relational database. The class diagram for the managed entities is depicted in Figure 7.1 and can be divided into two parts. The meta-data, shown in the upper part of the diagram, are defined by the dependencies definitions. For example, the dependency `roleAssignment` in Listing 4.2 defines that the `subjectId` is required to resolve `roles`. Here, the `AttrId` is `role`, and there is one `CtxAttr` with the `AttrId` `subjectId`. The dependency for the frame type `confirmedBrokenGlass:subject-patient` for stateful Break-Glass in Listing 4.8 (if the glass is already broken depends on the `subjectId` and the `patient`) is stored with the `AttrId` `confirmed⌐BrokenGlass:subject-patient` and two `CtxAttrs` `patientId` and `subjectId`. The dependency `activePolicies` from Listing 4.7 has no depending attribute and hence no `CtxAttr` assigned. Those data are meta-data in the sense that no concrete values are stored, but the `AttrTypes` are only templates for the effective assignments.

The effective assignments are stored in `AttrTypeAssign` and `CtxAttrAssign`, while those assignments have to follow the patterns defined by the meta-data, i.e., one can see those two as "instantiation" of the associated meta-data. `AttrTypeAssign` stores the assigned value and the validity of the assignment, e.g., `role` "nurse" is assigned from 1.1.2012 until ever. `CtxAttrAssign` stores the values of the required context attributes which are required to identify an assignment, e.g., `subjectId` "alice@myhostpital.de". One can see

CtxAttrAssign as constraint when an AttrTypeAssign is valid. This core component does some integrity checks, e. g., prohibiting a double role assignment at one point in time. As second part, the integration into the XACML PDP, the PolicyStateModule class is implemented as AttributeFinderModule and is responsible for retrieving attributes managed by the policy state, i. e., is functioning as context handler. If the PDP tries to resolve some attribute, the PolicyStateModule first checks if it responsible for the searched attribute by checking if there is a AttrType with an according AttrId If yes, the list of attributes which have to be resolved from the EvaluationCtx is returned, i. e., the CtxAttr attribute identifier associated with the found AttrType. This list of required attributes may be empty or have an arbitrary length. We have presented examples for zero (get the currently active policies), one (role assignment), or two (broken glass frame) attributes. In our current implementation, we expect that for every required context attribute exactly one value is returned (e. g., one and only one subjectId may be contained in an AC request), however, it may be possible to extend this behavior. Finally, with the resolved values from the evaluation context, the policy state can be queried, if valid assignments exist. This query always requires a time-stamp for when the assignment should exist. For the productive PDP this time-stamp is stored in the evaluation context once the request arrives at the PDP, and this timestamp is also stored in the logs. For the analysis PDP, this timestamp can be defined according to the use case. The result can be returned as resolved attributes to the PDP.

For example, if the PDP tries to resolve the values for the attribute role, the policy state will check for an AttrType with the AttrId role. This AttrType is defined with one CtxAttr with AttrId subjectId, and hence the PolicyStateModule will resolve the value "alice@myhostpital.de" as subjectId from the EvaluationCtx. This is used to query the effective assignments, i. e., if one or several AttrTypeAssign can be found for the given CtxAttrAssign value and temporal validity (i. e., validFrom <= now <= validTo).

The third part, a management component, is responsible for retrieving evaluation-IDs of AC requests and update the policy state with the herein constrained notifyPolicyState obligations. For this, the AC request is loaded from the log store, the attributes as defined in the dependency definition are loaded, and policy is updated according to the defined action, i. e., assignments are added or removed. Adding an assignment means to create an AttrTypeAssign entry with validFrom set to the current date and validTo to the "infinite date" 9999-12-31 23:59:59.999. Removing an assignment means to update the validTo field of the the corresponding AttrTypeAssign entry to the current date.

Policy Permissions Versioning

The versioning concept presented in subsection 5.2.1 requires not only the versioning of the policy state (already described in this section 7.1), but also the versioning of the policy permissions (described now) and the versioning of the log files (described next).

The most easiest way to store XACML policy permissions is to store them as text files. Although it would be possible to store every new version of a policy as new value for an attribute in the PDP state, we decided for a more elegant solution, i. e., use a system which is specialized to manage versions and changes of text files: Subversion (SVN). Here, not only the power and advantages of SVN, but also the existing tool support can be used for the management and development of policy permissions. For example, SVN branches can be used for developing and testing new versions of policies before they are used in a productive system, e. g., an analysis PDP can load a new test version of policies directly from SVN. Thus, for the maintenance and development of XACML policy permissions a SVN system is used.

SVN uses an integer number to unambiguous identify a version. This number is stored as attribute `policy-version` in the policy state. If a request has to be evaluated, the `SVNPolicyFinderModule` retrieves the `policy-version` from the context (i. e., from the policy state), loads the corresponding policy from the SVN store and returns the corresponding policies for evaluation to the PDP. The `SVNPolicyFinderModule` caches once retrieved policy versions or may even pre-load versions which will get active within a certain time frame to avoid the delay caused by the load of policies at evaluation time. Thus, the differentiation of policy state and policy permissions is also visible at implementation level, with the policy permission version number being stored as policy state.

Log Server

Policy state and policy permissions versioning allow to reconstruct the policy state in every point in time, but for an investigation we also need to store the information about the system state retrieved by the PDP, the information contained in the request and response and some other basic information (e. g., when was the request executed). For this, we want to capture all information which is retrieved from the PDP and store it, associated with the actual request, in the versioning log storage.

To implement such a logging, we have to capture all attributes that are resolved and store them associated to a unambiguous request, which requires

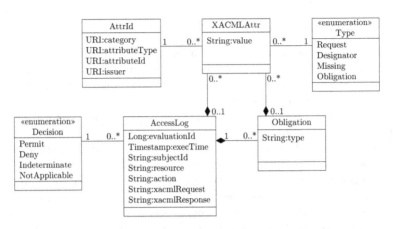

Figure 7.2: Class diagram: log server implementation.

a unique Identifier (ID) for every request. Also, we do not want to decrease the performance during evaluation, i.e., the collected information should not be written to the persistent storage in the same thread as the evaluation is running.

When a request arrives at the PDP, the request gets assigned a unique ID. All information (including the request, the collected information, and the AC decision) is collected and put onto a queue, where another thread is responsible for writing the collected data to a database, i.e., the AC request can be processed with only minor overhead.

Both the collection and storing of information has to be thread safe as requests are executed in parallel. Out of this, the collected information is, during evaluation, collected within the evaluation context (`EvaluationCtx`) which implements an `IRecordEvaluationContext` interface to retrieve all resolved information and an `IEvaluationIdContext` interface which returns an evaluation ID. When a request arrives at the PDP, a `RecordEvaluationContext`, implementing both interfaces, is created, receiving a unique evaluation ID. After the evaluation, the collected information is put on a queue and the result can be returned. Another thread processes the collected information, i.e., transforms the data so that they can be written to a database using hibernate (hibernate.org).

The used database schema is depicted in Figure 7.2. Every `AccessLog` entry can be identified along its evaluation ID and be assigned to a policy version along its `execTime` (the timestamp used to retrieve attributes and stored as access time is retrieved from the `SVNPolicyFinderModule` to avoid race conditions). An `XACMLAttr` can be either assigned to an `AccessLog` or be part of an `Obligation` and has to have an `AttrId`. The `Decision` type is an enumeration. So is the `Type` of an `XACMLAttr` with four possible values. `Request` means that the attribute was part of the XACML request, `Designator` that the attribute has been resolved at runtime, `Missing` that it was requested by the PDP but could not be resolved, and `Obligation` that it is assigned to an `Obligation`.

To collect the information at runtime, the `IRecordEvaluationContext` has to be provided with the required information. AspectJ (eclipse.org/aspectj) allows to set pointcuts on every `AttributeFinderModule` when it resolves some attribute. As the pointcuts are defined over the `AttributeFinderModule` (which has to be used to resolve attributes), all possible existing and future implementations resolving attributes from the environment are covered as with aspectJ the required code is waved into the byte code (i. e., no source code of the modified classes is needed). We will discuss aspectJ in more detail in the next section.

Finally, the PDP provides an API to log actually executed Break-Glass accesses, In more details, it receives an evaluation-ID and an optinal message, and stores it into a separate table within the log storage.

7.2 Analysis Workbench

Runtime Information – XACML Core Modifications

To enable analysis, we enhanced the XACML core implementation to keep track of runtime information, which contains both location information (i. e., in which line of which file the element is located) and information about the calling object, i. e., to be able to construct the current "call stack" at runtime. For this, two types of XACML elements and their representation as Java objects can be differentiated:

Locatable are objects where a XACML element has a directly representing Java object, e. g., for every `<Rule>` element one Java object of type `com.sun.xacml.Rule` is created. Thus, those objects can hold some location information.

Indirectly Locatable are objects which are referenced multiple times, i. e., functions and combining algorithms. As such objects are used in different contexts (e. g., in Listing C.1 p. 216, the function `string-equal` is used in the `<ActionMatch>` in line 63 and in the `<Condition>` in line 45), the location information has to be determined at runtime.

For implementation, we added three additional types to the XACML core implementation (see Listing 7.1). The class RuntimeInfo is used to store the location and call stack information. The interface Locatable is implemented by all locatable objects and allows to retrieve a RuntimeInfo object. The IndirectLocatable interface extends the Locatable interface and allows to set and unset the RuntimeInfo object at runtime. Thus, if a function or combining algorithm is evaluated, the setRuntimeInfo() function is called, with the unsetRuntimeInfo() function being called when the function or combining algorithm returns its result.

Every XACML object contains a reference to a RuntimeInfo object. Locatable XACML objects retrieve their location information at start-up when the policies are loaded: the static helper function getRuntimeInfo(), using the XML DOM node as argument, creates a RuntimeInfo object if analysis is active or null if not. Indirectly locatable objects retrieve their information at runtime via the setRuntimeInfo() function. For this, classes encapsulating functions (i. e., Apply, TargetMatch, and HigherOrderFunction) and combining algorithms (i. e., AbstractPolicy) have to create a RuntimeInfo object for those indirectly locatable objects, by calling getIndirectRuntimeInfo() on their own RuntimeInfo object, passing the called XACML object as argument.

At runtime, the evaluation functions of all XACML objects are "hooked," i. e., before and after the evaluation function is executed, some monitoring action can be executed. This is needed for two things. First, some runtime information about the call stack is injected via the functions setCalled⏎From() and unsetCalledFrom() into the RuntimeInfo objects of all XACML elements. Second, it is used to generate and distribute evaluation events via the EvaluationEventHub which can be subscribed by, e. g., analysis tools.

To implement this, we use aspectJ and the concept of pointcuts which allow to define, first, patterns identifying moments in the execution of a program[2], and, second, which actions before and after such a pointcut should be executed. For the definitions of those pointcuts, XACML classes can be divided along the interfaces they are implementing into the following groups: 1. PolicyTreeElement is implemented by Policy, PolicySet, Policy⏎Reference, and Rule 2. Evaluatable is implemented by AttributeDesignator, AttributeSelector, VariableReference, Condition, Apply, and Attribute⏎Value (and all thereof derived classes, e. g., StringAttribute) 3. Function is implemented by all functions 4. CombiningAlgorithm is implemented by

---

[2]One can think of pointcuts as a syntax dependent dialect of regular expressions for Java programs

```
   package com.sun.xacml.debug;
   interface Locatable{
3    RuntimeInfo getRuntimeInfo();
   }
   interface IndirectLocatable extends Locatable {
6    void setRuntimeInfo(RuntimeInfo src);
     void unsetRuntimeInfo();
   }
9  class RuntimeInfo {
     /* called at startup time for
        Locatable XACML objects */
12   static RuntimeInfo getRuntimeInfo(
         org.w3c.dom.Node xmlNode, Locatable xacmlObject);
     /* called at runtime to create a RuntimeInfo
15      for IndirectLocatable XACML objects */
     RuntimeInfo getIndirectRuntimeInfo(
         IndirectLocatable xacmlObject);
18   // where the XACML was read from the policy
     int getLineNumber();
     String getFileName();
21   // the XACML object this RuntimeInfo is valid for
     Locatable getXACMLObject();
     /* the runtimeInfo of the calling element or null,
24      if not part of the current call stack */
     RuntimeInfo getCalledFrom();
     /* called from the runtime
27      to maintain the call stack information */
     void setCalledFrom(RuntimeInfo o);
     void unsetCalledFrom(RuntimeInfo o);
30 }
```

Listing 7.1: Anaysis modifications to the core XACML implementation.

all combining algorithms 5. `MatchElement` was introduced by us to conflate `Target`, `TargetMatch`, `TargetMatchGroup`, and `TargetSection`

The effort to implement those changes in the XACML core are reasonable. The new introduced interfaces and classes (`RuntimeInfo`, `Locatable`, `IndirectLocatable`, and `MatchElement`) have about 70 lines of code (including some code to generate location statements for error and analysis messages).

To implement the `Locatable` interface, a `RuntimeInfo` instance variable has to be accessible with the `getRuntimeInfo()` function. As described above, the `RuntimeInfo` is retrieved at startup during the parsing of the policies, using the static `getRuntimeInfo()` function. For this, three interfaces have to extend the `Locatable` interface, causing modifications in eighteen classes. One special case is the `AttributeValue`, as the parsing is done by the `BaseAttributeFactory`, hence, this class sets the `RuntimeInfo`. Overall, this introduced about 100 lines of new code, using the available `RuntimeInfo` for more meaningful error messages caused changes to about 100 lines of existing code.

The implementation of the `IndirectLocatable` required changes in one interface and two classes, and caused changes in classes encapsulation functions and combining algorithms, i. e., the four above mentioned classes. Overall, this introduced about 50 lines of new code. The definition of the pointcuts and the required actions before and after the pointcuts has about 150 lines of code. All changes introduced less than 500 lines of code (with more than 100.000 lines code for the whole XACML implementation).

We explicitly want to mention that this is owed to the fact that the SUN XACML implementation is well designed and allows, through the sound usage of interfaces and abstract classes, a clean implementation of the presented concepts. We did not have to change major parts of the existing implementation to introduce our modifications.

Storing and associating the runtime information directly into the XACML objects allows for an easy implementation, however, comes with the drawback that the implementation is not thread-safe, i. e., one analysis PDP can be used for only one analysis in parallel. However, the implementation is intended as prototype, and with the policies discussed here a new analysis PDP load in less than 200 milliseconds.

Abstract Evaluation

As noted in subsection 6.2.2, all code implementing lazy operations have to be re-implemented in an abstract-aware version, i. e., all combining algorithms and the functions `and` and `or`. As we do not want to re-implement all other functionality which has to handle attributes (and hence possibly abstract values), we have to implement two things. First, we introduce abstract data types, which extend the regular attribute types and implement an `Abstract‑Attribute` interface. A factory can create such abstract attributes to be injected into the evaluation. By this, an, e. g., `AbstractStringAttribute` can be used as a regular `StringAttribute` when evaluating the policy, however, abstract-aware code will be able to check if a value is abstract by checking if the value is an instance of `AbstractAttribute`. Second, we have to keep track if the result of a target, a condition, or from a sub-element (i. e., sub rule, policy, or policy set) is abstract. To handle this, one could re-implement all functions and return an abstract value if one of its inputs is abstract. To avoid this re-implementation, we build a parallel structure which keeps track if in the current evaluation context abstract values are used. This allows to implement abstract-aware functions and combining algorithms as described in subsection 6.2.2.

XACML Analysis Configuration

The configuration of the PDP is part of the policy. This configuration contains the information which attribute designators, data types, functions, and combining algorithms have to be used. However, for the analysis some of those parameter have to be changed. To omit the need to define for every productive configuration an analysis equivalent, we implemented an `AnalysisConfig` which can be constructed with a regular configuration (`PDPConfig`) and used to initialize the PDP. In more detail, the `AnalysisConfig`

- Replaces all combining algorithms and the **and** and **or** functions with the version for abstract evaluation
- Removes all `AttributeFinderModules` and sets `AnalysisFinderModule` as the only finder module. This finder module retrieves its values from the analysis workbench.
- Enables the parser feature to keep track of the source lines
- Removes the log server from the configuration

This allows to load the XACML configuration and all policies as used for the productive environment into the analysis PDP and use it for the analysis evaluation.

8 Related Work

In this chapter, we will present an overview of the related work and demonstrate how the approaches presented there can be implemented with our generic Break-Glass model.

There are multiple approaches to and similar names for those approaches which are related to Break-Glass as it is discussed in this thesis. In 1990, Badger [7] states that it is "occasionally necessary to override security protection" when assets, for which security is provided, are threatened more directly than by a *Security Override*. The term *Override* [73, 75] is also used in *Overriding Access Control* [4, 89, 90] or *Policy Override* [11]. Apart from Break-Glass or Break-the-Glass (BTG) [5, 27, 50, 51, 66, 73, 76], further terms are *Optimistic Security* [87, 103], *posteriori compliance control* [48], or *exception-based access control* [91]. We have chosen the term "Break-Glass" to describe the general concept, and use "override" to describe the actual execution by the user.

Firozabadi and Sergot [52] distinguish between *power* vs. *permission*, i.e., if someone has the practical ability (e.g., the opportunity and the know-how) vs. if someone is allowed (e.g., it does not contradict with any rule) to do something. Just because someone has the power to do something, it does not mean he is permitted to do so, and if he does not have the power to do something this does not mean he should not be permitted to do so. To (try to) ensure that no one does something he is not permitted to do, one can choose two strategies: a *detective* or a *preventative* control mechanism (e.g., [25, p. 5]). Large parts of our daily life are following a detective control mechanism: crimes can be committed (i.e., the criminal has the power to commit the crime), but the crime might be detected, and the criminal might be made responsible for these actions. On the other hand, Access Control (AC) in computer systems implements a preventative control mechanism. An AC mechanism would be perfect if there was no mismatch between power and permissions. In order to reach this goal (as far as possible), most AC mechanisms follow the least privilege principle, i.e., give subjects only those privileges which are required to execute things they are needed to do. These privileges should be a subset of what is permissible for the user [65]. In this chapter, we will discuss approaches which introduce a detective character. This may imply that subjects have more power than might be permissible. In terms of power and permission, Break-Glass allows subjects to gain more power than what is (or can be) defined in machine-readable encoded form for the regular case, but apply a detective approach to discover if the gaining of power was incorrect.

We are only interested in the Break-Glass aspects of the cited papers, i.e., the presented papers may provide further contributions which are not discussed here. Furthermore, please note that we are not always using the original terms and notation, but applied the unified terminology as defined in Appendix A or introduced in the background discussion (chapter 2).

8.1 Pre-Staging Emergency Accounts and Roles

One common technique to allow users to extend their regular privileges is to distribute accounts with extended privileges. In [66] it is argued that authentication may fail in emergencies (e.g., forgotten passwords) and especially in the case of a health care system a delay could result in "patient discomfort, additional injury or worse." [66] They propose to provide emergency accounts for systems, where operators have to login via username and password, and four phases with different challenges are identified:

1. Pre-staging accounts, i.e., the before-hand creation of emergency accounts. User names for such accounts should be easily identified as such, and passwords should be hard to crack. Exceptional accounts should follow the least privilege principle.
2. Distributing accounts in a way that accounts are accessible when needed, but unintended usage can be prevented or at least punished.
3. Monitoring the use of accounts to enable audit trails.
4. Cleaning up after account usage, i.e., define procedures how to adjust the emergency procedure, e.g., disable used accounts.

SAP, market leader for enterprise applications software, offers a product for its standard suite which allows users to acquire emergency accounts, called "SAP GRC Superuser Privilege Management" (formerly "Firefighter"). It "allows personnel to take responsibility for tasks outside their normal job function [...] to perform tasks in emergency situations" [98]. So called super-users can get assigned the right to acquire special and specific privileges. Those privileges can be activated within the Superuser system. Once acquired, a new session with the extended privileges can be started, for which all actions are recorded for later audit. Thus, instead of pre-staging emergency accounts, users can acquire pre-staged emergency roles. This product is used for business software and demonstrates that Break-Glass is not limited to the health care domain.

Pre-staging emergency accounts and role can fulfill the requirements for Break-Glass as discussed in section 3.1 only to some extend. For governance, exceptional privileges cannot be bound to the accessing subject and hence to the access context. As consequence, nurses may get granted the same exceptional privileges as a physician or the station master. In terms of accessibility, users have to execute a procedure they are not used to, and may even have to understand technical details such as the system they want to get access to. As emergency accounts are not bound to the accessing subject, users cannot be informed which actions are covered by regular privileges and which extend their regular tasks to which amount. Finally, to assure accountability, the post-access investigation is a fully manual task, also the auditor has to figure out which tasks would have been covered by regular privileges, which have been exceptional and why.

There is no direct mapping to an exceptional AC model, as they do not define an AC model or an extension of an AC model. However, the requirements defined by [66] are similar to the fundamental principles of Break-Glass we discussed in section 3.1. The pre-staged accounts should follow the least privilege principle, and the usage of the accounts have to be audited, exceptional accounts have to be cleaned up, i. e., formulating governance. The exceptional accounts have to be accessible, i. e., formulating accessibility. When using exceptional accounts by, e. g., opening a sealed cover, users are aware that they are using exceptional privileges, i. e., implicitly formulating awareness. Finally, the distribution procedure requires that users who used an exceptional account can be identified, i. e., formulating accountability. Products offered by large software vendors such as SAP show the relevance and market need of exceptional access mechanisms.

8.2 Categorization of Permissions

Several approaches categorize permissions which are available in a system (or for a subject) or describe the boundaries between different types of permissions.

Access Control Spaces

Jaeger et al. [65] present a model of *Access Control Spaces*. In an ideal world there are two initial spaces: *specified* (positive permission assignments, i. e.,

PERMIT) and *prohibited* (permissions which are precluded, i. e., DENY). A third space, *permissible*, identifies the permissions which may be granted. An *obligated* space is needed for the correct operation of the system. Both, the obligated and specified space are a subset of the permissible space. Finally, an *unknown* space contains permissions which are neither covered by the permissible nor by the prohibited space. If the unknown space is empty, the policy is said to be complete. Thus, Jaeger et al. make a distinction what could be permitted without violating the prohibited space (permissible), and what is actually permitted (specified), e. g., to enforce the least privilege principle. In real systems spaces may be conflicting, i. e., overlaps of spaces with different authorization semantics (PERMIT, DENY, unknown) may exist. For example, the specified space may have an intersection with the unknown or even the prohibited space, e. g., some permissions are assigned although they should not, and some permissions should be assigned, but are not. The main contribution is a tool, which, based on a given access control model, allows to find conflicts between the different spaces and undefined subspaces, i. e., determine the permissions which are implicitly in the unknown space. With such a tool the administrator is able to develop and maintain more accurate, i. e., conflict-free and complete, policies. Furthermore, for a health care system, they propose "to permit a doctor to access [...] the unknown subspace [...] upon request by the doctor" [65], i. e., to override the system and use permissions from the unknown space, if the users requests this override and the system can assure that those requests are audited. Thus, Break-Glass should be possible as long as the access is not explicitly prohibited.

Jaeger et al. do not explicitly formulate a Break-Glass model, hence no definition of how the user can be notified about exceptional privileges given. The main contribution is a tool which allows to detect conflicts and underspecified areas between explicitly defined PERMIT and DENY policies. The underspecified area, i. e., neither permitted nor denied accesses, could be considered as exceptional permission. This approach can directly be modeled with our approach: the given positive permissions would define the regular PERMIT policy p^{reg} on ℓ_1, the negative permissions the DENY part of a p^{excp} policy on ℓ_2. The PERMIT part of p^{excp} would define a policy permitting all accesses executed by physicians, attaching the required Break-Glass obligations. As p^{excp} is not extended, the DENY part of p^{excp} would be non-overridable. Accesses not captured by the given positive or negative permissions and executed by a physician would be granted as exceptional privilege, all others denied (following the default deny principle).

Policy Spaces

Similar to Access Control Spaces, Ardagna et al. [5] present a model of *Policy Spaces*, with the goal to explicitly model override policies. They point out that for the health care industry the Care Comes First (CCF) principle requires some mechanism to bypass AC mechanisms in case of emergencies. In their assumption, existing systems define solely *Authorized Accesses* ($\mathscr{P}^+$) and that, to allow the implementation of the CCF principle, everything else has to be considered as *Unplanned Exception* ($\mathscr{E}^U$) which has to be overridable.

Based on this assumption they detect that there are accesses which cannot help in managing emergency situations and should therefore always be denied. In terms of Cheng et al. [40] and Bartsch [11], subjects can override a *soft boundary*, but the *hard boundary* cannot be overridden. For this, negative permissions defined in *Denied Accesses* ($\mathscr{P}^-$) can neither be overwritten by $\mathscr{P}^+$ nor by any override mechanism. Furthermore, there are accesses which do not fall into the normal routine, but can be foreseen and should be permitted as *Planned Exceptions* $\mathscr{E}^P$, for which obligations can be defined. Every request not falling into $\mathscr{P}^-$, $\mathscr{P}^+$, or $\mathscr{E}^P$ is considered as *Unplanned Exceptions* $\mathscr{E}^U$, which itself is divided into two sub-spaces: $\mathscr{E}^{U^+}$ permits requests happening in an emergency, whereas $\mathscr{E}^{U^-}$ denies requests if no such emergency can be detected. Permissions are defined in a language which is based on Role Based Access Control (RBAC) and supports the usage of context information on an attribute basis similar to XACML. When evaluating an AC request, the following steps are executed:

1. Evaluate $\mathscr{P}^-$ and return DENY, if a matching negative permission is found.
2. Evaluate $\mathscr{P}^+$ and return PERMIT, if a matching positive permission is found.
3. Evaluate $\mathscr{E}^P$ and return PERMIT with the according obligations if a matching positive permission is found.
4. If an exceptional situation can be detected return PERMIT, otherwise return DENY; in both cases, create an audit notification.

For both $\mathscr{E}^P$ and $\mathscr{E}^{U^+}$ the system has to be aware of an ongoing exception, e. g., it is assumed that every emergency situation can be detected by the component evaluating AC requests. In this model exceptional privileges are expressed implicitly, i. e., one can only define what should not be overridable.

Using our lingo, Ardagna et al. [5] define regular permissions (authorized accesses $\mathscr{P}^+$) and denied permissions (denied accesses $\mathscr{P}^-$). Planned exceptions $\mathscr{E}^P$ are an extension to regular permissions, and may have obligations attached. If an access does not fall into $\mathscr{P}^-$, $\mathscr{P}^+$, or $\mathscr{E}^P$, it is checked if an exceptional situation defined in $\mathscr{E}^{U^+}$ can be detected, otherwise the deny all policy $\mathscr{E}^{U^-}$ is applied. Regarding the combination of those policies, $\mathscr{P}^-$ dominate all other policies, i.e., cannot be overridden. $\mathscr{P}^+$ dominates $\mathscr{E}^{U^+}$, i.e., if a PERMIT without obligations can be found in $\mathscr{P}^+$, this PERMIT should be applied. Finally, $\mathscr{E}^{U^+}$ dominates $\mathscr{E}^{U^-}$.

There are three aspects which are special about this approach, both, regarding the other existing approaches and our own work. First, following Ardagna et al. [5], accesses denied by $\mathscr{E}^{U^-}$ have to be audited. It remains unclear why not executed accesses have to be audited, and how the user should be made responsible for not executed accesses. Second, it is assumed that exceptional situations can be detected by the system, what we consider to be impossible for all kinds of exceptions and is, for most approaches, the main argument for introducing Break-Glass. Third, it remains unclear if a user has to confirm the usage of exceptional permissions granted by $\mathscr{E}^{U^+}$ (note that no obligations can be defined for $\mathscr{E}^{U^+}$), i.e., if the BTG decision implicitly requires a user conformation or only requires a post-access investigation. Regarding the first and the third consideration, it seems to be an implicit assumption that the user has to know what is permitted regular situations and which tasks could only be executed with exceptional privileges.

For mapping the model of Ardagna et al. [5] to our model, we have to assume that the underlying AC model can define obligations attached to DENY decisions: in our model, no obligations for DENY decisions can be defined (this was a design decision, see subsection 10.3.1). However, $\mathscr{E}^{U^-}$ requires to define some obligations attached to a DENY decision. To implement such a behavior in our model, the PERMIT part of p^{reg} on ℓ_1 would be required to implement, as part of the underlying AC model, a default DENY strategy with the obligations attached to $\mathscr{E}^{U^-}$. The positive permissions of p^{reg} are defined by $\mathscr{P}^+$, the $\mathscr{E}^P$ is a PERMIT policy p^{ep} on ℓ_2. On ℓ_3, the policy p^{eu} contains as PERMIT part $\mathscr{E}^{U^+}$ and as DENY part $\mathscr{P}^-$. Except for the obligations of $\mathscr{E}^{U^-}$, this simulates the model of [5]. Assuming an underlying AC model which can implement a default DENY strategy and attach some obligations, the model can be simulated completely.

Overall, we do not follow the argumentation of Ardagna et al. [5] and Jaeger et al. [65] regarding DENY policies. As argued in section 3.4, DENY policies should not define an complement of PERMIT permissions: therewith the default deny and default permit principle would be implemented redundant. This would require first, double work and, second, the PERMIT and DENY part would have to be kept in sync when requirements for the policy change. Such an approach would also have the effect that exceptional permissions are defined implicitly. While exceptional accesses can be restricted, i.e., defining conditions when a situation has to be considered as exceptional, the exceptional access can only be executed if not denied by $\mathscr{P}^-$. Especially with powerful languages such as XACML it can be a complex task if a specific access matches $\mathscr{P}^-$ and hence implicitly model exceptional privileges.

Access Categories

Rissanen [89] argue that a policy cannot be specified completely, as not all situations are expressible in a machine readable language and not all situations can be predicted. There are approaches which allow to dynamically assign rights, e.g., delegation. But even then some authorizations have to be assigned in advance and the person able to delegate the required permissions has to be available. This leads to the following access categories:

1. Allowed and machine encodable, i.e., PERMIT.
2. Denied and machine encodable, i.e., DENY
3. Allowed and not machine encodable: the machine cannot decide if the unspecified condition is fulfilled or not.
4. Denied and not machine encodable: the machine cannot decide if the unspecified condition is fulfilled or not.
5. Unanticipated: accesses which have been forgotten or cannot be predicted.

Similar to the distinction between power and permissions [52], Rissanen et al. [90] propose to distinct what a subject is *permitted* to do, what it *can* do, and what it is *forbidden* to do. The intersection of *can* and *not permitted* is referred to as *possibility-with-override*. They propose a distinction of three access categories: *permitted*, *denied* (categorization 1 and 2 of Rissanen are equivalent to the specified and prohibited space of [65]), and *possible* accesses (categorization 3 to 5 are equivalent to the unknown space of [65]) where override is possible but has to be audited. To implement Break-Glass, one of the three combinations of the three access categories can be implemented:

1. Define permitted and possible accesses, everything else is denied.
2. Define permitted and denied accesses, everything else is possible.
3. Define denied and possible accesses, everything else is permitted.

They follow the first approach, although they do not exclude the others as they may make sense depending on the environment and the required properties, e.g., the second type corresponds to the model of Jaeger et al. [65].

We follow their general observation regarding the categorization of permissions but refine it in the sense that encoded permissions may be in conflict, and the policy engineer has to have a possibility to define how such conflicts have to be resolved. The first two approaches of Rissanen [89] (define regular and overridable/denied permissions) can be defined directly:

1. Define two PERMIT policies, on ℓ_1 the regular permissions in a p^{reg} policy, on ℓ_2 the overridable permission in a p^{excp} policy.
2. Define the regular permissions as p^{reg} policy on ℓ_1, the denied accesses as DENY policy on ℓ_2, and a match all PERMIT policy with the corresponding obligations on ℓ_2, i.e., the same approach as for Jaeger et al. [65].
3. For the third variant (define exceptional and denied permissions), one would define the exceptional permissions on ℓ_1 with the corresponding obligation, define the DENY policy on ℓ_2, and a match all PERMIT policy on ℓ_2. However, we see this variant as a variant of the default permit principle applied to Break-Glass and hence as rather exotic.

Soft vs. Hard Boundary

Cheng et al. [40] argue that AC policies are static although the environment is dynamic. For defining policies, the security engineer has to make a risk vs. benefit trade-off for accesses in the future, although the risk vs. benefit trade-off should be done according to the current situation and needs. Furthermore, even though there is always uncertainty in AC decisions, they have to be binary, i.e., PERMIT or DENY. They introduce a third AC decision ALLOW WITH RISK-MITIGATION in between PERMIT and DENY. The delimitation between PERMIT and ALLOW WITH RISK-MITIGATION is called *soft boundary*, the delimitation between ALLOW WITH RISK-MITIGATION and DENY is called *hard boundary*: users may override the soft boundary but cannot override the hard boundary.

Bartsch [11] motivates Break-Glass for small and mid size companies. Regular policies describe regular and most common work processes. Every once in a while higher privileges are needed, causing employees to behave inefficient (e.g., asking colleagues for help) or even risky and uncontrollable (e.g., asking colleagues for their credentials). Thus, allowing users to override AC enables a more efficient way to handle exceptions from regular processes. Permissions which are needed for regular work should be granted following the least-privilege principle, building a "soft boundary" [40] between regular and exceptional permissions. This boundary can be overwritten, using override permissions up to a "hard boundary", which follows the *most-*

tolerable-privilege principle, and cannot be overwritten. Furthermore, Bartsch provides an Break-Glass extension of a RBAC model and a calculus to define the hard boundary. Both [40] and [11] will be discussed in the context of other RBAC specific model later in this chapter.

Rumpole

Marinovic et al. [76] point out that "access control operates under the assumption that it is possible to correctly encode and predict all subjects' needs and rights" but that "it is hard if not impossible to encode all emergencies and exceptions, but also to imagine a priori all the permissible requests." They present Rumpole, a model which uses two categories to abstract from existing AC models: competence and empowerment. Fundamentally, AC models allow to assign permissions to categories of subjects (e.g., roles), which is referred to as *competence*. Constraints (such as Separation of Duty (SoD) or temporal constraints) restrict those permissions to ensure integrity, which is referred to as *empowerment*. Note that this is a conceptual distinction: technically, constraints can also be used for the definition of competence, i.e., the assignment of a permission to a (category of) subjects can be constrained. Both competence and empowerment can be positive, negative, or unknown for a triple (S, R, A). It is assumed that Rumpole can *query* competence and empowerment as knowledge base from the underlying policies.

For Break-Glass, Rumpole allows to use the knowledge base from existing AC models and policies for the definition of exceptional permissions. If a request cannot be permitted with regular permissions, Rumpole allows to define an exceptional policy which can be based on the knowledge base of underlying policies. For the definition of this exceptional policy, they present a policy model and language based on a four value logic. Beside the truth values *true* and *false*, two further elements are used: ⊥ represents *no knowledge*, and ⊤ represents *over-knowledge*. In terms of XACML, no knowledge ⊥ can be seen as the representation of NOTAPPLICABLE, and over-knowledge ⊤ is handled by combining algorithms and can therefore not occur. The language allows to define predicates which can be used to represent the knowledge base of domain and AC policy specific properties (e.g., test the assignment of a subject to a role), and to define predicates about obligations history (e.g., did a subject agree or violate a specific obligation).

The exceptional policy split into two parts. The first part defines PERMIT and DENY rules, based on the knowledge base of the underlying policies (i.e., competence and empowerment queried by Rumpole), on predicates defined in Rumpole, or on the obligations history. PERMIT and DENY rules can be positive or negative. Following the four value logic, ¬*true* does not mean *false*, i. e., a negative PERMIT rule does not mean DENY. This property is exploited in the second part, called resolution query, which defines how conservative or tolerant the override decision is. For example, a conservative resolution query could require at least one positive but no negative PERMIT rule and at least one negative but no positive DENY rule in the knowledge base. For such a resolution query, an override has to be exclusively and explicitly permitted, and exclusively and explicitly not be denied. A more tolerant resolution query could only require at least one positive PERMIT and no positive DENY rule to be in the knowledge base, i. e., there has to be some rule which permits, but no rule which denies the override. Both parts can be defined on a granularity for (S, R, A).

It is argued that the existing knowledge, which is used to formulate the regular policy, should be used to define exceptional privileges. They follow our approach, checking if the underlying policy would grant an access with regular privileges and only if not, Rumpole is applied to check for exceptional privileges. While our model fully abstracts from the underlying policy with the Access Control Function (ACF), Marinovic et al. define competence and empowerment as a concrete AC model and hence require a more intimate knowledge of underlying AC model.

The resolution query of Rumpole is in some sense the counterpart of our lattice evaluation algorithm. Our lattice evaluation algorithm has a fixed regulation that a DENY dominates a PERMIT, and does not support the notion of negative PERMIT or DENY policies (rules), but achieves its flexibility by structuring policies in the lattice. The resolution query of Rumpole allows for a flexible combination of PERMIT and DENY rules, i. e., allows to define how results (i. e., positive/negative PERMIT/DENY rule) should dominate each other per triple (*subject, resource, action*), however, does not allow to structure permissions within those categories.

While we see the abstraction of competence and empowerment as a way to define exceptional policies also in our model, we see the flexibility given by the resolution query as in some sense problematic: one can define resolution queries where redundant information is per construction required in the knowledge base. For example, the conservative example of a resolution query requires the security engineer to formulate a positive PERMIT rule and its negated equivalent, i. e., a negative DENY rule, into the knowledge base to make an override possible.

8.3 Break-Glass Models

8.3.1 Post-Access Models

Optimistic Security

Povey [87] proposes an AC scheme called "Optimistic Security" which allows for the implementation of Break-Glass. Povey motivates the need for Optimistic Security not only with the static nature of authorization schemes which are unable to handle dynamically changing environments, he also argues that it is risky *not* having access to a system or information, e. g., in health care scenarios. Povey defines five requirements for an optimistic security scheme:

Constrained entry points: Users have to be warned that they are using non-regular privileges and that misusing them will have consequences.

Accountability: Users have to be authenticated to be associated with executed actions.

Auditability: The executed actions and additional information such as the current system state have to be logged to enable an auditor to determine whether an access is legitimate or not.

Recoverability: Potentially illegitimate actions which modify the system state (e. g., write or update) or have effects on external systems have to be revertible. For [87] it is assumed that for every transformation there is a compensating transaction, reversing the transformation.

Deterrents: There has to be some form of punishment of incorrectly behaving users.

Based on the Clark-Wilson integrity model [41] (see subsection 2.2.2 p. 27), the traditional "pessimistic scheme" may exist to cover the regular case. Exceptional privileges may be defined as "inclusive or exclusive list of authorization," i. e., either as positive or negative permissions. For defining exceptional privileges, the underlying Clark-Wilson model is extended with the concept of a Partial Transformation Procedure (PTP). Unlike a Transformation Procedure (TP), which results in a valid Constrained Data Item (CDI), the PTP results in a Partially-Constrained Data Item (PCDI). An administrator can either verify that the PCDI does not violate integrity, or execute a Compensating TP. Hence, the general idea is to define transactions which can be rolled back (recoverability) so that illegitimate actions can be rolled back by the administrator.

The requirements presented by Povey [87] are similar to the principles presented in section 3.1 with one exception: recoverability, discussed in the context of underlying Clark-Wilson [41] integrity model. Here, two things have to be discussed. First, how the underlying integrity model can be extended with Break-Glass, which we will discuss in section 9.3 in the context of the Clark-Wilson model. Second, how privileges can be extended in exceptional situations. Here, [87] can directly be mapped to our approach: the authorization checks done by Clark-Wilson are based on lists, defining which subject is authorized to execute which TP on which CDI. Those remain to cover the regular case. For exceptional accesses, another list is maintained which is defining exceptional permissions, either explicit as positive list or implicit as negative list. This maps directly to an exceptional PERMIT or DENY policy and, consequently, allows to define positive or negative non-overridable permissions. Our approach allows to further refine this approach by introducing several policies, defining authorization lists as underlying AC policies. Overall, Povey demonstrates how an integrity model can be extended and used to handle illegitimate, especially write accesses and bring the system back to valid state after an illegitimate access.

Audit-Based Access Control

Dekker and Etalle [44] present a posteriori AC framework for an Electronic Health Record (EHR) scenario based on a delegation model. The model defines two basic actions *createRessource* and *delegatePermission* and one basic permission *own*. Based on those, application specific actions (e. g., *read*, or *giveDrug*), permissions (e. g., *mayRead*) and conditions (e. g., *isNurse*) and hence a basic policy can be defined, e. g., allow patients to read their own health records and delegate permissions to physicians. Subjects store delegated permissions in a log.

At runtime, no authorization checks are executed. Instead, auditors are doing posteriori checks by finding *proof* that executed accesses have been legitimate. For this, subjects have to provide parts of the log, containing received permissions and conditions, to the auditor. Here, tools are provided which allow to find and check such proof. The benefit of doing the posteriori AC is that permissions may be acquired after the actual access, e. g., if some physician is not available to delegate the required permissions before the access, it can be done after the access.

Dekker and Etalle [44] chose a complete different approach, as no at-access checks are executed, deferring the AC decision completely to the post-access phase. This has some consequences regarding the fundamental principles we identified for Break-Glass. First, there is no control of tolerated empowerment, i. e., violating the principle of governance. Second, users cannot be warned that they are using exceptional privileges, i. e., violating the principle of awareness. Hence, users are required to know what is legitimate and what is exceptional. We see the main contribution of their approach that, post-access, information which has not been available at-access can be used for audit in an automated manner. This approach is similar to our concept of post-access policies presented in section 6.3. In the example of Dekker and Etalle, permissions are delegated for a referral. Post-access it is checked, if the required permissions have been delegated at all, not necessarily before the access, e. g., if the referral or the confirmation from the patient was not entered to the system immediately. Similar, in our running example, a Treatment Relationship (TR) is automatically created if a patient is referred to another department or physician. In exceptional situations this may be done post-access. Given the policy state and the versioning thereof, our audit policies are able to execute a similar check on an automated basis.

8.3.2 RBAC Extensions

Exceptional Role-Upgrade

Bartsch [11] provides, based on his definition of soft vs. hard boundary discussed in section 8.2, an extension of a RBAC model, which allows the definition of exceptional permissions. For this, a new role association describing which role can be "upgraded" up to which role in "override mode" is introduced. In terms of standard RBAC, this override roles assignment (OR) relates a role the user is assigned to, to a role the user can activate in override mode. Bartsch also provides a calculus which helps an expert to define the hard boundary, i. e., define exceptional permissions. This calculus is based on established risk management techniques, i. e., balancing the risk of an access against its potential benefits, where risk is calculated based on *protection need* and *threat likelyhood* and benefit is calculated based on *frequency* and *benefit per override*. Applied to his Break-Glass RBAC model, the outcome of this calculus are suggestions how to set role associations for the override mode.

In our lingo, Bartsch allows to define exceptional privileges along a role-role relationship, describing which role can be upgraded to which role in override mode. Thus, the exceptional policy expresses which additional roles can be activated by the user. We will discuss how exceptional permissions can be defined in RBAC in section 9.3 in more detail.

Tees Confidentiality Model

Longstaff et al. [74] present the Tees Confidentiality Model (TCM), which is a mixture of RBAC, Identity Based Access Control (IBAC), and Attribute Based Access Control (ABAC). In TCM, subjects, actions, and resources are described by classifiers with single values (in XACML: attributes), ordered in hierarchies. Different types of "confidentiality permission" can be assigned to grant access rights, e. g., depending on a role or directly on the identity. Confidentiality permissions can make use of the hierarchical character of the classifiers, i. e., inherit the permissions upwards or downwards the hierarchy, or not at all. Also, negative (i. e., DENY) permissions can be assigned. The permissions are, depending on the type, evaluated in a defined order.

One of the proposed override mechanisms is to allow users to override DENY permissions, i. e., to break the glass if there is a PERMIT permission. Further override mechanisms are team-override (i. e., to allow emergency access if a team member has access), role-override (i. e., to allow emergency access if a senior role in the role hierarchy would grant access), or global override (i. e., remove all restrictions). It remains unclear, if and how override permissions can be defined (e. g., which DENY permissions can be overwritten, or up to which level in the role hierarchy permissions are checked), and how the availability of exceptional privileges is communicated to the users.

Longstaff et al. [74] do not propose a concrete Break-Glass model, but only discusses how the concepts of TCM could be used to define exceptional privileges. This fits perfectly into our model, i. e., TCM can be used as ACF implementation to define regular and exceptional privileges, and our model can be used for both assuring that exceptional privileges are only applied if no regular privileges can be found, and for the integration into the application, e. g., using obligations attached to exceptional privileges.

BTG-RBAC

Ferreira et al. [51] present a BTG RBAC model, i. e., a BTG approach based on the American National Standards Institute (ANSI) core RBAC model and an RBAC extension for obligations [112]. To support Break-Glass, the RBAC engine has to hold some state: BTG state variables define "areas" which "break" (i. e., are set to true) once a Break-Glass access is executed, and remain "broken" until set back to false. The areas of such a variable are role, resource and action, and wildcards can be used to give a variable a broader scope. As long as the BTG state variable is true, exceptional permissions may be used without the need to break the glass again. Thus, there are four types of permissions: regular permissions, permissions to set a BTG state variable to true, exceptional permissions which can only be used if a specific BTG state variable is set to true, and permissions to set a BTG state variable to false.

When evaluating an AC request, first, regular permissions are checked. If no PERMIT is found, it is checked if (with the current active BTG state variables) an exceptional permission is available. If no such exceptional PERMIT is found, it is checked if the user is permitted to set a BTG state variable to true. In all three cases obligations may be attached to the AC decision. If a BTG state variable can be set to true, the user is asked if he wants to break the glass. If yes, the BTG state variable is set to true, and, again, it is checked if an exceptional permission is available. A user may be able to break the glass, but not be able to use exceptional permissions, or he may be able to use exceptional permissions but not be able to set a required BTG state variable to true, i.e., if the security engineer wants a user to be able to break the glass and use exceptional permissions, he has to assure that both types of permissions are assigned. BTG state variables can be set back to false in three different ways: automatically (e.g., by a reset after 30 minutes or after a certain number of accesses), semi-automatically (i.e., same as automatically but triggered from outside the RBAC engine), or manually (i.e., as explicit action by a user).

Ferreira et al. [51] define a stateful Break-Glass approach similar to our Break-Glass as discussed in subsection 4.2.3: users can break the glass to activate exceptional privileges. However, compared to our approach, there are some limitations. First, the areas – or dimensions – which can freely be defined in our approach are limited to role, resource, and action, which is caused by the fact that [51] is based on and hence specific to RBAC. This also means that, second, the glass can only be broken for multiple subjects[1]. In conjunction with the fact that the user confirmation is tied to a third AC decision (which is used to break the glass and activate exceptional privileges but not to confirm the usage of exceptional privileges), third, users can get exceptional privileges granted without that they are notified or have to confirm exceptional privileges (which contradicts our principle

---

[1]One could argue that breaking the glass only for one subject can be implemented by breaking the glass, consuming the exceptional privileges, and restoring the broken glass. However, as for this multiple requests – set variable to true, consume exceptional permissions, set variable to false – are required, this would introduce race conditions. First, after the effect of the first but before the effect of the third takes place, exceptional permissions would be granted. Second, two subjects breaking the glass in parallel would influence each other.

of "awareness" we identified for Break-Glass in section 3.1). As discussed in subsection 4.2.3, one can easily think of use cases where, once an exceptional situation is confirmed by an authorized user, exceptional privileges can be granted without that further accesses have to be confirmed as exceptional by the user. However, we see this as application specific and argue that the underlying Break-Glass approach has to support both a stateless and stateful approach and hence allow the security engineer to model what is required by the use case. Fourth, breaking the glass for a single action, i.e., in a state-less way, is not possible as a Break-Glass AC decision always inherently contains the obligation to update a policy state variable, hence requires a state and hence does not allow for stateless Break-Glass. Finally, users who have regular access (e.g., a physician) cannot break the glass to allow other users for exceptional access (e.g., for a nurse), although such persons are likely to be in the position to decide if exceptional privileges should be permitted.

8.3.3 Process-Based Approaches

The following approaches also make usage of RBAC, however, focus – especially regarding Break-Glass – on the handling of SoD and Binding of Duty (BoD) constraints.

Workflow-RBAC with Overriding Constraints

Wainer et al. [105] extend the RBAC model for workflow management systems, i.e., support the definition of Dynamic Separation of Duty (DSoD) and BoD constraints. In this model, a workflow consists of tasks, subjects are assigned to roles, roles contain a set of permissions to execute tasks. DSoD and BoD constraints can be defined on a workflow-instance basis, or system wide. Furthermore, within their model it is possible to provide a list of users which are most appropriate for a specific task.

They observe that there may be unanticipated, exceptional situations, or the system may come to a "dead end," i.e., tasks cannot be executed without violating constraints, e.g., caused by unfortunate choices in the assignment of tasks. To allow a controlled override of such constraints, levels are assigned to constraints. Levels can be seen as priorities, e.g., a BoD constraint defined to ensure that a customer will communicate with only one employee throughout the workflow will receive a lower level (priority) than a constraint that has to be enforced due to legal regulations. The right to override constraints up to a specific level is modeled as permission assigned to roles, where the maximum level assigned is the relevant one. Typically, users with more powerful roles will have the right to override higher-level constraints.

The override mechanism of Wainer et al. [105] does not extend regular RBAC permissions, but allows to override SoD and BoD constraints. This can be mapped to our constraints model, i. e., regular permissions defined with RBAC are expressed in the regular policy p^{reg} on ℓ_1 using positive permissions. Constraints are expressed as DENY policies on higher levels, where the priorities of constraints directly map to the levels in our model.

UML Extension for Break-Glass

In our paper [27] we present a Break-Glass extension of Unified Modeling Language (UML) with support for hierarchical RBAC. Extending our paper, Schefer-Wenzl and Strembeck [101] support the definition of SoD and BoD constraints. Roles have permissions to execute tasks in processes. Dynamic Separation of Duty (DSoD), Static Separation of Duty (SSoD) and BoD can be defined for tasks. They allow to override the herewith defined regular permissions to be overridden in three ways. First, during override the constraints do not have to evaluate to true, i. e., can be ignored. Second, roles, and third, subjects, can have assigned *breakable* permissions, i. e., additional permissions which are active during override. For processes allowing for override, an audit process has to be defined which, beyond others, contains the definition who is permitted to approve the override. The paper focuses on the modeling aspect and hence only describes the definition of regular and exceptional permissions but not the runtime evaluation, e. g., how the user gets notified about the need to override. Furthermore, it is not clear if and how regular and exceptional permissions have to be free of conflict, e. g., if a role has the regular permissions and a derived exceptional permissions to executed some task.

Schefer-Wenzl and Strembeck [101] focus on the modeling aspect of Break-Glass in Business Process (BP) models. What is defined about the Break-Glass model can directly be mapped to our model: constraints which can be overridden with Break-Glass would be attached to p^{reg} on level ℓ_1 and hence would not be enforced by the exceptional policy on level ℓ_2. The exceptional permissions would be expressed in the exceptional policy on level ℓ_2. In fact, our approaches could complement each other. Applying our runtime integration and lattice combining algorithm and therewith avoid the question if regular and exceptional permissions have to be free of conflict could enhance the work of [101]. In return, we did not discuss Break-Glass in the context of business processes, where [101] demonstrates how the audit can be made part of the business process modeling.

Break-Glass for Business Process Models

von Stackelberg et al. [104] present a framework to support Break-Glass for Business Process Models (BPMS). Tasks are annotated with permissions required for regular access, whereas constraints can be formulated with a BP constraint language using context information available within the BPM, e.g., get owner, or start time of a task. Exceptional permission can have attached obligations as compensation for a Break-Glass access. Additional to pre-obligations ("synchronous" obligations), they introduce use post-obligations ("asynchronous" obligations) which add additional tasks to be executed with in a process, i.e., dynamically add additional tasks to a process. For Break-Glass, they differentiate between three Break-Glass roles: BTG activator, access, and compensator role. If no regular permission can be found, but Break-Glass can be applied, the access role has to ask for exceptional access. If the access role is equals the activator role, the Break-Glass access is automatically activated, otherwise, Break-Glass has to be activated by the activator, e.g., a patient confirming a Break-Glass access to his health record. The compensator is responsible for executing obligations attached to exceptional permissions.

von Stackelberg et al. [104] focus, similar to Schefer-Wenzl and Strembeck [101], on Break-Glass in BP models. For this, both regular and exceptional permissions can be expressed with a BP specific language. This could be directly mapped to our model, i.e., defining a regular and an exceptional policy. As BP specific extensions, they introduce two further concepts. First, with the notion of the three roles: BTG activator, accessor, and compensator role. With those, a concept similar to delegation is introduced: before exceptional permissions can actually be used by the BTG access role, the BTG activator role has to activate a BTG case. In terms of delegation, an authorized user (being in the role of the BTG activator role) has to delegate exceptional permissions on request, i.e., activate a BTG case for the BTG accessor role. It is possible to model cases where a user is both the activator and accessor role. Second, asynchronous obligations allow to define the required audit process or other post-access tasks, i.e., allow to dynamically add additional tasks to be executed within the process where the Break-Glass access was executed. Regarding the AC aspects, the BTG activator and accessor role are comparable to our stateful Break-Glass approach, i.e., one subject activating exceptional permissions for another user. As for [101], we see that our generic approach can represent the generic Break-Glass concepts, while the BP specific concepts contribute how the audit can be handled within BP environments.

8.3.4 Multi-Level Security Adoptions

Relaxation Lattices

Badger [7] defines a model which can give guarantees to forestall specified *information flow*. In more detail, the model defines subjects $\mathscr{S}$ and resources $\mathscr{R}$, being entities $e \in \{\mathscr{S} \cup \mathscr{R}\}$, where a subject $S \in \mathscr{S}$ can execute actions (read r and write w) upon a resource $R \in \mathscr{R}$. Every entity e has a security level $L \in \mathscr{L}$. It can be defined which information flows between entities assigned to labels may happen.

This allows to formulate Multi-Level Security (MLS) models, e. g., constraints as the ss- and $\star$-property from the Bell-La Padula model. The constraints defined for a system are called *security policy* and can be seen as negative permissions. Constraints and hence the security policy can be *relaxed*. For example, while the regular security policy may define a constraint ensuring a "no writes down" property, for an exceptional security policy this may be relaxed and allow information flow from "secret" to the lower level "confidential."

Different security policies can be ordered in a lattice, with the most constraining security policy being on top, and security policies getting relaxed towards the bottom. At runtime, subjects can, using another security policy, change the security policy which must be satisfied, i. e., relaxing the constraints the system should follow. In this relaxed state, subjects can start actions they would not be allowed under the more strict constraints. In general, information flow between entities which already have experienced information flow in a relaxed state may continue even after a more constrained automaton is put in place, i. e., to not halt progress which has been started in relaxed mode. The idea is that guarantees which have been violated do not need to be enforced any more. As exception to this rule, constraints which may not be violated even if it halts progress started in relaxed mode (e. g., prohibit publication of data which have been relabeled in relaxed mode), are marked as "strong" constraints.

Badger [7] proposes, similar to our model, to define multiple security policies, where relaxed constraints (i. e., increasing privileges) are used to model the need for override according to the current state of the system. Those constraints correspond to DENY policies in our model. However, there is only one active security policy. A separate security policy (i.e., what we call an administrative policy) defines how the active security policy can be set by subjects. Furthermore, the formulation of information flow is intended to model MLS systems; if a security policy relaxes another cannot be guaranteed by the model but needs to be shown separately.

The model of Badger is based on the definition of information flow, where the transitivity of information flow together with the change of the security policy raises the question, how information can flow after an override when the security policy is switched back to normal operation, i.e., constraints are not relaxed any more. The proposed solution to define "strong" constraints (where information flow started in relaxed mode is prohibited) implies that the system state reached in override mode cannot be simply switched back. The solution of strong constraints is theoretic in the sense that it is not defined how the system can be transformed when changing the security policy. For example, if the regular security policy does strongly not allow information flow from e_x to e_z, but in a relaxed mode information was flowing from e_x to e_y, it is unclear how the system should behave when information is flowing from e_y to e_z.

Fuzzy Multi-Level Security

Cheng et al. [40] present, based on the notion of soft vs. hard boundary as discussed in section 8.2, a *Fuzzy* MLS model. The region within the soft and hard boundary is divided into risk bands, i.e., the closer the used risk band is to the hard boundary the more risk is associated with the access. The risk bands between the soft and the hard boundary are computed based on the information given with a MLS system such as the Bell-La Padula model, i.e., the classification and categories assigned to subjects and resources. As the risk of one access has to be treated relative to the (potential) benefit, they propose a credit card similar system: every user has some "risk credit" she can spend. Accesses in a low (i.e., close to the soft boundary) risk band are cheaper than in a high risk band. The credit a user has is defined by the return of investment the user achieves. Each use of risk credit is logged so that the users behavior can be reviewed.

In fuzzy MLS, exceptional policies are be computed automatically, giving a list (i.e., a specific instance of a lattice) of policies which are activated all the time. Who can use which exceptional policy is decided along a risk credit, which could be modeled as policy state. We will discuss the MLS aspects of those Break-Glass approach in section 9.3 in more detail.

8.3.5 Delegation-Based Models

Authority Resolution

Based on their categorization of accesses [89] discussed in section 8.2, Rissanen et al. [90] provide a technique they call *authority resolution*. The general idea is that the subject who granted a permission is able to audit and approve an override. Based on a delegation framework [8] where authorizations are expressed as delegation certificates, it is possible to determine the sources of authorization along the authorization chain.

As extension to the original model, not only permissions (*perm*) can be delegated, but also possibility-with-override (*can*), where *can* is a weaker privilege than *perm* and can therefore be delegated whenever a *perm* could be delegated. During evaluation, it is first searched for (regular) *perm* permissions, and only if no such permission can be found, a possibility-with-override *can* permission is used to answer an AC request with a "require override" response. If neither a *perm* nor a *can* is found, the access is denied. Overrides are logged and have to be audited. For searching an authority who can audit and approve the access (i. e., the authority resolution), not only for subjects in the delegation chain is searched, but for all persons who could permit (i. e., delegate a *perm* permission) the request, i. e., along the whole delegation graph. The found persons are ordered, the person who delegated the *can* permission is a prime candidate, and the source of authority will be the last as it is the highest authority. For subjects between the prime and the last candidate, a heuristic on top of the delegation graph is presented.

For Rissanen et al. [90], the underlying AC model is a delegation based model. First a regular PERMIT is searched, and only if no such regular PERMIT can be found, exceptional privileges are checked, i. e., implicitly implementing our lattice evaluation algorithm. The authority resolution is based on the underlying AC model and hence cannot be adopted to our approach. Furthermore, the approach is based on the assumption that an authority who could grant permissions for regular access is also in the position to approve a Break-Glass access. We are not sure if this can always be a valid assumption, as the delegator is likely to be "near" and hence in a personal relation to the delegatee, which may cause the delegator to decide more on a personal than on a professional basis. Hence, we see this approach as problematic in cases where an independent third party has to approve an override. Eventually a random examination by a third party may reduce the risk of incorrectly behaving delegators.

Auto-Delegation Mechanism

Crampton and Morisset [43] provide a delegation based approach to handle exceptional situations. Delegation allows to enhance the access rights at runtime, but still the possibility to delegate (e. g., the permission to delegate) has to be planned beforehand, and hence a user has to be available who is willing and able to delegate. To circumvent those problems, they provide an automated delegation mechanism, which delegates access rights automatically to one of the most qualified available person. This requires, first, that the system is able to determine the set of available persons (e. g., by keeping track of logged in users), and, second, to define which of the available ones are the most qualified.

For this, the presented model defines a partial order of subjects, where the order is defined along the qualification of the subjects (in respect to a specific resource). This model is instantiated for information flow policies and RBAC. For RBAC, a distance function $\delta_{rbac}(s_1, s_2)$ defines the similarity of two subjects, where the distance is based on the given permissions, user-role and role-permission assignments. Given a set of subjects S_o which are considered to be most qualified to access a specific object (i. e., resource), one can order all available subjects in respect to the minimal distance δ_{rbac} to one of the most qualified subjects $s \in S_o$. Crampton and Morisset [43] do not define how S_o has to be derived, but it could be, for example, the set of subjects which have regular access. This gives, for RBAC, a total order of most qualified subjects, and, naturally, all subjects $s \in S_o$ head the order, followed by subjects which have the most similar permissions as one of the subjects $s \in S_o$. When using the automated delegation mechanism for an exception mechanism, the automated delegation mechanism implements an extension for the Policy Enforcement Point (PEP): when a users is denied the regular access, the automated delegation mechanism can be queried, if the accessing user is the most qualified, available one, i. e., if there is no users available with regular permissions and he is the one with the closest permissions in respect to δ_{rbac}. By this construction, users which do not have regular permissions, but are nonetheless the most qualified ones, can be granted access.

The approach of Crampton and Morisset [43] is not a Break-Glass approach in terms of the fundamental principles we identified for Break-Glass, as none of the four principles can be fulfilled. However, the main contribution of [43] is an algorithm to find the most competent available person, which could also be applied for a Break-Glass approach as we define it. If users have to explicitly ask for auto-delegation instead of automatically triggering it, the principles of accessibility, awareness, and accountability could be fulfilled. The "auto" of auto-delegation would in this case describe what can when be automatically delegated, but not when this automatism is triggered. The ability to fulfill the principle of governance would require a deeper change, as there will always be a most competent user to execute a task (as long as there is any user competent to execute this task and another user is available) and hence every access will be accessible for someone. If the governance principle has to be fulfilled in the targeted scenario, this could be mitigated by roughly defining – implicitly or explicitly – what should never be happen even with auto-delegation. The auto-delegation mechanism could then be used as fine-grained constraint, who shall be able to effectively override a denied access.

8.3.6 XACML-Based Approaches

Obligation Combining Algorithm in XACML

Alqatawna et al. [4] argue that XACML as general purpose language should be enabled to express Break-Glass policies, implementing the model as presented in [90]. They introduce *override obligations* which express that the PEP has to ask the user for confirmation, notify the authority for approval, and log the override access before granting access. Those override obligations should only be applied, if no regular permit (with or without other obligations) is available. As XACML does not define a structure or order over obligations, they propose to enhance XACML by replacing the existing policy combining algorithms with effects-combining and obligations-combining algorithms[2].

The *effects-combining algorithms* replace the standard algorithms, i. e., evaluate the sub-policies, and has as output not only a single AC decision, but also a set of obligations (the obligations attached to the policy, matching the AC decision) and a list of sets of obligations from the sub-policies. This output is the input for (a chain of) *obligation-combining algorithms*, further algorithms may be defined for other purposes. In case of the Break-Glass algorithm, it is checked if a "regular" permit (i. e., without override-obligation) can be found. If yes, the override-obligations are removed from the result. This ensures that no override-obligations are returned if a regular permit can be found.

---

[2]Those algorithms operate at `PolicySet` level, as in XACML 2.0 used by Alqatawna et al. [4], obligations can only be defined for policies.

Alqatawna et al. [4] demonstrated that yet powerful languages such as XACML have problems with expressing different "types" of permissions, e. g., that exceptional permissions, attached with exceptional obligations, should always be dominated by regular permissions. The proposed obligation-combining algorithm of Alqatawna et al. [4] allows to define a domination of obligations in XACML and hence a domination of permissions. In the shown example, there is only one type of domination, i. e., exceptional obligations shall be removed if a PERMIT without exceptional obligations can be found. The presented approach would allow to implement more sophisticated algorithms and hence could be used to implement a similar structure as we define with our policy lattice.

The obligation-combining algorithm as proposed in [4] would require an integration into the underlying AC model. In exchange, their approach does not have some of the limitations of ours (discussed in subsection 10.3.1), e. g., could handle obligations attached to DENY decisions more flexible. However, this flexibility comes with some drawbacks. First, it is specific to XACML and hence lacks the generality of our approach. Second, it requires to extend the existing XACML standard, whereas our approach can be fully implemented using existing XACML concepts, as shown in chapter 7. Although the paper and hence the proposal was published in 2007 for XACML 2.0, it was not included in XACML 3.0 which is available since end 2010. This may be caused by, third, the fact that no lazy evaluation in combining algorithms could be applied. For example, the XACML standard allows to stop the `first-applicable` algorithm whenever a matching element was found. Following [4], all further elements would have to be evaluated as only the obligation combining algorithm can decide if the result of first element or the result of another element should be returned, resulting in a worse performance and making optimization of policies harder.

OASIS XACML – Break the Glass Profile

Based on the work presented by Ferreira et al. [51], OASIS is working on a break the the glass profile for XACML, a preliminary version is available from Chadwick and Lievens [38]. Here, the Policy Decision Point (PDP) has a state, maintained by an own component, queried through the Policy Information Point (PIP). If the user is not permitted to access a resource with regular permissions, the PDP returns a BTG response back to the PEP, i. e., a DENY decision with an <Advice> in XACML 3.0 and an <Obligation> in XACML 2.0. The user is informed by the PEP about the possibility to break the glass. Thus, first, the user can request to break the glass (which

modifies the state of the PDP), and, in a second request, can try to access
the protected resource with exceptional privileges. It is in the responsibility
of the security engineer to assure that a user which retrieves an <Advice> is
permitted to do so. For a discussion of the concepts, see the discussion of
Ferreira et al. [51] above.

8.4 Field Tests

Application Specific Break-Glass

Ferreira et al. [50] present an Electronic Medical Record (EMR) system for
a university hospital with more than 500 physicians. They state that the
assumption that permissions are known in advance does not hold for real
environments, where in unanticipated situations access to information is
essential. Hence, they implement a BTG mechanism to override AC whilst
providing some non-repudiation mechanisms, following the requirements
defined by health care professionals: allow subjects to override denied
accesses on request (i. e., notify the user that exceptional privileges are about
to be used), but record and monitor the users actions (i. e., users must
be authenticated), notify responsible parties (i. e., define a responsibility
hierarchy) and make subjects responsible for their actions. They note
that a BTG mechanism in place may mean that patient confidentiality
is breached, but this breach is known by responsible parties and can be
analyzed afterwards.

The basic AC model for regular permissions is defined with a mixture of
RBAC and IBAC, and IBAC is used to model, e. g., relationships between
patients and physicians. There are no explicit exceptional permissions
defined, i. e., every user which is able to search for medical data can make use
of Break-Glass, however, they note that restricting exceptional permissions is
considered to be a required mechanism. Following the BTG mechanism, if the
regular AC decisions evaluates to DENY, the Graphical User Interface (GUI)
shows a corresponding error message, but presents the possibility to break
the glass in case of an emergency situation. If the user breaks the glass, he
has to provide a reason, a superior is notified about the emergency access,
and the access will be logged for later audit.

Non-electronic EMR systems, where only physical mechanisms can be used
to protect patient data, e. g., lock rooms or filing cabinets, do not allow for
fine-grained AC or non-repudiation. In comparison, electronic EMR systems
with Break-Glass allow to protect patient data in a better way, as BTG

assures non-repudiation in case of exceptional situations and can enforce a fine-grained regular policy.

Domain-Specific Models

Hafner et al. [60] model AC policies for Electronic Health Record (EHR) following an usage control approach. They adapt a framework which allows to model policies in a domain-specific language. Also, exceptional permission can be modeled within this framework, e. g., define, beside the regular visit, an emergency visit. The emergency visit has an audit obligation attached, and allows to do execute emergency visits, but requires a post-hoc audit.

Exceptional Treatment Relationships

Denley and Smith [45] present a case study of British hospitals, where, for accessing a patients health record, a relationship between subject and patient has to exist. As the system will occasionally not be aware of such an ongoing TR, it implements an override mechanism which allows some subjects to access patients health records even if the, for regular access required, relationship is missing. This causes around 50 override per day, especially from departments where the required information about subject-patient relationships are missing, or from departments where the "lack of computerization means that the clinical information system has no data."

Inter-Organizational Collaboration

Stevens and Wulf [103] present a case study of an inter-organizational scenario, where, for organizations cooperating in projects, external partners require access to internal data. They note that traditional AC, which only allows to define *"allowed"* and *"forbidden"* beforehand, does not comply to organizational requirements. Concerning this, they propose that AC systems should be aware of three mechanisms, when access control decisions are made:

- *ex-ante* (before access) corresponds to traditional AC, i. e., AC policies are defined before the access.
- *uno-tempore* (at access) is a form where the decision is done as manual task at access time, i. e., a competent person decides upon the access, e. g., when data are requested per mail or fax
- *ex-post* (after access) defers the decision to some later point in time, however, this approach is only applicable if misuse can be detected and sanctioned.

Both uno-tempore and ex-post can be used to compensate problems resulting from ex-ante, and meccanisms can be combined. Stevens and Wulf develop a system where external subjects can request internal documents, and a policy decides which of the access mechanisms should be applied, assuring that ex-post checks are done.

Healthcare Audit Trails

Røstad and Edsberg [91] present a case study on audit trails of Norway hospitals using DocuLife EPR of Siemens Medical Solutions for managing patient records. Here, Break-Glass mechanisms for handling dynamic and unplanned events are implemented. For the study, the audit trails of eight hospitals collected during one month were examined. To ensure that the exception mechanisms are not misused, audits have to be performed on a regular basis. The audit should teach how AC mechanisms should be changed to "eliminating or at least minimizing the use of exception mechanism," and, should also teach if information is missing in audit trails. However, the system makes audit hard, e. g., only exceptional accesses are logged as exceptional access, follow-up accesses enabled by initial Break-Glass have to be retrieved from regular log, which makes it hard to retrieve all relevant accesses which have to be monitored. Also, the information should be available through a usable interface and contain sufficiently information to get a picture of what happened.

The health records of 54% of those patients which have been in contact with a hospital were at least once accessed with Break-Glass, and 17 % of the overall accesses. The authors conclude that this can rarely be called an exception mechanism. They conclude that Break-Glass is not a replacement of accurate regular policies, but should be used as real exception mechanism for situations which cannot be handled otherwise. Break-Glass should not be generally available, but only for, e. g., specific roles. Thus, Break-Glass does not invalidate the need for accurate regular policies or AC models able to define such accurate policies.

9 Evaluation

We are presenting four lines of evaluation. First, in order to demonstrate that the requirements as they are demanded for a Break-Glass solution are fulfilled by our approach, in section 9.1 we will compare the requirements listed in section 3.1 with the properties of our solution. To show the generalizability of our approach, second, we have shown how existing approaches can be modeled along our Break-Glass model (chapter 8) and will present an approach to classify existing Break-Glass approaches along our Break-Glass model in section 9.2. Third, we will show how to model Break-Glass on top of a selected set of Access Control (AC) models in section 9.3. Fourth, to demonstrate the feasibility of the presented approaches, we have described a prototypic implementation in chapter 7.

9.1 Requirements vs. Properties

In section 3.1 we identified four basic principles which make up Break-Glass: governance, accessibility, awareness, and accountability. We will now discuss how those requirements are fulfilled by our Break-Glass approach. As noted in section 3.1, the more properties can be fulfilled by the Break-Glass model itself, the less has to be fulfilled within the following pre-, at-, and post-access phases. We will now discuss that most requirements can already be fulfilled by the model and the pre-access phase.

Governance

Our Break-Glass model allows to define what is permitted, what should never be permitted, and what could be permitted in exceptional situations, i. e., define positive, negative and exceptional permissions. Using the policy lattice, our model can guarantee that exceptional privileges are only applied if no regular privilege can be granted.

We do not dictate how exceptional privileges have to be defined: as our model is defined on top of existing AC models, the expressiveness of the used policy language defining exceptional privileges is not restricted and depends on the used AC model. This includes that we do not require the exceptional situation to be modeled for defining exceptional privileges.

Using the lattice, exceptional privileges can be structured into policies, which can be activated and deactivated by persons in charge. For the this activation process no deep knowledge is required. Exploiting stateful Break-Glass, fine grained Break-Glass mechanisms as they are demanded for Health Insurance Portability and Accountability Act (HIPAA) can be implemented.

Accessibility

For using Break-Glass, users do not need to posses specific knowledge: our concept of Break-Glass allows to notify and ask users when exceptional privileges are available. This contributes to fulfill both the accessibility and awareness property. Our approach does not dictate how Break-Glass is integrated in the Graphical User Interface (GUI), or which obligations have to be used (for both stateless or stateful Break-Glass).

The separation of regular and exceptional privileges also guarantees that users are only asked to confirm the usage of exceptional privileges if no regular but only exceptional privileges are available.

Awareness

The structuring of exceptional privileges into policies allows to define messages to users using exceptional privileges, i. e., making them aware of what they are about to do. An override measurement can be requested by the users to get further information about the granted exceptional privileges.

Accountability

Our logging mechanism ensures that a Break-Glass access is only executed if it has been logged centrally to a log storage. Furthermore, it is ensured that only actually used exceptional privileges are logged as Break-Glass accesses and can be separated from regular ones post-access. Modeling Break-Glass on top of existing AC models, the authentication of the user can be done as for the underlying AC.

We presented techniques to log information at-access to be available post-access, and thereon proposed techniques for the post-access evaluation of Break-Glass accesses.

9.2 Classification of Break-Glass

We now present a classification of Break-Glass approaches which is based on our own experiences in developing and applying Break-Glass as well as the result of the intensive study of the existing body of literature in chapter 8. Based on our analysis, we identified the following dimensions for classifying approaches for implementing exceptional access control:

1. *Structuring of permissions:* How regular, exceptional, and negative permissions are defined, which permission types are known by existing approaches, and how conflicts between different permission types are handled.

2. *Type of Break-Glass Decision:* How exceptional AC decisions are modeled, i. e., using a third AC decision versus using obligations.

3. *Adherence to the Requirements of Break-Glass:* To which extend the different approaches adhere to the fundamental principles of Break-Glass as described in section 3.1.

The characterization of existing approaches will be done along the identified dimensions as shown in Table 9.1, where one of the following values can be assigned to those categories (except for the first two columns "contribution category" and "defined permissions" which will be discussed separately):

"-" for not applicable, i. e., the paper does not make any explicit or implicit statement,

"y" for yes: the paper contributes (at least to some extent) to this issue,

"r" for requirement: this issue is identified as requirement,

"n" for no: this issue is either explicitly or implicitly excluded, and

"e" for extendible: the paper does not make any explicit or implicit statement, however, the core contribution could be adapted with minor changes to contribute to this issue.

Contribution Category

The column *contribution* shows which kind of contribution is provided by the presented approach, where the following values can be assigned:

Requirements *R* define (only) requirements (and do not fall into one of the following categories)

Case study *C*, field test, prototypic or application specific implementation

Model *M* define access control models which allows to express Break-Glass policies

Model Extension E define extensions to access control models (or policy language based on some AC model) which allows to express Break-Glass policies

Generic Model G Define generic Break-Glass models (independently from any AC model)

G_i define a generic Break-Glass model and demonstrate along one "instantiation" with a specific AC model or policy language

Structuring of Permissions

In Break-Glass models, permissions can conceptually be separated into three general categories: regular (R, i. e., PERMIT), negative (D, i. e., DENY), and exceptional (E) permissions, grouped into policies. This gives a wide variety of patterns which permissions are defined in Break-Glass policies. In our table, *defined permissions* are those which are defined explicitly.

It depends on the model which category dominates which other category. There is a common understanding that exceptional permissions policies should not dominate the regular policy, i. e., if a subject has regular access, no exception mechanisms should be triggered. However, there are different strategies how positive and exceptional relate to negative permissions. This can be expressed with two sub categories of negative permissions: D^o are negative permissions which are overridable, either by regular or exceptional permissions, and D^n are not overridable by any other positive permission. Finally, E^d denotes a sub category for exceptional permissions, i. e., when exceptional permissions can be derived (with no or minor additional input) from the other (e. g., regular) permissions.

Some approaches allow to *structure exceptional permissions* according to varying strategies and granularities, e. g., into policies or levels. Such structures can be used to, e. g., assign different obligations to different types of exceptional AC decisions. Moreover, these structures can be used for the *activation of exceptional permissions*, i. e., activating and de-activating – at runtime – parts of the exceptional permissions.

Type of Break-Glass Decision

By introducing, beneath positive and negative, exceptional permissions as third type of permissions, it seems natural to introduce, beneath PERMIT and DENY, a *third access control decision* for exceptional permissions. Other approaches model Break-Glass accesses using *obligations* (see discussion in subsection 10.3.3, why we have chosen obligations for our model).

Adherence to the Requirements of Break-Glass

A Break-Glass model may only partially fulfill the principles discussed in section 3.1. To be able to compare different Break-Glass models, we will derive rather abstract requirements which can be applied to Break-Glass models, leaving some aspects which concern a holistic Break-Glass approach out of scope.

Governance can be split into two technical requirements. First, it has to be possible to *restrict Break-Glass* privileges of users, i. e., even with Break-Glass users must not be able to do everything. Second, if persons in charge without technical knowledge are able to *control the empowerment* of users at runtime.

Accessibility is both a requirement on the actual runtime implementation (e. g., the integration into the user interface) as well as the actual Break-Glass model. A model fulfills the accessibility requirement, if regular users can directly override denied access. If overriding a denied access requires significant additional effort such as the execution of a complicated procedure or a separate login, we call an access control model inaccessible.

Awareness requires that a break-glass access is a conscious decision, e. g., by requiring a *user confirmation* before applying exceptional privileges. While, e. g., the integration into the user interface is not in the scope of discussing the Break-Glass model itself, the different approaches may differ in model extensions – as well as specific algorithms – that allow for computing the seriousness of an exceptional access.

Accountability requires to authenticate the accessing subject. In general we assume that the authentication used for decision of a regular access is also sufficient for exceptional accesses, e. g., if the authentication using a pseudonym is sufficient for regular access, we consider this authentication as sufficient for Break-Glass accesses. As technical requirements, it is required to *log exceptional accesses* or mark exceptional accesses in the regular log as exceptional. Finally, *post-access analysis* has to be possible.

9.3 Generalized Break-Glass Models

With the Access Control Function (ACF) (see Equation 2.1) we characterized AC models along the evaluation of AC requests. For our Break-Glass model we only rely on this ACF and do not make any assumptions, e. g., how privileges for concrete AC models need to be defined, or how the ACF is implemented. Our Break-Glass model can be seen as yet another implementation of an ACF, however, for the evaluation of permissions it

Table 9.1: Classification and contributions: exceptional access control models.

	SPC [66]	SAP [98]	Jaeger et al. [65]	Ardagna et al. [5]	Rissanen [89]	Marinovic et al. [77]	Povey [87]	Dekker and Etalle [44]	Bartsch [11]	Longstaff et al. [74]	Ferreira et al. [51]	Wainer et al. [105]	Brucker and Petritsch [27]	Schefer-Wenzl et al. [101]	von Stackelberg et al. [104]	Badger [7]	Cheng et al. [40]	Rissanen et al. [90]	Crampton et al. [43]	Alqatawna et al. [4]	This thesis
Post-access analysis	r	y	r	r	r	–	y	y	r	r	r	–	r	y	y	–	y	y	–	y	y
Log excep. access	y	y	r	y	r	–	r	y	r	r	y	–	y	y	y	–	y	y	–	y	y
User confirmation	y	y	r	–	r	–	r	n	y	r	y	–	y	y	y	–	–	y	–	y	y
Accessibility	n	n	–	–	–	–	–	–	y	y	–	y	–	y	–	–	y	y	y	y	y
Control empowerment	n	n	n	n	n	n	n	–	n	n	y	n	y	n	y	n	n	y	–	n	y
Restrict Break-Glass	y	y	y	y	y	y	y	n	y	y	y	y	y	y	y	y	y	y	y	y	y
Obligations	–	–	–	y	–	y	–	–	n	–	y	–	y	–	y	–	–	n	–	y	y
Third AC decision	–	–	–	y	–	n	–	–	n	–	y	–	n	–	n	–	y	y	–	n	n
Activation of excep. perm.	–	–	n	n	n	n	n	–	y	n	y	n	y	n	y	y	n	y	–	n	y
Structurable excep. perm.	–	–	n	n	n	n	n	–	n	n	y	y	y	n	n	y	y	n	–	n	y
Defined permissions	E	E	R,D	R,E,D^n	R,E,D	R,E,D	R,E	R	R,E^d	R,E^d,D^o	R,E	R,E	R,E	R,D^o,E	R,E	D^o	R,E	R,E	R,E^d	R,E	$R,E,D^{o,n}$
Contribution	R	C	G	G_i	G	G_i	R	M	E	M	E	E	G_i	E	M	M	E	E	E	M	G_i

relies on another, given AC model which implements an ACF. Hence, our model is abstract, as it requires another, concrete ACF. Furthermore, our Break-Glass approach is generic as it allows to be defined on top of every AC which follows the ACF.

When implementing Break-Glass on top of a specific AC model, one needs to define regular and exceptional privileges. As noted in subsection 2.2.2, providing a comparison of all existing AC model would exceed the scope of this work. Hence, showing how Break-Glass can be defined on top of all existing AC models is not feasible. Instead, we selected a (subjective) list of AC models which are commonly referenced in research, while having different proprieties.

Access Control Matrix

In an access control matrix [58] (discussed as representative for Discretionary Access Control (DAC) models) permissions onto resources are directly assigned to subjects. The matrix holding those permission defines the regular case and hence p^{reg}. As exceptional policy p^{excp} another instance of the access control matrix is created, defining additional, exceptional entries in the matrix. When delegating permissions from the regular matrix, the delegator is allowed to chose if the permissions should be delegated as regular or as exceptional permission, i. e., if the copied permissions should be entered into the regular or the exceptional matrix. Providing this choice to the delegator is similar to what Rissanen et al. [90] propose. Permissions from the exceptional matrix can only be copied to the exceptional matrix. Not only a user confirmation but also a "notify owner" obligation is defined, i. e., the owner of a resource would receive notifications about executed actions on his resources (not that this also includes the delegation of exceptional permission).

Role Based Access Control

Role Based Access Control (RBAC) is a very common AC model in both industry and research. There are multiple extensions which, commonly, allow to define different types of constraints, e. g., location [3, 21] or temporal [3, 20] constraints, or constraints (e. g., Separation of Duty (SoD)) for workflow systems, e. g., [105]. Common to such RBAC models, permissions are assigned to roles (PA), and roles are assigned to users (UA).

Regular permissions are defined in p^{reg}, where constraints (if defined for the RBAC model) might constrain those assignments. To define Break-Glass, exceptional permissions might be introduced in exceptional policies extending p^{reg}, e. g., assume one exceptional policy p^{excp} with a user conformation obligation attached. For the definition of exceptional permissions, the following strategies with increasing granularity may be chosen (this list is not necessarily complete):

- Define an additional role-role relationship for p^{excp} which denotes which role can be upgraded to which role in case of Break-Glass (e. g., [11, 74]), i. e., users have additional roles when searching for Break-Glass permissions.
- Define additional UA assignments for p^{excp}, i. e., users have additional roles when searching for Break-Glass permissions.
- Define additional PA assignments for p^{excp}, i. e., an assigned role has more permissions when searching for a Break-Glass permission, e. g., [51, 101]
- Define weaker constraints (in RBAC models supporting constraints), e. g., [74, 101, 105]. Constraints can be defined within DENY policies of our lattice and hence use the guaranteed refine property our lattice provides.

Multi-Level Security – Bell-La Padula

Another group of AC models which are not so obvious candidates for Break-Glass are Multi-Level Security (MLS) models with Bell-La Padula as the most prominent example. For Bell-La Padula, two types of Break-Glass can be defined. First, overriding the DAC part, i. e., the access control matrix. Second, overriding the Mandatory Access Control (MAC) (or MLS) part. As we already discussed the access control matrix, we will focus on the MLS part.

The MLS model of Bell-La Padula does not define permissions as RBAC or the access control matrix. Instead, constraints (ss- and ⋆-property) define, based on labels assigned to subjects and resources, which accesses should *not* be granted. To grant exceptional permissions, those constraints need to be relaxed – directly or indirectly. Obviously, when doing so, the herewith guaranteed properties of the MLS model (subjects can read information only from their security level or below, information flow from higher to lower levels is forestalled) cannot be guaranteed any more. For example, relaxing the ⋆-property (directly or indirectly) has also some effect after the exceptional access: when information is flowing to a lower level with exceptional permissions, users with a lower level can access those information with regular privileges. Depending on how the ss-property is relaxed, information may be declassified only for the accessing subject, but the ⋆-property (no write-up) may still be in place. Thus, relaxing the ss- or ⋆-property provides means for a (controlled) declassification of information.

When introducing Break-Glass to Bell-La Padula, two things can be achieved: some resources should be readable for more users in exceptional situations (i. e., relaxing the ss-property), and to some resources it should be possible to write more confidential information than the regular label would allow (i. e., relaxing the ⋆-property). To achieve this, one can choose out of two strategies:

1. Directly relaxing the constraints guaranteed by the MLS model, e. g., as proposed by [7].
2. Assigning exceptional labels to subjects and resources and hence indirectly relax the constraints.

In terms of our ACF definition, one can interpret the constraints of the MLS model (e. g., the ss- and ⋆-property in Bell-La Padula) as part of the ACF implementation and hence not as part of the security state σ_{sec} passed to the ACF. Consequently, relaxing those constraints implies changing the ACF and hence the underlying AC model. To implement such a system, a policy language which allows to express the ss- and ⋆-property as part of the security state σ_{sec} is needed. Given such a language, relaxed constraints can be defined, e. g., as part of DENY policies and be relaxed along the lattice. Our model will guarantee the refinement between the elements of the lattice.

Badger [7] provides such a language, i. e., constraints and their relaxation can be expressed. Our lattice evaluation algorithm can guarantee the refinement between relaxed security policies. Cheng et al. [40] implements a similar relaxation, where the amount of relaxation is divided into risk bands which can be computed based on the classification and categories of both subjects and resources. Also, our concept of the policy state can be exploited to hold the labels assigned to resources and subjects, and policy permissions (e. g., using XACML) can be used to implement the policy permissions, i. e., expressing the ss- and ⋆-properties, and their relaxed derivatives. However, this requires a change to the underlying AC model. In this thesis we want to demonstrate how Break-Glass can be added on top of an existing AC model. Hence, we will now discuss the indirect relaxation of constraints by assigning exceptional labels.

The relaxation of the ss-property can indirectly be implemented by assigning higher exceptional levels to subjects, or lower exceptional levels to resources where information should be read from. This allows subjects to read resources they for usual do not have access to. Assigning higher levels to subjects should be preferred, as this only allows to read subjects from higher levels, but does not annul the control implemented by the $\star$-property. When resources have a lower exceptional level, it will be possible for subjects to read this information, but also the $\star$-property will not forestall a write operation from the "lowered level" and hence will not forestall the declassification of this information.

The relaxation of the $\star$-property can be implemented by assigning higher exceptional levels to resources where information should be written to. This allows to write information to resources which are for usual not writable. As for the implementation of indirectly relaxed ss- and $\star$-properties both higher and lower exceptional levels can be assigned, this should be defined in separate exceptional policies.

Hence, for implementing Break-Glass on Bell-La Padula without directly relaxing constraints, one would define three policies. Policy p^{reg} on ℓ_1 constraints the regular label assignments. In the policies p^{ss} and $p^\star$ on ℓ_2 some of the regular label assignments are replaced with exceptional assignments to implement the relaxed ss- and $\star$-properties as described above. Such exceptional policies could be generated and do not necessarily be created by hand. Furthermore note that this approach allows to define Break-Glass on top of Bell-La Padula without the need to change the underlying AC model.

Clark-Wilson

The Clark-Wilson integrity model defines both authorization and integrity concepts. We discussed how the authorization parts of the Clark-Wilson model can be extended with Break-Glass in the context of Povey [87] in subsection 8.3.1. Regarding integrity, our model does not make any statement and hence, when extending the capabilities for integrity checks, one has to extend the capabilities of the underlying integrity model. One can see that our model is a pure authorization model and cannot guarantee integrity (see Definition 7 p. 17: integrity is as superset of authorization).

How this can be done was demonstrated by Povey [87] and hence we will give only a rough overview of the approach proposed there. The "Break-Glass" idea for integrity is that, as for authorization, it cannot be decided pre-access if the execution of a Transformation Procedure (TP) will result in a valid state, which is the ultimate goal of the underlying model. Hence, to relax this, the concept of Partial Transformation Procedure (PTP) are introduced. Those do not guarantee that the system comes to a valid state, but require a post-hoc audit of an administrator. Here, it has not only to be decided if the access can be authorized in a post-hoc fashion, but also if the system (or, the Constrained Data Item (CDI)) is (or can be brought to) a valid state again. If either the post-access authorization fails or the CDI cannot be brought to a valid state, the administrator has to execute a compensating TP, which will roll back the PTP and hence, bring the CDI back in a valid state. For a detailed description, please refer to [87].

Attribute-based Encryption

Attribute-based Encryption (ABE) allows to implement sticky Attribute Based Access Control (ABAC) policies with cryptographic means, i. e., AC model, AC policies and the enforcement thereof are aggregated into one. In Brucker et al. [33], we demonstrated how ABE can be extended with Break-Glass. Due to space limitations, we will only sketch the presented approach, for details please refer to [33].

The general idea is to introduce *emergency attributes* representing the policies of our lattice. The usage of such emergency attributes is bound to obligations as defined within the lattice, e. g., require user confirmation and log for later audit. For encryption, the policies of the lattice (in case of ABE a logical expression of attributes) is combined with a logical and ∧ with the corresponding attribute representing the policy. All policies are, ordered according to the order of the lattice, combined with a (lazy) logical or ∨, i. e., implementing our lattice evaluation algorithm in ABE.

10 Discussion and Conclusion

10.1 Contributions

The general idea of Break-Glass is not new, on the contrary, a lot of research has been done (as we have shown in chapter 8). The overall goal of this thesis was to provide a generic Break-Glass model and to demonstrate along the whole life cycle of a Break-Glass access that Break-Glass can contribute to the improvement of both the security and the usability of Information Technology (IT) systems. We see five main contributions.

First, we defined a generic Break-Glass model which allows, first, to implement Break-Glass independently from the underlying Access Control (AC) model as well as, second, to represent a wide range of existing Break-Glass models. We have chosen a fundamentally different approach compared to existing work and build Break-Glass as extension to existing AC models, and hence do not rely on the properties of an underlying AC model. We presented our generic representation of AC models in subsection 2.2.2 and our generic Break-Glass model in chapter 3. We discussed how this model can be used to model most existing Break-Glass models with the related work in in chapter 8 and how our model can be applied to existing AC models in section 9.3.

Second, we introduced a conceptual distinction between *policy permissions* and *policy state* and the management thereof in section 4.1, which allow to model a security relevant system state as part of the security policy. This allows, for example, to model policies controlling changes to the security relevant system state, i. e., administrative controls. Using our approach it becomes transparent for applications if a request has to be considered as administrative or regular access.

Third, we showed how it can be ensured that exceptional privileges are only granted if not regular privilege is available, and how the user can be informed about exceptional privileges. This can be done by structuring privileges into policies of our lattice and attach according messages as shown in section 4.3. Furthermore, we presented a technique which gives the user an appropriate understanding of what they are about to do and enable them to make a reasonable decision in section 5.1.

Fourth, we introduced the concept of *versioning* of policies (subsection 5.2.1). This concept is used to support post-access analysis of Break-Glass accesses by aims of an analysis framework which is both extendible with domain or application specific analysis techniques, and allows for policy-driven analysis of Break-Glass accesses in chapter 6.

Fifth, we described both a language and an infrastructure which supports the definition, evaluation, and enforcement of Break-Glass policies and allows to record the information required for the post-access phase. The policy language, based on XACML [80], is described in subsection 4.1.4. Based on the language we showed how health care policies as they have been modeled by Becker [14] in a formal language can be expressed in XACML in subsection 4.1.5. Policies can be evaluated in the authorization infrastructure described in section 4.1.

Furthermore, we provided a survey (chapter 8) and categorization (section 9.2) for existing Break-Glass approaches. This gives an overview of existing approaches, common concepts and allows to compare Break-Glass approaches, their weaknesses and strengths.

Overall, we demonstrated how to implement the whole life cycle of an Break-Glass access using just one model and one technical infrastructure validating that all phases of Break-Glass can be implemented. We are the first who present an approach which targets the overall Break-Glass life cycle.

10.2 Research Questions

This thesis was started to solve five research questions presented in a thesis proposal [85]. We will now present the initial research questions and discuss where and how those questions are answered within this thesis. During research, some of the questions turned out to be misleading, e. g., question two has partially been answered together with question one. Hence, there is now direct mapping between questions and Chapters. The thesis proposal is written in German, hence, the here presented questions are a translation of the original questions.

Question 1 – Access Control Model for Exceptional Situations

Is it possible to define an AC model so that it can adapt at runtime to exceptional situations, especially that a decision under incomplete information can be found? The focus shall be on the question, if the user can be part of this decision process, e. g., by making him aware of the situation and allow him, to some extent, to override AC decisions.

We presented a generic Break-Glass model in chapter 3. The presented model allows a security engineer to define what could be permitted in exceptional situations, without the need to define all possible exceptional situations or relate them to the regular privileges. User can be involved into the AC decision by offering the possibility to override an AC decision, while at the same time making him aware that misuse can and will be punished. The requirements for such an approach have been defined in section 3.1.

Question 2 – Policy Language

How should policy languages (e. g., XACML [80]) be designed or adapted so that a policy engineer can express privileges which should only be applied in exceptional situations? A stepwise enhancement of exceptional privileges should be possible. It is important that exceptional privileges should not influence the applicability of regular privileges, e. g., exceptional privileges should not restrict what is possible in regular situations. Which policy analysis techniques (e. g., refinement of policies [6]) have to be developed to assure such properties?

Is the defined approach restricted to the used AC model and policy language, or can it be applied for other AC models? Possible further models could be Role Based Access Control (RBAC) [97], Bell-La Padula [17], Attribute Based Access Control (ABAC) [107], or Attribute-based Encryption (ABE) [86].

It turned out that some parts of question two can already be answered with the answer to question one, i. e., the chosen model. The model is generic in the sense that it, first, can be guaranteed that exceptional permissions do not influence regular permissions, invalidating the need for analysis techniques for a specific policy language. Second, the model does not rely on a specific AC model or policy language, but can be applied to a wide range of AC models. For the stepwise enhancement of exceptional permissions, both the policy lattice or the stateful Break-Glass approach (subsection 4.2.3) can be used. The policy language defined in subsection 4.1.4 is a subset of XACML, where we introduced an approach to structure policies in XACML. In respect to

research question two and the Break-Glass model, no restrictions of XACML
are required.

We discussed how our Break-Glass model can be defined on top of the
listed possible models in section 9.3, including the list of AC models listed
in the proposal, i. e., RBAC, Bell-La Padula and ABE. As XACML is an
ABAC based language, we did not discuss ABAC in section 9.3 separately.

Question 3 – Modeling and Definition of Policies

The concept of Break-Glass introduces a further dimension to the already
complex task of defining policies. To be able to keep a good overview of
the provided privileges, clear concepts and structures for expressing both
regular and exceptional privileges are required. Especially if privileges are
not directly assigned, but complex conditions have to be met (e. g., if the
creation of a Treatment Relationship (TR) implicitly assigns privileges to
both the creating and other subjects), a clear overview is essential.

Our Break-Glass model allows to separate regular from different levels
of exceptional policies. Hence, the additional complexity of exceptional
permissions can be split into separate problems or policies.

The concept of policy state and policy permissions (subsection 4.1.2)
allows to structure complex policies in a natural way. As basis, policy
state assignments allow to define the AC model and the policy state which
can then be used by the policy permissions at runtime. How this state
can be changed can be defined in the administrative part of the policies
(subsection 4.1.3), while this state can be used in the policy permissions
without having to consider how this state can be reached. Thus, for the
policies itself one can define the conditions which have to be fulfilled before
access can be granted (e. g., is there a TR between patient and physician)
without having to consider all the possible ways how a TR can be created.

We have shown that policies – once used to the chatty notation of XACML –
can be formulated in a rather natural way, using policy and variable references
to re-use once defined elements (e. g., is there a TR between the accessing
subject and the patient, what are the regular permissions of a nurse, etc.).
We have presented a way to structure policies along the running example in
subsection 4.1.5 and section 4.2.

Question 4 – Information for the User

A fundamental concept of exceptional accesses is that the user has a better
understanding of the benefit or avoided damage of an exceptional access

than the IT system. To make a well founded decision, the user has to put this benefit in relation to the extent of his override, i. e., the potential risk of the override [40, 47, 110]. How can the user be supported in making such a decision, i. e., which information has to provided to him in which way. It has to be considered that the user may have a limited or no technical understanding, and is in a stressful, exceptional situation. Thus, not only the question which information sources should be used has to be answered, but also how the information can be prepared so that the user can get maximal knowledge out of it.

The subject can be provided with two types of information. First, to every `userConfirmation` obligation a message is attached, which allows the policy engineer to attach a message explaining the kind of override (section 4.3). Second, we developed a technique called "override measurement" (section 5.1), which allows to present a list of users to the subject which would have access to the requested resource and are "near" to and known by the accessing subject, allowing the subject to estimate how large his override is.

Question 5 – Analysis

Both regular and exceptional policies have to be created, administrated and analyzed. Analyzing tasks could be, e. g., find redundancies in policies, proof compliance, and show required properties such as Static Separation of Duty (SSoD).

Another important analysis question is how the auditor can be supported in analyzing Break-Glass accesses. This includes the question how the auditor will be able to acquire all for the audit relevant information. Also, Break-Glass accesses can be exploited to improve the system and the accuracy of AC policies.

As we did not define our own policy language, we hence did not develop techniques to analyze this language. Furthermore, some of the properties which where intended to be shown with such tools can be guaranteed by the model, e. g., Separation of Duty (SoD) constraints can be defined as part of a non-overridable DENY policy. Furthermore, a lot of existing work discusses such topics. In the context of Break-Glass, the most urgent questions are those of post-hoc analysis, i. e., how can the auditor be supported in evaluating Break-Glass accesses. Hence, we focused on the post-access analysis. For this, we, first, showed how the information for the post-access investigation can be collected at-access in section 5.2. Second, we proposed some techniques which allow for a more efficient analysis of Break-Glass accesses and how knowledge acquired during post-access investigations can be used to improve regular policies and make future investigations more efficient in chapter 6. Overall, the proposed techniques allow for a more efficient analysis of Break-Glass accesses and hence can contribute to the successful implementation of Break-Glass in real-world application.

10.3 Discussion

We want to discuss some aspects which help in better understanding our Break-Glass approach. The properties of our Break-Glass model are discussed in subsection 10.3.1, and how it could also be applied for non-Break-Glass applications in subsection 10.3.2. Also, we want to discuss why we did not follow some existing approaches to introduce a third AC decision (subsection 10.3.3), if and how non-overridable DENY decisions should be used and how they relate to constraints (subsection 10.3.4), and how our abstract model could, beside the core and constraints model, be refined (subsection 10.3.5).

10.3.1 Properties of the Break-Glass Model

Generic. Our model is an extensions to existing AC models, i.e., allows to define Break-Glass on top of existing AC models, Access Control Function (ACF) and Policy Decision Point (PDP) implementations, and the reuse of policies for, e.g., the regular case. The policies used in our model can be implemented with any policy language following the ACF definition in Equation 2.1 (subsection 2.2.2).

Obligations for compensation. Obligations are used to implement the typical Break-Glass scenario, i.e., attaching a user confirmation obligation to a policy will require the user to confirm an exceptional situation before access is granted. However, obligations can also be used to model more complex compensation actions which have to be triggered when using exceptional privileges. This allows for a smooth integration of Break-Glass into a given environment – on application side only the Policy Enforcement Point (PEP) has to be extended with support for obligations. We avoid the definition of a third AC decision due to reasons discussed in subsection 10.3.3.

Regular, exceptional and negative permissions. Our model allows to define positive (regular and exceptional) and negative permissions. The default deny all principle should be applied, i.e., everything not explicitly permitted is denied per default. In the core model, negative permissions can only be defined implicitly, i.e., by not defining positive permissions.

Positive permissions can be separated into regular and exceptional, whereas exceptional permissions are commonly identified along obligations attached to them.

Conflict resolution. As we do not define which AC models are used to define those permissions, there may be conflicts within defined policies, i. e., a permissions defined in one policy may have an overlap with a permission in another policy, eventually with another effect (DENY or PERMIT) or different obligations (from the underlying or from the Break-Glass model). To handle such conflicts, it has to be defined which type of policy dominates which other policy. Following the requirement that exceptional permissions are never applied if regular privileges can be permitted, in our model policies on higher levels are always dominated by policies refining them. For negative permissions, a security engineer can use our model to define which negative permissions should override which positive (regular and exceptional) permission.

Default deny principle. Our model follows the default deny principle. Everything not explicitly permitted – as regular or exceptional PERMIT– should be denied per default. Negative permissions in the constraints model can be used to constrain positive permissions, however, should not be used to define the complementary of positive permissions (see subsection 10.3.4 for further discussion).

Privilege activation at runtime. At runtime, policies can be activated and deactivated. For this activation, the security state has to be modified. Here, the same techniques as for other parts of the security state configuration (e. g., role assignment for users) should be used, i. e., an administrative policy protecting the security state. We present a detailed solution how this can be done in section 4.1, which is also the basis for stateful Break-Glass (subsection 4.2.3), allowing to model "broken glass," requiring some state in the PDP to remember which glass is in a broken state.

Based on those properties, we will, first, discuss some modeling aspects of our model, including a discussion why we explicitly and intentionally excluded some possible further features from our model, and how they can or could be mitigated. Second, we will sketch some patterns which should be considered when defining Break-Glass policies.

Modeling Aspects

Our model is designed to help policy engineers in modeling regular and exceptional policies along once central idea: the more privileges are granted in exceptional situations, the higher the potential compensation has to be and hence the stronger the obligations attached to privileges should get. Thus, obligations are attached to exceptional privileges, or, obligations attached to positive permissions make them exceptional. We do not make any assumption about the properties or the inner structure and meaning of obligations, hence we do not enforce the refinement of obligations.

This approach has two implications. First, obligations are only attached to positive AC decisions, i. e., PERMIT decisions. Within our model, obligations cannot be attached to DENY decisions. (Note that this does not prohibit the underlying AC model to attach obligations to DENY decisions.) Second, as obligations are attached to permissions, the domination of obligations is bound to the domination of permissions they are assigned to, i. e., in our model there is no concept which would allow to define a separate domination of obligations.

Those two properties can be interpreted as limitations, as some use cases can either not or not directly be modeled. For example, one may want to model obligations attached to DENY decisions which is not supported within our Break-Glass model. For obligations attached to DENY decision, the policy engineer is required to define them within the underlying AC model (in subsection 10.3.5 we will discuss how this can be done). However, we see only a limited set of use cases for obligations attached to DENY decision such as, e. g., in Linux, if a users is not allowed to execute the *sudo* command (i. e., to get root privileges), the administrator gets a notification of a possible attempt to break into the system. Consequently, we see even less use cases for obligations attached to DENY decision which should change with the activation of exceptional privileges. Furthermore, we see such obligations as specific to permissions (e. g., notify the administrator about a failed sudo attempt) and not bound to a (intended to be coarse-grained) exceptional policy. Hence, such obligations should be covered by the underlying AC model and should not be defined on the level of the lattice modeling Break-Glass privileges.

Another use case which cannot directly be modeled is a domination of obligation contradicting the domination of privileges, e. g., if increasing privileges with increasing exception level should reduce the compensation level. Our model does not allow to modify a given PERMIT on extending policies. This includes that obligations attached to a PERMIT cannot be altered. For example, one could want to reduce the logging level with increasing exceptional level to enable the auditor to focus on the major overrides post-access, or prevent the mail notification of every single exceptional access to avoid a flooding of the responsible persons mail box. Also here, we see it as questionable if such scenarios are a major use case. For the first example, we see it as questionable if the decision which override should be audited post-access should be answered at any other point in time than post-access. Instead, we would argue that all information available at-access has to be recorded at-access, and the decision which override should be examined in detail should be done post-access. The analysis framework could help in filtering out those privileges granted by a lower policy. For the second example, not flooding a mail box should be part of the used alerting service, e. g., summarize the overrides of one hour into one mail, or send an Short Message Service (SMS) alert only every ten minutes.

In our experience use cases requiring a separate domination order of obligations should be implemented by components being in a better position to handle the required functionality. If, despite the discussed considerations, such a use case has to be implemented by the Break-Glass model, there are two alternatives. First, one could use what our model provides with the incomparable feature given by the lattice, and define two policies (which may grant the same privileges), but are incomparable regarding the lattice, i. e., they do not refine/extend each other, and define different types of obligations. At runtime, only one of them shall be active, e. g., the activation of the "higher" one automatically deactivates the "lower" one. This allows to simulate the required behavior, however, is not elegant as the dominance of obligations has to be implicitly encoded with dominance of permissions. Second, one could define, similar to the approach of Alqatawna et al. [4], beneath the existing lattice evaluation algorithm which is responsible for combining permissions (i. e., implementing the refinement relationship) a separate obligations combining algorithm which allows to define a dominance of obligations.

We are aware of the fact that with the given model not all use cases can be modeled. However, we see the described two properties not as limitations, but rather as characterization of the fundamental principle of Break-Glass: extending privileges requires more sensitive handling and hence more compensation actions for granted exceptional accesses. Our model is intended to enable policy engineers in writing Break-Glass policies following this concepts. Including further concepts would increase both the complexity of the Break-Glass model, and would also affect the runtime behavior. For example, if a PERMIT from a higher policy could alter a given PERMIT, all active policies would have to be evaluated instead of being able to abort evaluation after the first PERMIT is found.

Patterns

The given model is very powerful and does not forestall the definition of inefficient, inaccurate or useless policies. Hence, when implementing Break-Glass policies with our model, one should follow some patterns.

When defining permissions, one should avoid redundancy, i. e., permissions should only be defined once. If two types of policies have a set of permissions in common, this common set of permissions should be wrapped into one separate policy which refines the two others. Hence, the extension property of the lattice should be used: new policies should only define additional permissions.

Our model follows the default deny all principle, i. e., permissions should be defined with positive permissions. Negative permissions in the constraints model are intended to define constraints over given positive permissions, e. g., SoD or Binding of Duty (BoD). This technique is intended to help avoiding redundancy, i. e., defining constraints within positive permissions multiple times. As all negative policies extending a policy have to be evaluated, regardless if exceptional policies are active or not, DENY policies should only be defined if they allow to circumvent a redundant definition of constraints within PERMIT policies. We will discuss this property in more depth in subsection 10.3.4.

The lattice structure of our model allows to define policies which are incomparable. This allows to express powerful concepts, but also introduces a complexity which may be hard to understand and analyze, both when defining policies and when investigating policies or system behavior. When using this property, the policy engineer should have a clear concept for the separation of policies into incomparable branches. For example, incomparable policies could be defined in a way that allows to make them easily comparable on AC level, e. g., specify permissions only for a specific role or resource, or, separating exceptional privileges for departments. Or, policies may be only exclusively active, e. g., as we will discuss in subsection 10.3.2 along Figure 10.1. Here, the administrative policy will ensure that incomparable polices are only exclusively active.

One of the requirements we identified for Break-Glass in section 3.1 is that no exceptional permission is applied if a regular permissions would be available. Given the lattice and the fact that our model does not make any statement about the refinement of obligations, this property cannot be fulfilled by the model itself. However, it can give support and can easily be checked for every instance of a lattice that no exceptional policy is defined on a lower or equal level than any active regular policy. The best pattern to fulfill this property is to define exceptional policies on a strictly higher level than all regular policies, eventually using empty policies (e. g., deny all PERMIT policies) to push exceptional policies to higher levels. If this cannot be applied to a given use case, this property has to be checked and enforced by the administrative policy.

The DENY policies as defined in our constraints model are overridable, i. e., a policy extending a policy defining a constraint will override a defined DENY. However, a policy engineer is free to define non-overridable DENY permissions by not defining any extending policy or forestall with an administrative policy that extending policies can get activated.

10.3.2 Applications of the Break-Glass Model

In this thesis, we used a specific instantiation of the core model: in our running example presented in section 1.2 we do not have to model constraints and hence had no need to use the constraints model. Furthermore, we did not limit but only extend privileges in exceptional situations, i. e., regular privileges are modeled in the policy p^{reg}, which is always active and the only policy on level ℓ_1. Policies on the levels ℓ_2 and higher are exceptional policies. They have, e. g., a *user confirmation obligation* attached, which defines the privileges to be exceptional privileges which can only be used if the users confirm an exceptional situation (see the discussion in subsection 10.3.3 why we use obligations instead of introducing a third access control decision). Access which is granted by p^{reg} we called regular access, whereas access which is only granted by an exceptional policy on level ℓ_2 or higher was called *override access*.

Our Break-Glass model is a generic in the sense that existing AC models can be extended, but also that it could be used for other problems than Break-Glass. For example, if parts of a policy should be enabled or disabled in an ad-hoc way, or, if an order onto obligations is needed. For example, the policy which models the regular case does not have to be on the first level. Policies on lower levels than p^{reg} may model an operation mode where less privileges should be available, e. g., limit regular access during an investigation after, e. g., a break-in, or during a quiet period. For our running example, we define p^{reg} to be the only policy in ℓ_1 which is always active, and all policies in ℓ_2 and higher are exceptional policies and have at least a user confirmation obligation attached. This is intended to keep a focus on Break-Glass and have a definite vocabulary, i. e., differentiate between regular privileges in p^{reg} and exceptional privileges on higher levels. However, our model can also be applied to other problems, but not all of them may be summarized under the term Break-Glass. For example, regular privileges may be divided into several policies instead of only one and structured into different "types of operation." This, for example, could be used to limit (and not extend) regular privileges in exceptional cases, e. g.,

- When there is some error detected but the root cause has still not to be detected, it may be needed to restrict normal business until the problem is solved.
- For compliance reasons, an incorporated company has to follow a quiet period where specific business processes or actions are forbidden.
- In periods which are temporally but well defined and where specific actions would interrupt or invalidate an ongoing process, e. g., inventory.

In such cases, p^{reg} may be in level ℓ_2 and inherit all privileges from a skeleton policy p^{skel} (which grants only rudimentary privileges) in ℓ_1 as shown in see Figure 10.1. Also, an exceptional "out of turn" policy p^{oot} may be defined which allows a small set of users to execute the required out of turn actions to return to normal behavior (e. g., check the logs to detect the error, do the inventory, etc.). Both p^{reg} and p^{oot} would inherit the privileges from p^{skel}. If regular privileges have to be restricted, p^{reg} is deactivated and p^{oot} is activated, preventing unwanted behavior and enabling a set of people to start their out of turn

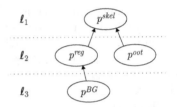

Figure 10.1: A policy lattice allowing to restrict regular access: p^{reg} on ℓ_2 may be deactivated, restricting access to what is defined in p^{skel}.

actions. Note that this does not prevent to also use Break-Glass, i. e., exceptional privileges may be modeled into one or several policies, e. g., p^{BG} in Figure 10.1. Also, one may want p^{oot} as Break-Glass policy or attach an obligation to increase the logging level to enable an investigation of actions done under p^{oot}.

The activation and deactivation of policies is a feature of the model which does not have to be used in practice, i. e., it may be the case that all policies are always active. If and how policies are and can be activated or deactivated (e. g., internal or external triggers, authorized persons, etc.) depends on the application the model is implemented in and the privileges which are granted by a policy. For example, in case of a health care system, a medical director may be permitted to activate a low exceptional policy for his department, whereas a commission is required to approve the activation of a policy which gives broader access to a central authority in case of a pandemic. Thus, as the activation and deactivation is done via the Policy Administration Point (PAP), according administrative AC policies have to be defined which neither make the system vulnerable nor prevent an appropriate functioning of the Break-Glass mechanism. Such an administrative policy may also include further rules about the state of active policies, e. g., it may be forbidden to activate two policies at the same time.

10.3.3 Obligations vs. Third Access Control Decision

Obligations are a way to tie conditions to an AC decision and are therefore a natural choice to express exceptional privileges, i. e., privileges which are only active if the users confirms an exceptional situation. However, in policy languages such as XACML, which already support obligations, those obligations can also be used for other purposes. This causes a problem (e. g., reported by Alqatawna et al. [4]): There is no obligation combining algorithm available which would allow to define a precedence of one obligation over the other, obligations are simply collected during evaluation. This makes it hard to distinguish between a regular permissions (potentially with a "non Break-Glass" obligation attached) and an exceptional permissions, having a user conformation obligation attached. For example, suppose a hierarchical RBAC policy with two roles *physician* and *nurse*, where *physician* as senior role inherits all permissions from the junior role *nurse*, i. e., *phsician* $\geq$ *nurse*. To the role *physician* regular permissions with some obligation are granted. To the role *nurse* the same permissions, marked as exceptional permissions, are granted. As role *physician* inherits all permission from role *nurse*, a subject assigned to role *physician* will have the permissions assigned both as regular and as exceptional permissions. The system has to be able to "prefer" the regular permissions over the exceptional permissions.

To distinguish those two types of permissions, some approaches introduce a third access control decision, e. g., POSSIBILITY-WITH-OVERRIDE [90], ALLOW WITH RISK-MITIGATION [40], or BTG [5, 51] to distinguish between a regular AC decision and an AC decision which allows for the usage of Break-Glass. On a first glance, such a third AC decision is a very elegant solution for this problem: for the evaluation engine and the security engineer its easy to distinguish regular and exceptional permissions, obligations can be used as without Break-Glass: one can assign obligations to PERMIT and BTG decisions without any interference. The evaluation engine would be enabled to apply the Break-Glass decision (and its obligations) exclusively if no regular PERMIT is available.

However, while obligations are an existing concept and hence supported at least partially, a third AC is a completely new element, causing additional overhead to be introduced in all implementing components. Furthermore, a third AC decision only allows only to separate regular and exceptional permissions. If one wants to distinguish in between exceptional permissions, one has the same problem as with the distinction between PERMIT (with or without user conformation obligation) and DENY permissions. For example, accessing some data outside the working hours (although only granted during working hours) may have other consequences than an accessing a system where the user does not have any regular privileges. Therefore, other obligations may be used to notify the user, or start some other actions, e. g., one may want to differentiate between only logging the exceptional access vs. sending an automated e-mail alert to a superior vs. having to notify a federal commission. Thus, if one is only able to distinguish between regular and exceptional permissions, the same problem as between regular and exceptional permissions occurs: the system may apply "harder" or simply wrong obligations for the Break-Glass access. Equal to the distinction between regular and exceptional permissions (or obligations), one would like to have the least or weakest obligation to be applied. Thus, if there is a regular permissions available, do not use Break-Glass permissions; if a notification of a superior is sufficient for a specific request, do not send an alarm to a federal commission.

Our model is the generalization of the idea of introducing a third AC decision: one can freely define exceptional permissions, without the need to think about overlapping regular and exceptional permissions. If both, regular and exceptional permissions would allow an access, automatically the regular permission is chosen. However, our model does not only support the distinction between regular and exceptional permissions, but also the distinction in between exceptional permissions. Furthermore, our model does not require the introduction of new primitives such as a further AC decision or control codes. This allows a more smooth introduction of Break-Glass into existing system landscapes, as wide parts of both the AC infrastructure and AC policies can be re-used and extended instead of completely restructured.

The underlying AC model may itself support obligations. Hence, obligations from the underlying AC model and the Break-Glass model are combined, i. e., the PERMIT decision from the underlying AC model is combined with the Break-Glass obligations from the granting policy from the lattice. For the core model, the obligations from the underlying AC model and the

Break-Glass model are simply combined (see line 8 in Listing 3.1), i.e., once a PERMIT is found in the underlying policy, this PERMIT is enhanced with the obligations defined by the Break-Glass model on top

For the constraints model, DENY policies have to be taken into account, i.e., as noted in section 3.4, the Break-Glass obligations from the policy effectively permitting the request are attached to the AC result. For example, let us assume that for some request, policy $p_P^{1,1}$ from Figure 3.3 returns PERMIT with an obligation $oblg_{AC}^{1,1}$ attached. Furthermore we assume that $p_D^{1,1}$ denies the request, but $p^{2,1}$ is active. This implies that only $p^{2,1}$ can grant exceptional privileges and hence the Break-Glass obligation $oblg_{BG}^{2,1}$ attached to $p^{2,1}$ would have to be applied. Hence, a PERMIT attached with two obligations $oblg_{AC}^{1,1}$ and $oblg_{BG}^{2,1}$ is returned.

10.3.4 Non-Overridable DENY Decisions vs. Constraints

In general, we follow the argumentation that access has to be restricted even in exceptional situations. In our core model, this is done *implicitly*: every access which is not permitted (neither by a regular, nor by an exceptional policy) should be denied per default, i.e., following the default deny principle. The *explicit* definition of (non-overridable) negative permissions as in the constraints model gives the policy engineer the certainty that, if there is an overlap between PERMIT and DENY policies, DENY permissions will dominate PERMIT permissions from extended policies.

However, the application of such negative permissions should be done with special care, i.e., should only be used to formulate constraints explicitly contradicting positive permissions. If negative permissions are used as complementary to positive permissions as, e.g., by [5, 65], the main reason for the need of DENY policies is to provide a runtime assurance that if there is an overlap in the two policy types, i.e., the "guarantees" given by the DENY policy will hold. Or, phrased in another way, the goal of DENY policies applied in such a way would be to detect, at runtime, potential design errors within the policies. This makes DENY policies not an elementary part of the approach, but rather a control mechanism to detect and handle errors and bugs in the policy. As such, DENY policies represent redundant information. If the policy changes, both the PERMIT and the DENY policies have to be changed, i.e., both representations of the redundant information. This causes higher effort and introduces a new source of error. Furthermore, both PERMIT and DENY policies may contain errors. If both PERMIT and DENY policies have the same or similar errors, they may remain undetected, i.e., only inconsistencies between PERMIT and DENY can be detected. Thus, even with the DENY model in place one has to apply other techniques to detect errors within the policies.

We think that design errors should not be detected at runtime but at design time, e. g., by applying tools which help an security engineer to resolve conflicts in policies. In chapter 6 we discussed a framework which allows to re-execute already executed AC requests against another policy, e. g., a DENY policy. This allows to detect such conflicts in a post-hoc fashion.

Hence, we see the application of DENY policies for situations, where an intended conflict between positive and negative permissions allows for an easier understanding and a more efficient evaluation. For example, SoD constraints are naturally expressed as negative permissions, and there has to be a conflict between PERMIT and DENY policies as SoD only make sense if there are conflicts with positive permissions.

10.3.5 Possible Model Variants

For the definition of our model, we had to make some design decisions. We argued why we see a clear decision for using obligations instead of introducing a third AC decisions. However, there are some further decisions where a slight variant of our model may be support even more use cases. In general, we wanted to keep the model as "simple" as possible. There would have been technical possibilities to integrate even more features or properties into the model, however, this would have made the model more complex or the evaluation less efficient or both.

Obligations for non-PERMIT Decisions

Our model focuses on the definition of exceptional privileges and uses obligations to bind exceptionally granted privileges to some condition. However, our model does not directly support obligations for DENY decisions. With the lattice evaluation algorithms, the first DENY decision which is found is returned if no PERMIT could be found, eventually returning also the obligations attached to this DENY. In cases where p^{reg} is the only policy on ℓ_1, obligations to DENY decisions can be defined "as usual" in p^{reg} and hence meet the expected behavior. However, those assumptions may not always be true and hence may not fulfill the requirements for all scenarios. Our algorithm would need to be adopted to support other requirements. A – not necessarily complete – list of possible other approaches regarding DENY obligations are:

- Return a plain DENY, i. e., do not even store found DENY decisions. This approach is best if the underlying AC model does not support obligations for DENY decisions or no obligations for DENY decisions are used.
- Make p^{reg} a special policy: return what p^{reg} returns, except for a PERMIT return a plain DENY. Thus, if p^{reg} would permit the access, but is not active, return a plain DENY. Otherwise return DENY obligations only if they are defined by p^{reg}. This approach may make sense if p^{reg} is not the only policy on ℓ_1.
- Return the result of the policy which is active and closest to p^{reg}. Thus, if p^{reg} is not active, then a policy refining p^{reg} provides the obligations, otherwise, similar to the last approach, return DENY obligations if they are defined by p^{reg} (if p^{reg} is active, p^{reg} is always the closest active policy to p^{reg}).
- Collect all found DENY obligations.
- Return the last DENY decision which was found (instead of the first).

AC Decisions beside PERMIT and DENY

Underlying AC models may define further AC decision beside PERMIT and DENY. For example, XACML returns INDETERMINATE to signal an error state, and NOTAPPLICABLE to signal that no definite decision could be found. We think that there is no general pattern how such AC decisions have to be handled, instead, the lattice evaluation algorithm has to be adapted for additional AC decisions to fit to the required properties.

For our prototypic implementation we use XACML and hence had to define how the two additional AC decisions are handled. In subsection 4.2.1 we have shown how the core model from section 3.3 can be implemented using existing XACML techniques, i. e., using an `ordered-permit-overrides` policy combining algorithm to implement the lattice evaluation algorithm from Listing 3.1. Hence, we adopt the behavior as defined for `ordered-permit-⌐` `overrides`: an error state (INDETERMINATE) is only returned if no PERMIT or DENY can be found. NOTAPPLICABLE is only returned if none of the policies matches or returns INDETERMINATE. For the constraints model and the corresponding lattice evaluation algorithm (Listing 3.3), we implemented an XACML policy combining algorithm discussed in subsection 4.2.4 which has, regarding additional AC decisions, the same behavior.

Activation of Policies

Another design decision was to implicitly activate all extended policies once a policy is activated. Another choice could be to only evaluate the extended policies and let the actually active policy return the first found PERMIT, i. e., attaching the obligations defined by the active policy. However, this would make the combining algorithm more complex and hence the behavior would be harder to understand.

10.4 Future Work

We see several lines of future work.

The model discussed in this thesis is a pure authorization model. When considering write operation executed with exceptional privileges[1], one has to think about the integrity of the modified data, i. e., the system has to be kept in a valid state. If a write operation turns out to be illegitimate, it has to be clarified how actions influenced by the illegitimate data have to be handled. The adoption of the Clark-Wilson model [41] for Break-Glass as done by Povey [87] is one approach, i. e., also moving the decision of integrity to the post-access phase. However, it should be investigated how a more generic solution – as possible extension to our generic Break-Glass model – could look like.

Similar, when looking at the information flow point of view, it is unclear how, e. g., a switch back from an exceptional policy back to a regular policy has to be handled. Badger [7] proposes two types of information flow properties: the first allows to do things which remain after the override, i. e., such information flow properties do not have to be transitive over several security policies. The current security policy only enforces its own properties and does not consider the (information flow) history before getting activated. For the second "strong" type of information flow property, the system requires knowledge about the flow path of information to enforce those properties, or there may be some transformation when the security policy is changed.

Although research about Break-Glass in Business Process (BP) models has already been executed , there are open questions how Break-Glass effects the execution of a BP, especially in regards to SoD and BoD constraints. A

---

[1]Following the definition of *information flow* as used for Multi-Level Security (MLS) models, this includes write operations executed with regular permissions if the written data have been read with exceptional permissions

possible scenario which should be investigated is, e. g., consider one task is executed with exceptional permissions, but for this task a BoD constraint is defined for another task where the subject does not have regular permissions. Here, it is unclear if the BoD constraint dominates the permissions to execute the task, i. e., access should be granted automatically, if the subject has to break the glass for both tasks at once, or if yet another strategy should be chosen.

We have shown how the concepts of post-access policies can be used for automated investigations and preserving analysis knowledge for access specific questionnaire, using our analysis workbench and hence providing the technical foundations for the evaluation of such post-access policies. However, further research has to be done how such policies can be written and maintained, e. g., changes in the regular policy may also effect the post-access policies.

For the evaluation of Break-Glass accesses, we proposed some basic techniques, however, further research has to be done how the basic techniques can be implemented in a toolset to be easy to use.

10.5 Conclusion

We see three main learnings from this thesis.

First, Break-Glass is a generic concept that can be applied to any AC model following our abstract definition of an ACF given in subsection 2.2.2. Our goal was to distill the concepts of existing approaches and combine them into a generic Break-Glass concept. We have shown that Break-Glass is an orthogonal concept and can be defined independently of a specific AC model. Our Break-Glass model obviously cannot solve all problems regarding AC. However, we think our approach includes the results that research efforts in the past years have detected to be required for Break-Glass, and allows to model what can be considered as best practice.

Second, Break-Glass is an approach to make a system more secure. At first glance, granting additional, exceptional permissions seams to make the systems more vulnerable for misuse. However, having Break-Glass as exception mechanism at hand allows to make regular permissions more restrictive and precise. This also shows that Break-Glass does not invalidate the need for AC, which allows to define fine-grained permissions. Users can use the Break-Glass mechanism and react in exceptional situations. Hence, there is no risk if regular permissions are made more restrictive, as this is balanced by the possibility of exceptional privileges granted through the

Break-Glass mechanism. Using solely traditional AC mechanisms, a security engineer may be made responsible for damage caused by too restrictive policies: especially if the life of a patient is at risk, regular policies are likely to be defined more permissive than for the regular case required.

Third, Break-Glass is not "static." Instead, we see Break-Glass as an incremental approach which allows to learn from the system and refine AC policies over time: along concrete accesses executed within a concrete situation, it is easier to make a decision about the access and derive more accurate and fine-grained AC policies than what is possible on the drawing table during the design or installation and setup phase of a software component. Such an incremental learning approach allows companies to react faster in case of new situations without having to define too lax regular policies. This means one can e. g., learn from effectively occurring accesses during the setup phase of a new process or product in order to accurately define AC policies. Hence, Break-Glass can be used as a mechanism to constantly increase the quality of AC policies.

Bibliography

[1] ISO/IEC 27001: Information technology - Security techniques - Information security management systems - Requirements, 2005. URL http://www.iso.org/iso/iso_catalogue/catalogue_tc/catalogue_detail.htm?csnumber=42103.

[2] American National Standards Institute (ANSI). Role Based Access Control. Technical Report ANSI INCITS 359-2004, American National Standards Institute, 2004.

[3] Dana Al Kukhun. *Steps towards adaptive situation and context-aware access: A contribution to the extension of access control mechanums within Pervasive Information Systems.* PhD thesis, Universite de Toulouse, 2012. URL http://www.irit.fr/publis/SIG/These_Dana_Al_Kukhun.pdf.

[4] Ja'far Alqatawna, Erik Rissanen, and Babak Sadighi. Overriding of access control in XACML. In *Proceedings of the Eight IEEE International Workshop on Policies for Distributed Systems and Networks*, POLICY '07, pages 87–95. IEEE Computer Society, 2007. ISBN 0-7695-2767-1. DOI: 10.1109/POLICY.2007.31.

[5] Claudio A. Ardagna, Sabrina De Capitani di Vimercatia, Sara Forestia, Tyrone W. Grandison, Sushil Jajodiac, and Pierangela Samaratia. Access control for smarter healthcare using policy spaces. *Computers & Security*, 29(8):848–858, 2010. DOI: 10.1016/j.cose.2010.07.001.

[6] Michael Backes, Günter Karjoth, Walid Bagga, and Matthias Schunter. Efficient comparison of enterprise privacy policies. In *Proceedings of the 2004 ACM symposium on Applied computing*, SAC '04, pages 375–382. ACM Press, 2004. ISBN 1-58113-812-1. DOI: 10.1145/967900.967983.

[7] Lee Badger. Providing a flexible security override for trusted systems. In *Proceedings Computer Security Foundations Workshop III*, pages 115–121. IEEE Computer Society, 1990. ISBN 0-8186-2071-4. DOI: 10.1109/CSFW.1990.128192.

[8] Olav Bandmann, Babak Sadighi Firozabadi, and Mads Dam. Constrained delegation. In *Proceedings of the 2002* IEEE *Symposium on Security and Privacy*, pages 131–140. IEEE Computer Society, 2002. ISBN 0-7695-1543-6. DOI: 10.1109/SECPRI.2002.1004367.

[9] Ezedin Barka and Ravi Sandhu. Framework for role-based delegation models. In *Proceedings of the 16th Annual Computer Security Applications Conference*, ACSAC '00, pages 168–176. IEEE Computer Society, 2000. ISBN 0-7695-0859-6. DOI: 10.1109/ACSAC.2000.898870.

[10] Steve Barker. The next 700 access control models or a unifying meta-model? In *Proceedings of the 14th ACM symposium on Access control models and technologies*, SACMAT '09, pages 187–196. ACM Press, 2009. ISBN 978-1-60558-537-6. DOI: 10.1145/1542207.1542238.

[11] Steffen Bartsch. A calculus for the qualitative risk assessment of policy override authorization. In *Proceedings of the 3rd international conference on Security of information and networks*, SIN '10, pages 62–70. ACM Press, 2010. ISBN 978-1-4503-0234-0. DOI: 10.1145/1854099.1854115.

[12] Basel Committee on Banking Supervision. Basel II: International convergence of capital measurement and capital standards. Technical report, Bank for International Settlements, Basel, Switzerland, 2004. URL http://www.bis.org/publ/bcbsca.htm.

[13] David A. Basin, Jürgen Doser, and Torsten Lodderstedt. Model driven security: From UML models to access control infrastructures. ACM *Transactions on Software Engineering and Methodology*, 15(1):39–91, 2006. ISSN 1049-331X. DOI: 10.1145/1125808.1125810.

[14] Moritz Y. Becker. A formal security policy for an NHS electronic health record service. Technical Report 628, University of Cambridge, 2005. URL http://www.cl.cam.ac.uk/techreports/UCAM-CL-TR-628.html.

[15] D. Elliott Bell and Leonard J. La Padula. Secure computer systems: Mathematical foundations. Technical Report MTR-2547, Volume I, MITRE, 1973.

[16] D. Elliott Bell and Leonard J. La Padula. Secure computer system: Unified exposition and multics interpretation. Technical Report MTR-2997, Rev. 1, MITRE, 1976.

[17] D. Elliott Bell and Leonard J. LaPadula. Secure computer systems: A mathematical model, volume II. In *Journal of Computer Security 4*, pages 229–263, 1996. An electronic reconstruction of *Secure Computer Systems: Mathematical Foundations*, 1973.

[18] David Elliott Bell. Looking back at the bell-la padula model. In *Proceedings of the 21st Annual Computer Security Applications Conference*, ACSAC '05, pages 337–351. IEEE Computer Society, 2005. ISBN 0-7695-2461-3. DOI: 10.1109/CSAC.2005.37.

[19] Berliner Beauftragter für Datenschutz und Informationsfreiheit. Datenschutz und Informationsfreiheit, 2009. URL http://www.datenschutz-berlin.de/attachments/669/Jahresbericht_2009.pdf.

[20] Elisa Bertino, Piero Andrea Bonatti, and Elena Ferrari. TRBAC: A temporal role-based access control model. *ACM Transactions on Information and System Security*, 4(3):191–233, August 2001. ISSN 1094-9224. DOI: 10.1145/501978.501979.

[21] Elisa Bertino, Barbara Catania, Maria Luisa Damiani, and Paolo Perlasca. GEO-RBAC: a spatially aware RBAC. In *Proceedings of the tenth* ACM *symposium on Access control models and technologies*, SACMAT '05, pages 29–37. ACM Press, 2005. ISBN 1-59593-045-0. DOI: 10.1145/1063979.1063985.

[22] John Bethencourt, Amit Sahai, and Brent Waters. Ciphertext-policy attribute-based encryption. In IEEE *Symposium on Security and Privacy*, pages 321–334. IEEE Computer Society, 2007. ISBN 0-7695-2848-1. DOI: 10.1109/SP.2007.11.

[23] Claudio Bettini, Sushil Jajodia, Xiaoyang Sean Wang, and Duminda Wijesekera. Obligation monitoring in policy management. In *Proceedings of the 3rd International Workshop on Policies for Distributed Systems and Networks*, POLICY '02, pages 2–12. IEEE Computer Society, 2002. ISBN 0-7695-1611-4. DOI: 10.1109/POLICY.2002.1011288.

[24] K.J. Biba. Integrity considerations for secure computer systems. Technical Report MTR-3153, Rev. 1, MITRE, 1977.

[25] Matthew A. Bishop. *The Art and Science of Computer Security*. Addison-Wesley Longman Publishing Co., Inc., Boston, MA, USA, 2002. ISBN 0201440997.

[26] David F.C. Brewer and Michael J. Nash. The chinese wall security policy. In *Proceedings of the 1989* IEEE *Symposium on Security and Privacy*, pages 206–214. IEEE Computer Society, 1989. ISBN 0-8186-1939-2. DOI: 10.1109/SECPRI.1989.36295.

[27] Achim D. Brucker and Helmut Petritsch. Extending access control models with break-glass. In *Proceedings of the 14th* ACM *symposium on Access control models and technologies*, SACMAT '09, pages 197–206. ACM Press, 2009. ISBN 978-1-60558-537-6. DOI: 10.1145/1542207.1542239.

[28] Achim D. Brucker and Helmut Petritsch. Idea: Efficient evaluation of access control constraints. In *International Symposium on Engineering Secure Software and Systems*, ESSOS '10, number 5965 in LNCS, pages 157–165. Springer-Verlag, 2010. ISBN 978-3-642-11746-6. DOI: 10.1007/978-3-642-11747-3_12.

[29] Achim D. Brucker and Helmut Petritsch. A framework for managing and analyzing changes of security policies. In IEEE *International Symposium on Policies for Distributed Systems and Networks*, POLICY '11, pages 105–112. IEEE Computer Society, June 2011. ISBN 978-0-7695-4330-7/11. DOI: 10.1109/POLICY.2011.47.

[30] Achim D. Brucker and Burkhart Wolff. Symbolic test case generation for primitive recursive functions. In *Formal Approaches to Testing of Software*, number 3395 in LNCS, pages 16–32. Springer-Verlag, 2004. ISBN 3-540-25109-X. DOI: 10.1007/b106767.

[31] Achim D. Brucker and Burkhart Wolff. HOL-TESTGEN: An interactive test-case generation framework. In *Fundamental Approaches to Software Engineering*, number 5503 in LNCS, pages 417–420. Springer-Verlag, 2009. DOI: 10.1007/978-3-642-00593-0_28.

[32] Achim D. Brucker, Helmut Petritsch, and Andreas Schaad. Delegation assistance. In IEEE *International Symposium on Policies for Distributed Systems and Networks*, POLICY '09, pages 84–91. IEEE Computer Society, 2009. ISBN 978-0-7695-3742-9. DOI: 10.1109/POLICY.2009.35.

[33] Achim D. Brucker, Helmut Petritsch, and Stefan G. Weber. Attribute-based encryption with break-glass. In *Information Security Theory and Practices. Security and Privacy of Pervasive Systems and Smart Devices*, WISTP *2010*, volume 6033 of LNCS, pages 237–244. Springer-Verlag, 2010. ISBN 978-3-642-12367-2. DOI: 10.1007/978-3-642-12368-9_18.

[34] Achim D. Brucker, Lukas Brügger, Paul Kearney, and Burkhart Wolff. An approach to modular and testable security models of real-world health-care applications. In *Proceedings of the 16th* ACM *symposium on Access control models and technologies]*, SACMAT '11, pages 133–142. ACM Press, 2011. ISBN 978-1-4503-0688-1. DOI: 10.1145/1998441.1998461.

[35] Lukas Alexander Brügger. *A Framework for Modelling and Testing of Security Policies*. PhD thesis, ETH Zürich, February 2012.

[36] Jery Bryans. Reasoning about XACML policies using CSP. In *Proceedings of the 2005 workshop on Secure web services*, SWS '05, pages 28–35. ACM Press, 2005. ISBN 1-59593-234-8. DOI: 10.1145/1103022.1103028.

[37] Anna Carlin and Frederick Gallegos. IT audit: A critical business process. *Computer*, 40(7):87–89, July 2007. ISSN 0018-9162. DOI: 10.1109/MC.2007.246.

[38] David Chadwick and Stijn Lievens. Break the glass profile for xacml v2.0 and v3.0 (draft), 2011. URL http://lists.oasis-open.org/archives/xacml/201106/doc00002.doc.

[39] Liang Chen, Jason Crampton, Martin J. Kollingbaum, and Timothy J. Norman. Obligations in risk-aware access control. In *Tenth Annual International Conference on Privacy, Security and Trust*, PST, pages 145–152. IEEE Computer Society, 2012. ISBN 978-1-4673-2323-9. DOI: 10.1109/PST.2012.6297931.

[40] Pau-Chen Cheng, Pankaj Rohatgi, Claudia Keser, Paul A. Karger, Grant M. Wagner, and Angela Schuett Reninger. Fuzzy multi-level security: An experiment on quantified risk-adaptive access control. In *Proceedings of the 2007 IEEE Symposium on Security and Privacy*, SP '07, pages 222–230. IEEE Computer Society, 2007. ISBN 0-7695-2848-1. DOI: 10.1109/SP.2007.21.

[41] David D. Clark and David R. Wilson. A comparison of commercial and military computer security policies. In IEEE *Symposium on Security and Privacy*, pages 184–194. IEEE Computer Society, 1987. ISBN 0-8186-0771-8. DOI: 10.1109/SP.1987.10001.

[42] Jason Crampton and Hemanth Khambhammettu. Delegation in role-based access control. In *Computer Security – ESORICS 2006*, volume 4189 of LNCS, pages 174–191. Springer-Verlag, 2006. ISBN 978-3-540-44601-9. DOI: 10.1007/11863908_12.

[43] Jason Crampton and Charles Morisset. An auto-delegation mechanism for access control systems. In *Security and Trust Management*, volume 6710 of LNCS, pages 1–16. Springer-Verlag, 2011. ISBN 978-3-642-22443-0. DOI: 10.1007/978-3-642-22444-7_1.

[44] Marnix A. C. Dekker and Sandro Etalle. Audit-based access control for electronic health records. In *Proceedings of the Second International Workshop on Views on Designing Complex Architectures*, volume 168 of *Electronic Notes in Theoretical Computer Science*, pages 221–236. Elsevier Science Publishers, February 2007. DOI: 10.1016/j.entcs.2006.08.028.

[45] Ian Denley and Simon Weston Smith. Privacy in clinical information systems in secondary care. *British Medical Journal (BMJ)*, 318(7194):1328–1331, May 1999. URL http://www.bmj.com/content/318/7194/1328.full.pdf.

[46] Jeremy Dick and Alain Faivre. Automating the generation and sequencing of test cases from model-based specifications. In *Formal Methods Europe 93: Industrial-Strength Formal Methods*, volume 670 of LNCS, pages 268–284. Springer-Verlag, 1993. ISBN 978-3-540-56662-5.

[47] Nathan Dimmock, Andrá Belokosztolszki, David Eyers, Jean Bacon, and Ken Moody. Using trust and risk in role-based access control policies. In *Proceedings of the ninth ACM symposium on Access control models and technologies*, SACMAT '04, pages 156–162. ACM Press, 2004. ISBN 1-58113-872-5. DOI: 10.1145/990036.990062.

[48] Sandro Etalle and William H. Winsborough. A posteriori compliance control. In *Proceedings of the 12th ACM symposium on Access control models and technologies*, SACMAT '07, pages 11–20, New York, NY, USA, 2007. ACM. ISBN 978-1-59593-745-2. DOI: 10.1145/1266840.1266843.

[49] David F. Ferraiolo and D. Richard Kuhn. Role-based access controls. In *Proceedings of the 15th National Computer Security Conference*, pages 554–563, 1992.

[50] Ana Ferreira, Ricardo Cruz-Correia, Luis Antunes, Pedro Farinha, E. Oliveira-Palhares, David W. Chadwick, and Altamiro Costa-Pereira. How to break access control in a controlled manner. In *19th IEEE International Symposium on Computer-Based Medical Systems*, pages 847–854. IEEE Computer Society, 2006. ISBN 0-7695-2517-1. DOI: 10.1109/CBMS.2006.95.

[51] Ana Ferreira, David Chadwick, Pedro Farinha, Ricardo Correia, Gansen Zao, Rui Chilro, and Luis Antunes. How to securely break into RBAC: The BTG-RBAC model. In *Proceedings of the 2009 Annual Computer Security Applications Conference*, ACSAC '09, pages 23–31. IEEE Computer Society, 2009. ISBN 978-0-7695-3919-5. DOI: 10.1109/ACSAC.2009.12.

[52] Babak Firozabadi and Marek Sergot. Power and permission in security systems. In *Security Protocols*, volume 1796 of LNCS, pages 48–53. Springer-Verlag, 2000. ISBN 978-3-540-67381-1. DOI: 10.1007/10720107_6.

[53] Babak Sadighi Firozabadi, Marek Sergot, and Olav Bandmann. Using authority certificates to create management structures. In *Security Protocols*, volume 2467 of LNCS, pages 134–145. Springer-Verlag, 2002. ISBN 978-3-540-44263-9. DOI: 10.1007/3-540-45807-7_21.

[54] Kathi Fisler, Shriram Krishnamurthi, Leo A. Meyerovich, and Michael Carl Tschantz. Verification and change-impact analysis of access-control policies. In *Proceedings of the 27th international conference on Software engineering*, ICSE '05, pages 196–205. ACM Press, 2005. ISBN 1-58113-963-2. DOI: 10.1145/1062455.1062502.

[55] Ludwig Fuchs, Günther Pernul, and Ravi S. Sandhu. Roles in information security - a survey and classification of the research area. *Computers & Security*, 30(8):748–769, 2011. DOI: 10.1016/j.cose.2011.08.002.

[56] Craig Gentry. *Handbook of Information Security*, volume 2, chapter IBE (Identity-Based Encryption), pages 575–592. John Wiley & Sons, January 2006. ISBN 0-471-64833-7.

[57] Anindya Ghose. Information disclosure and regulatory compliance: Economic issues and research directions. http://ssrn.com/abstract=921770, July 2006.

[58] G. Scott Graham and Peter J. Denning. Protection: principles and practice. In *Proceedings of the spring joint computer conference*, AFIPS '72 (Spring), pages 417–429. ACM Press, 1972. DOI: 10.1145/1478873.1478928.

[59] Lionel Habib, Mathieu Jaume, and Charles Morisset. A formal comparison of the Bell & LaPadula and RBAC models. In *Fourth International Conference on Information Assurance and Security*, ISIAS '08, pages 3–8. IEEE Computer Society, 2008. ISBN 978-0-7695-3324-7. DOI: 10.1109/IAS.2008.18.

[60] Michael Hafner, Mukhtiar Memon, and Muhammad Alam. Modeling and enforcing advanced access control policies in healthcare systems with SECTET. In *Models in Software Engineering*, volume 5002 of LNCS, pages 132–144. Springer-Verlag, 2008. ISBN 978-3-540-69069-6. DOI: 10.1007/978-3-540-69073-3_15.

[61] Alan R. Hevner, Salvatore T. March, Jinsoo Park, and Sudha Ram. Design science in information systems research. *MIS Quarterly*, 28(1):75–105, March 2004. ISSN 0276-7783. URL http://dl.acm.org/citation.cfm?id=2017212.2017217.

[62] HMISS Analytics. 2012 HMISS analytics report: Security of patient data, 2012. URL http://www.krollcybersecurity.com/media/Kroll-HIMSS_2012_-_Security_of_Patient_Data_040912.pdf.

[63] Vincent C. Hu, David Ferraiolo, Rick Kuhn, Adam Schnitzer, Kenneth Sandlin, Robert Miller, and Karen Scarfone. Guide to attribute based access control (ABAC) definition and considerations. Technical Report SP 800-162, National Institute of Standards and Technology (NIST), 2014.

[64] Michael Jackson. The meaning of requirements. *Annals of Software Engineering*, 3:5–21, 1997. ISSN 1022-7091. DOI: 10.1023/A:1018990005598.

[65] Trent Jaeger, Xiaolan Zhang, and Antony Edwards. Policy management using access control spaces. ACM *Transactions on Information and*

System Security (TISSEC), 6(3):327–364, August 2003. ISSN 1094-9224. DOI: 10.1145/937527.937528.

[66] Joint NEMA/COCIR/JIRA Security and Privacy Committee (SPC). Breakglass: An approach to granting emergency access to healthcare systems. White paper, NEMA, COCIR, and JIRA, 2004.

[67] Jan Kolter, Rolf Schillinger, and Günther Pernul. A privacy-enhanced attribute-based access control system. In *Data and Applications Security XXI*, volume 4602 of LNCS, pages 129–143. Springer-Verlag, 2007. ISBN 978-3-540-73533-5. DOI: 10.1007/978-3-540-73538-0_11.

[68] Leonard J. La Padula and D. Elliott Bell. Secure computer systems: A mathematical model. Technical Report MTR-2547, Volume II, MITRE, 1973.

[69] Butler W. Lampson. Protection. In *Proceedings of the fifth Princeton Symposium on Information Sciences and Systems*, pages 437–443, 1971. Reprinted in Operating Systems Review, 8,1, January 1974, pp. 18–24.

[70] Ninghui Li, Ji-Won Byun, and Elisa Bertino. A critique of the ANSI standard on role-based access control. IEEE *Security and Privacy*, 5(6): 41–49, November 2007. ISSN 1540-7993. DOI: 10.1109/MSP.2007.158.

[71] Dan Lin, Prathima Rao, Elisa Bertino, and Jorge Lobo. An approach to evaluate policy similarity. In *Proceedings of the 12th* ACM *symposium on Access control models and technologies*, SACMAT '07, pages 1–10, 2007. ISBN 978-1-59593-745-2. DOI: 10.1145/1266840.1266842.

[72] Steven B. Lipner. Non-discretionery controls for commercial applications. In IEEE *Symposium on Security and Privacy*, volume 0, page 2. IEEE Computer Society, 1982. ISBN 0-8186-0410-7. DOI: 10.1109/SP.1982.10022.

[73] Jim Longstaff and Tony Howitt. Extensions to sealed envelope and break glass authorization. In AHIC: *Advances in Health Informatics Conference*, 2010. URL http://www.scm.tees.ac.uk/TeesConfidentialityModel/Longstaff_AHIC_apr10.doc.

[74] Jim Longstaff, Mike Lockyer, and John Nicholas. The tees confidentiality model: an authorisation model for identities and roles. In *Proceedings of the eighth* ACM *symposium on Access control models and technologies*, SACMAT '03, pages 125–133. ACM Press, 2003. ISBN 1-58113-681-1. DOI: 10.1145/775412.775428.

[75] J.J. Longstaff, M.A. Lockyer, and M.G. Thick. A model of accountability, confidentiality and override for healthcare and other applications. In *Proceedings of the fifth* ACM *workshop on Role-based access control*, RBAC '00, pages 71–76. ACM Press, 2000. ISBN 1-58113-259-X. DOI: 10.1145/344287.344304.

[76] Srdjan Marinovic, Robert Craven, Jiefei Ma, and Naranker Dulay. Rumpole: a flexible break-glass access control model. In *Proceedings of the 16th* ACM *symposium on Access control models and technologies*, SACMAT '11, pages 73–82. ACM Press, 2011. ISBN 978-1-4503-0688-1. DOI: 10.1145/1998441.1998453.

[77] Srdjan Marinovic, Robert Craven, Jiefei Ma, and Naranker Dulay. Rumpole: a flexible break-glass access control model. In *Proceedings of the 16th ACM symposium on Access control models and technologies*, SACMAT '11, pages 73–82. ACM Press, 2011. ISBN 978-1-4503-0688-1. DOI: 10.1145/1998441.1998453.

[78] Rebecca T. Mercuri. On auditing audit trails. *Communications of the* ACM, 46(1):17–20, January 2003. ISSN 0001-0782. DOI: 10.1145/602421.602436.

[79] OASIS. Core and hierarchical role based access control (RBAC) profile of XACML v2.0, 2005. URL http://docs.oasis-open.org/xacml/2.0/access_control-xacml-2.0-rbac-profile1-spec-os.pdf.

[80] OASIS. eXtensible Access Control Markup Language (XACML), version 2.0, 2005. URL http://docs.oasis-open.org/xacml/2.0/XACML-2.0-OS-NORMATIVE.zip.

[81] Department of Defense Standard. Trusted computer system evaluation criteria. Technical Report DoD 5200.28-STD, US Department of Defence, 1985. URL http://www.fas.org/irp/nsa/rainbow/std001.htm.

[82] U.S. Department of Health and Human Services Office for Civil Rights. HIPAA administrative simplification, 2006.

[83] Oracle. Oracle role manager, 2009. URL http://www.oracle.com/technetwork/articles/oracle-role-manager-wp-1-128095.pdf.

[84] Ken Peffers, Tuure Tuunanen, Marcus Rothenberger, and Samir Chatterjee. A design science research methodology for information systems research. *Journal of Management Information Systems*, 24(3):45–77, December 2007. ISSN 0742-1222. DOI: 10.2753/MIS0742-1222240302.

[85] Helmut Petritsch. Exposé zur Anmeldung des Promotionsvorhabens, 2009. URL http://www-sec.uni-regensburg.de/news20/upload/upload_538be2dd87e9be91b66c1bd42eb3657e.pdf.

[86] Matthew Pirretti, Patrick Traynor, Patrick McDaniel, and Brent Waters. Secure attribute-based systems. In *Proceedings of the 13th* ACM *conference on Computer and communications security*, CCS '06, pages 99–112. ACM Press, 2006. ISBN 1-59593-518-5. DOI: 10.1145/1180405.1180419.

[87] Dean Povey. Optimistic security: A new access control paradigm. In *Proceedings of the 1999 workshop on New security paradigms*, NSPW '99, pages 40–45. ACM Press, 1999. ISBN 1-58113-149-6. DOI: 10.1145/335169.335188.

[88] Torsten Priebe, Wolfgang Dobmeier, Björn Muschall, and Günther Pernul. ABAC - ein Referenzmodell für attributbasierte Zugriffskontrolle. In *Sicherheit 2005: Sicherheit - Schutz und Zuverlässigkeit, Beiträge der 2. Jahrestagung des Fachbereichs Sicherheit der Gesellschaft für Informatik e.v. (GI)*, volume 62 of *LNI*, pages 285–296. GI, 2005. ISBN 3-88579-391-1.

[89] Erik Rissanen. Towards a mechanism for discretionary overriding of access control (transcript of discussion). In *Security Protocols*, number 3957 in LNCS, pages 320–323, March 2006. DOI: 10.1007/11861386_39.

[90] Erik Rissanen, Babak Firozabadi, and Marek Sergot. Discretionary overriding of access control in the privilege calculus. In *Formal Aspects in Security and Trust*, volume 173 of IFIO *International Federation for Information Processing*, pages 219–232. Springer-Verlag, 2005. ISBN 978-0-387-24050-3. DOI: 10.1007/0-387-24098-5_16.

[91] Lillian Røstad and Ole Edsberg. A study of access control requirements for healthcare systems based on audit trails from access logs. In *Proceedings of the 2006 Annual Computer Security Applications Conferenc*, ACSAC '06, pages 175–186. IEEE Computer Society, 2006. DOI: 10.1109/ACSAC.2006.8.

[92] Amit Sahai and Brent Waters. Fuzzy identity-based encryption. In *Advances in Cryptology – EUROCRYPT 2005*, number 3494 in LNCS, pages 457–473. Springer-Verlag, 2005. DOI: 10.1007/11426639_27.

[93] Jerome H. Saltzer. Protection and the control of information sharing in multics. *Communications of the* ACM, 17(7):388–402, 1974. ISSN 0001-0782. DOI: 10.1145/361011.361067.

[94] Jerome H. Saltzer and Michael D. Schroeder. The protection of information in computer systems. *Proceedings of the* IEEE, 63(9):1278–1308, 1975. ISSN 0018-9219. DOI: 10.1109/PROC.1975.9939.

[95] Ravi Sandhu and Jaehong Park. Usage control: A vision for next generation access control. In *Computer Network Security*, volume 2776 of LNCS, pages 17–31. Springer-Verlag, 2003. ISBN 978-3-540-40797-3. DOI: 10.1007/978-3-540-45215-7_2.

[96] Ravi S. Sandhu, Edward J. Coyne, Hal L. Feinstein, and Charles E. Youman. Role-based access control models. *Computer*, 29(2):38–47, February 1996. ISSN 0018-9162. DOI: 10.1109/2.485845.

[97] Ravi S. Sandhu, David F. Ferraiolo, and D. Richard Kuhn. The NIST model for role-based access control: towards a unified standard. In *Proceedings of the fifth* ACM *workshop on Role-based access control*, RBAC '00, pages 47–63. ACM Press, 2000. DOI: 10.1145/344287.344301.

[98] SAP. SAP GRC superuser privilege management, 2006. URL http://scn.sap.com/docs/DOC-1608.

[99] P. Sarbanes, G. Oxley, et al. Sarbanes-Oxley Act of 2002. 107th Congress Report, House of Representatives, 2nd Session, 107–610, 2002.

[100] Andreas Schaad, Jonathan Moffett, and Jeremy Jacob. The role-based access control system of a european bank: a case study and discussion. In *Proceedings of the sixth* ACM *symposium on Access control models and technologies*, SACMAT '01, pages 3–9. ACM Press, 2001. ISBN 1-58113-350-2. DOI: 10.1145/373256.373257.

[101] Sigrid Schefer-Wenzl and Mark Strembeck. A UML extension for modeling break-glass policies. In *Proc. of the 5th International Workshop on Enterprise Modelling and Information Systems Architectures (*EMISA*)*, volume 206 of *Lecture Notes in Informatics (*LNI*)*. Gesellschaft für Informatik, 2012.

[102] Lineke Sneller and Henk Langendijk. Sarbanes oxley section 404 costs of compliance: a case study. *Corporate Governance: An International Review*, 15(2):101–111, 2007. URL http://econpapers.repec.org/RePEc:bla:corgov:v:15:y:2007:i:2:p:101-111.

[103] Gunnar Stevens and Volker Wulf. A new dimension in access control: studying maintenance engineering across organizational boundaries. In *Proceedings of the 2002* ACM *conference on Computer supported cooperative work*, CSCW '02, pages 196–205. ACM Press, 2002. ISBN 1-58113-560-2. DOI: 10.1145/587078.587106.

[104] Silvia von Stackelberg, Klemens Böhm, and Matthias Bracht. Embedding 'break the glass' into business process models. Technical report, Faculty of Informatics, Karlsruhe Institute of Technology, 2012. URL http://dbis.ipd.uni-karlsruhe.de/1860.php.

[105] Jacques Wainer, Paulo Barthelmess, and Akhil Kumar. W-RBAC - a workflow security model incorporating controlled overriding of constraints. *International Journal of Cooperative Information Systems*, 12(4):455–485, 2003. DOI: 10.1142/S0218843003000814.

[106] Lingyu Wang, Duminda Wijesekera, and Sushil Jajodia. A logic-based framework for attribute based access control. In *Proceedings of the 2004* ACM *workshop on Formal methods in security engineering*, FMSE '04, pages 45–55. ACM Press, 2004. ISBN 1-58113-971-3. DOI: 10.1145/1029133.1029140.

[107] Janice Warner, Vijayalakshmi Atluri, Ravi Mukkamala, and Jaideep Vaidya. Using semantics for automatic enforcement of access control policies among dynamic coalitions. In *Proceedings of the 12th* ACM *symposium on Access control models and technologies*, SACMAT '07, pages 235–244. ACM Press, 2007. ISBN 978-1-59593-745-2. DOI: 10.1145/1266840.1266877.

[108] Phebe Waterfield and John Casey. The governance of compliance: Putting policies into practice. Yankee Report, April 2005.

[109] Paul Watzlawick. *How real is real? Confusion, disinformation, communication.* Vintage Books, 1977. ISBN 0394722566.

[110] Lei Zhang, Alexander Brodsky, and Sushil Jajodia. Toward information sharing: Benefit and risk access control (barac). In *Seventh* IEEE *International Workshop on Policies for Distributed Systems and Networks*, POLICY 2006, pages 45–53. IEEE Computer Society, 2006. ISBN 0-7695-2598-9. DOI: 10.1109/POLICY.2006.36.

[111] Xinwen Zhang, Sejong Oh, and Ravi Sandhu. PBDM: a flexible delegation model in RBAC. In *Proceedings of the eighth* ACM *symposium on Access control models and technologies*, SACMAT '03, pages 149–157. ACM Press, 2003. ISBN 1-58113-681-1. DOI: 10.1145/775412.775431.

[112] Gansen Zhao, David Chadwick, and Sassa Otenko. Obligations for role based access control. In *21st International Conference on Advanced Information Networking and Applications Workshops*, AINAW '07, pages 424–431. IEEE Computer Society, 2007. ISBN 0-7695-2847-3. DOI: 10.1109/AINAW.2007.267.

[113] Xia Zhao and M. Eric Johnson. Managing information access in data-rich enterprises with escalation and incentives. *International Journal of Electronic Commerce*, 15(1):79–112, 2010. DOI: 10.2753/JEC1086-4415150104.

A Glossary

There are different names and terms for the same or similar concepts in use. We used one term for one concept throughout this thesis wherever possible, i. e., using one common terminology, even when citing and discussing foreign work where other terms are used.

Subject describing the identity executing an access. We will use the term *user* if we explicitly refer to a human.

Resource describing the accessed object.

Action describing a specific task executed on a resource.

Permitted or Authorized are commonly used as equivalents, where *permitted* is commonly used for a concrete access executed by a concrete subject, whereas *authorized* is be used in a rather abstract context.

Permissions vs. Privilege are commonly used as equivalents, however, we use them to express slightly different concepts. We use "permission" to describe a rather technical concept, e. g., a rule in a policy. In contrast, we use "privilege" as the effective right a subject has. For example, permissions can be positive and negative, and a subject may be defined to have some privilege if a positive but no negative rule is found.

Obligation expressing conditions which have to be enforced by the decision-enforcing authority. See subsection 2.2.1 for details.

Policy is used for AC policy defining privileges, e. g., in form of a set of rules. The policy is what is passed as security state σ_{sec} to the ACF. See subsection 2.2.2 for details.

Access Control Function is used as abstraction from concrete AC models, see subsection 2.2.2 for details.

Policy State Assignment describing an assignment within the policy state, see subsection 4.1.3 for details.

Dependency Definition describing the definition of a policy state assignment.

Versioning expressing a concept as introduced in subsection 5.2.1.

B Acronyms

ABAC   Attribute Based Access Control

ABE   Attribute-based Encryption

AC   Access Control

ACF   Access Control Function

ACL   Access Control List

ACM   Association for Computing Machinery

ANSI   American National Standards Institute

API   Application Programming Interface

BoD   Binding of Duty

BP   Business Process

BPM   Business Process Model

BTG   Break-the-Glass

CCF   Care Comes First

CDI   Constrained Data Item

DAC   Discretionary Access Control

DOM   Document Object Model

DoS   Denial of Service

DSoD   Dynamic Separation of Duty

IEEE   Institute of Electrical and Electronic Engineers

EHR   Electronic Health Record

EMR	Electronic Medical Record
ERP	Enterprise Resource Planning
GRC	Governance, Risk Management, and Compliance
GP	General Practitioner
GUI	Graphical User Interface
HIPAA	Health Insurance Portability and Accountability Act
HR	Human Resources
IBAC	Identity Based Access Control
IBE	Identity-based Encryption
ID	Identifier
IDP	Identity Provider
IEEE	Institute of Electrical and Electronics Engineers
IEC	International Electrotechnical Commission
ISO	International Organization for Standardization
IT	Information Technology
IVP	Integrity Verification Procedure
LNCS	Lecture Notes in Computer Science
MAC	Mandatory Access Control
MLS	Multi-Level Security
NHS	National Health Service
OASIS	Organization for the Advancement of Structured Information Standards
OS	Operating System
PAP	Policy Administration Point
PCDI	Partially-Constrained Data Item

PDP	Policy Decision Point
PEP	Policy Enforcement Point
PIN	Personal Identification Number
PIP	Policy Information Point
PTP	Partial Transformation Procedure
RBAC	Role Based Access Control
RBAC96	RBAC defined in [96]
REST	Representational State Transfer
ROI	return of investment
SACMAT	Symposium on Access control Models and Technologies
SAML	Security Assertion Markup Language
SAP	www.sap.com
SAT	Boolean Satisfiability Problem
SCIM	System for Cross-domain Identity Management
SMS	Short Message Service
SOAP	Simple Object Access Protocol
SoD	Separation of Duty
SOX	Sarbanes-Oxley Act
SPM	Superuser Privilege Management
SSO	Single Sign On
SSoD	Static Separation of Duty
SUN	Sun Microsystems
SVN	Subversion
TCSEC	Trusted Computer System Evaluation Criteria

TP	Transformation Procedure
TR	Treatment Relationship
UDI	Unconstrained Data Item
UI	User Interface
UML	Unified Modeling Language
URI	Uniform Resource Identifier
US	United States
XACML	eXtensible Access Control Markup Language
XML	Extensible Markup Language
TCM	Tees Confidentiality Model

C Code Samples

C.1 XACML Sample Policy

This Listing C.1 represents the full XACML code from the reduced representation in Listing 2.1 in subsection 2.2.4.

```
   <PolicySet
     xmlns="urn:oasis:names:tc:xacml:2.0:policy:schema:os"
3    PolicySetId="health-record"
     PolicyCombiningAlgId="urn:oasis:names:tc:xacml:1.0:⏎
   policy-combining-algorithm:permit-overrides">
6    <Description>PolicySet for health records</Description>
     <Target>
      <Resources>
9      <Resource>
        <ResourceMatch MatchId="urn:custom:uri-starts-with">
         <ResourceAttributeDesignator AttributeId=
12         "urn:oasis:names:tc:xacml:1.0:resource:resource-id"
          DataType="http://www.w3.org/2001/XMLSchema#anyURI"
          MustBePresent="true"/>
15        <AttributeValue
           DataType="http://www.w3.org/2001/XMLSchema#anyURI">
           urn:health-record</AttributeValue>
18       </ResourceMatch>
       </Resource>
      </Resources>
21   </Target>
     <Policy PolicyId="health-record:physician"
       RuleCombiningAlgId="urn:oasis:names:tc:xacml:1.0:⏎
24  rule-combining-algorithm:first-applicable">
      <Description>Policy for role physician</Description>
      <Target>
27     <Subjects>
        <Subject>
         <SubjectMatch MatchId=
30         "urn:oasis:names:tc:xacml:1.0:function:string-equal">
          <SubjectAttributeDesignator
           AttributeId="urn:custom:subject:role"
33         DataType="http://www.w3.org/2001/XMLSchema#string"/>
          <AttributeValue
           DataType="http://www.w3.org/2001/XMLSchema#string">
```

```
36             physician</AttributeValue>
           </SubjectMatch>
         </Subject>
39      </Subjects>
      </Target>
      <VariableDefinition VariableId="treating-physician">
42      <Apply FunctionId=
            "urn:oasis:names:tc:xacml:1.0:function:any-of-any">
          <Function FunctionId=
45            "urn:oasis:names:tc:xacml:1.0:function:string-equal"/>
          <SubjectAttributeDesignator AttributeId=
            "urn:oasis:names:tc:xacml:1.0:subject:subject-id"
48          DataType="http://www.w3.org/2001/XMLSchema#string"
            MustBePresent="true"/>
          <ResourceAttributeDesignator AttributeId=
51            "urn:runEx:patient:treating-subject"
            DataType="http://www.w3.org/2001/XMLSchema#string"/>
        </Apply>
54      </VariableDefinition>
      <Rule Effect="Permit"
          RuleId="health-record:physician:010">
57      <Description>allow read if patient
            gave consent</Description>
        <Target>
60       <Actions>
          <Action>
           <ActionMatch MatchId=
63           "urn:oasis:names:tc:xacml:1.0:function:string-equal">
            <ActionAttributeDesignator AttributeId=
              "urn:oasis:names:tc:xacml:1.0:action:action-id"
66            DataType="http://www.w3.org/2001/XMLSchema#string"/>
            <AttributeValue
              DataType="http://www.w3.org/2001/XMLSchema#string">
69            read</AttributeValue>
           </ActionMatch>
          </Action>
72       </Actions>
        </Target>
        <Condition>
75       <Apply
          FunctionId="urn:oasis:names:tc:xacml:1.0:function:or">
          <!-- check if subject is treating physician -->
78        <VariableReference VariableId="treating-physician"/>
          <!-- check if physician is assigned to a workgoup
               where the patient has given his consent -->
81        <Apply FunctionId=
              "urn:oasis:names:tc:xacml:1.0:function:any-of-any">
            <Function FunctionId=
84            "urn:oasis:names:tc:xacml:1.0:function:string-equal"/>
            <SubjectAttributeDesignator AttributeId=
```

```
              "urn:runEx:subject:department"
87            DataType="http://www.w3.org/2001/XMLSchema#string"/>
          <ResourceAttributeDesignator AttributeId=
              "urn:runEx:patient:treating-department"
90            DataType="http://www.w3.org/2001/XMLSchema#string"/>
          </Apply>
          </Apply>
93        </Condition>
        </Rule>
      </Policy>
96    <PolicyIdReference>health-record:nurse</PolicyIdReference>
      <Policy PolicyId="health-record:final"
          RuleCombiningAlgId="urn:oasis:names:tc:xacml:1.0:⌐
99  rule-combining-algorithm:first-applicable">
        <Description>Final Deny policy for health records
        </Description>
102     <Target/>
        <Rule Effect="Deny"
          RuleId="health-record:final:010">
105       <Target/>
        </Rule>
      </Policy>
108 </PolicySet>
```

Listing C.1: An XACML policy: physicians are permitted to read a health
record if the patient gave his consent to the physician or the
physician's department.

C.2 Lattice Evaluation Algorithm in Java

Listing C.2 represents the lattice evaluation algorithm from Listing 3.3 as
implementation for XACML.

```
    public Result combine(EvaluationCtx evalCtx,
                          List<CombinerParameter> combParam,
3                         List<CombinerElement> combElem) {
        /* store the first  deny we get, we will return it in
           case we do not find a permit */
6       Result firstDeny = null;
        /* store the first indeterminate */
        Result firstIndeterminate = null;
9
      /* create a cache where all permits are stored;
         we may need the result itself to get the obligations */
12    Map<String, Result> permitCache =
                            new HashMap<String, Result>();
      /* create a cache where the results of all deny policies
15       are storeddeny policies could be executed several time,
```

```
         i.e., remember both the result and if we executed it */
      Map<String, Result> denyCache =
18                                   new HashMap<String, Result>();

         /* get the active policies from the context once */
21    Set<String> activePolicies = getActivePolicies(evalCtx);

         /* create (or get from cache) the policy lattice
24                                    we want to evaluate */
      PolicyLattice lattice =
                    getLattice(evalCtx, combParam, combElem);
27
         /* iterate over the lattice (i.e., level per level) */
      for ( LatticeElem elem : lattice ) {
30     /* check if current element is an active policy */
       if ( isActive(elem, lattice, activePolicies) ) {
       boolean permitted = false, denied = false;
33
        /* store a permit if we find it in this policy */
        Result permit = null;
36      /* first, check for an inherited permit,
                                 then for a permit */
        LatticeElem inhPermit =
39                      getInheritedPermit(elem, permitCache);
        if ( inhPermit != null ) {
         permitted = true;
42      } else if (elem.getPermitPolicy() != null ) {
         /* no inherited permit,
                 we have to evaluate the current permit policy */
45       Result res = evaluate(elem.getPermitPolicy(), evalCtx);
         if ( res.getDecision() ==
                            Result.DECISION_INDETERMINATE ) {
48        if ( firstIndeterminate == null ) {
          firstIndeterminate = res;
         }
51       /* this policy will not provide a result,
                 go to next */
         continue;
54      } else if ( res.getDecision() ==
                            Result.DECISION_PERMIT ) {
         /* we found a permit, store it to cache (in the
57          current policy it may be overwritten by a deny) */
         permitCache.put(elem.getIdentifier(), res);
         permit = res;
60       permitted = true;
        } else if ( res.getDecision() == Result.DECISION_DENY
                     && firstDeny == null) {
63        firstDeny = res;
         continue; /* we do not need to evaluate the deny
                       policies if we do not have a permit */
```

```
66        }
        }

69     if ( permitted ) {
         /* check if there is an inherited deny: iterate over
            all extending policies, i.e, downwards */
72       for ( LatticeElem extending : elem.downwards() ) {
           /* check if extending policy
              has a deny policy defined */
75         if ( extending.getDenyPolicy() != null ) {
           Result res;
           /* check if we already evaluated this policy */
78         if ( denyCache.containsKey(
                                  extending.getIdentifier())) {
             res = denyCache.get(extending.getIdentifier());
81         } else {
             /* else, evaluate it and store it into the cache */
             res = evaluate(extending.getDenyPolicy(), evalCtx);
84           denyCache.put(extending.getIdentifier(), res);
           }
           /* check if the current deny policy
87             denies this request */
           if ( res.getDecision() ==
                                  Result.DECISION_INDETERMINATE ) {
90           if ( firstIndeterminate == null ) {
             firstIndeterminate = res;
           }
93         } else if ( res.getDecision() ==
                                  Result.DECISION_DENY ) {
           denied = true;
96         if ( firstDeny == null ) {
             firstDeny = res;
           }
99         break; /* we have found a deny,
                      do not need to look further */
           }
102      }
        }
        /* we end up here only if we found a permit,
105         check if we also found a deny */
        if ( ! denied) {
          /* if we did not find a permit for this policy */
108       if ( permit == null ) {
            /* we got an inherited permit: we have to remove the
               lattice obligations from this permit and attach
111            the lattice obligations of the current policy */
            permit = permitCache.get(inhPermit.getIdentifier());
            AbstractPolicy curPolicy =
114                           (AbstractPolicy) elem.getPermitPolicy();
            AbstractPolicy inhPolicy =
```

```
                            (AbstractPolicy) inhPermit.getPermitPolicy();
117         Set<Obligation> obligations = permit.getObligations();

            /* remove obligations defined by inhPolicy */
120         for ( Obligation oblgRm : inhPolicy.getObligations()){
             for ( Obligation oblg : obligations ) {
              if ( oblg.getId().equals(oblgRm) ) {
123            obligations.remove(oblg);
               break;
              }
126          }
            }
            /* add obligations from current policy */
129         for ( Obligation oblg : curPolicy.getObligations() ) {
             obligations.add(oblg.evaluate(evalCtx));
            }
132         permit = new Result(permit.getDecision(),
                                            evalCtx, obligations);

            }
135        return permit;
          }
         }
138      }
        }
       if ( firstIndeterminate != null ) {
141     return firstIndeterminate;
       } else if ( firstDeny != null ) {
        return firstDeny;
144    } else {
        return new Result(Result.DECISION_DENY, evalCtx);
       }
147   }
```

Listing C.2: The lattice evaluation algorithm implemented as XACML
policy combining algorithm in Java; full Java code for Listing 3.3.